The
Erotic History
of Advertising

The
Erotic History
of Advertising

Tom Reichert

 Prometheus Books
59 John Glenn Drive
Amherst, New York 14228-2197

Published 2003 by Prometheus Books

Inquiries should be addressed to
Prometheus Books, 59 John Glenn Drive, Amherst, New York 14228–2197
VOICE: 716–691–0133, ext. 207; FAX: 716–564–2711
WWW.PROMETHEUSBOOKS.COM

07 06 05 04 03   5 4 3 2 1

Library of Congress Cataloging-in-Publication Data

Reichert, Tom.
    The erotic history of advertising / Tom Reichert.
        p. cm.
    Includes bibliographical references.
    ISBN 1–59102–085–9
    1. Sex in advertising. I. Title.

HF5827.85.R45 2003
659.1'042—dc21

                                                            2003043207

Printed in the United States of America on acid-free paper

Contents

PART 2: REACHING MATURITY?
CONTEMPORARY CAMPAIGNS

Acknowledgments

First, I extend my sincere appreciation to America's advertisers for providing me with an interesting topic. My goal was to describe and make sense of the patterns and examples of sexual content in marketing over the last 150-plus years—not to criticize. It's too easy for commentators sitting offstage to sermonize and harangue, while you are in the spotlight for all the world to see. You're the ones taking the risks as you fight to survive in a fast-changing and increasingly competitive marketplace. I also want to thank the many advertisers—both brands and agencies—for granting permission to reprint their ads. The ads contribute much to the value of the book, and help to illustrate relevant points much better than my words.

Second, I want to thank the people who've contributed to making this project a reality. I want to thank my agent, Edward Knappman, and all those at New England Publishing Associates. They saw promise in this project and put me in touch with the perfect publisher. I'm sincerely indebted to my editor at Prometheus Books, Linda Regan, who also saw the potential of this book and has helped me to express my ideas as cogently and thoughtfully as possible. I want to thank others at Prometheus such as Jackie Cooke and Christine Kramer for making these ads look spectacular and keeping the 100-plus images in order. Without you all, this project would not have been possible.

No person is an island, and the following have helped with this project either directly, indirectly, or both. To my wife, Jill, and to my mother and grandmother Beverly and Christamae—my biggest supporters. To my family. To my dear friend Jacque Lambiase for telling me I was crazy for embarking on this project. Jacque has influenced so much of my thinking with regard to sex in advertising that she haunts many pages in this book ("sex-tinged" is her word). Other close friends and research associates include: Art Ramirez, Susan Morgan, Mike LaTour, Steve Gould, Eusebio Alvaro, Kevin Maly, Kay Colley, and Susan Zavoina.

Many others helped with research and support. At the University of Alabama, I wish to thank my colleagues in the Advertising and Public Relations Department for their support, specifically to Karla Gower, David Sloan, Jeremy Butler, Mike Little, Matt Bunker, Bill Gonzenbach, and the ladies in the office—Jade and Cheryl. Sincere indebtedness is in store for student researchers Ignatius Fosu, Lei Chen, Aimee Edison, Beth Dolin, Christen Lewis, Saskia Badgewell, Eric Sims, Ben Grover, and Trent Warsham. Their assistance pulling articles and thinking and writing about advertising strategy provided invaluable background research for this book.

Susan Strange at Smithsonian's National History Museum was extremely helpful, as were Jacqueline Reid and Ellen Gartrell at the J. Walter Thompson archives at Duke University. And to all those along the way: Hank Kenski, Harvey and Sandy Asher, Sally Jackson, Susan Heckler, Michael Durney, Lisa Delaney, Chris Puto, David Williams, Walid Afifi, Bill Key, Kay Colley, Paul Brothers, and Dale Brashers.

Preface

Iundertook this project to better understand if and how sex in advertising works. While conducting research for *The Erotic History of Advertising*, I examined hundreds of instances in which companies have used—and continue to use—sex to promote their products. My conclusion? Not surprisingly, they weren't wasting their money. It's clear that sex in advertising works. Not always, but sex has generated sales and saved companies from the brink of bankruptcy.

Despite its effectiveness, I discovered that only a few sources have seriously considered whether sex can sell or not. As I reviewed articles written about sex in advertising and spoke with advertising professionals in New York, Dallas, and Atlanta, it became clear that sex in advertising is typically dismissed as amateurish and sophomoric: a desperate—not to mention ineffective—attempt to rescue plummeting sales. On the other hand, many real-life examples from the 1800s to the present exist to suggest that it has worked, and does work, to inflame not only consumers' libidos but their motivations and desires to make purchases. In some cases, sex in advertising contributes to the building of strong, vibrant, and long-lasting brands. As such, it's my hope that this book can make a sizable contribution to the seemingly discordant dialogue about sex in advertising.

I also undertook this project to fill a void. Surprisingly, no single source fully documents the use of sex in advertising over a substantial period of time. Marvelous books and essays exist that describe the use of sex appeal in the 1920s, 1930s, or 1960s, but nothing weaves it together from the beginning of modern advertising to today and beyond. I believe it's important to provide a long-term view because perspective has the advantage of revealing trends that are masked if one examines only a relatively short period of time.

In addition, advertising campaigns that share many similarities—namely, sexual content—have never been grouped together for analysis. I think it's important for anyone interested in sex in advertising to have a convenient resource that includes provocative campaigns in the 1880s through today. I wanted to supply a resource that provides a context showing that sex in advertising is not a contemporary invention.

Research for this book wasn't done overnight. It involved over a decade of study. During that time, I was involved in a range of advertising investigations that analyzed sexual content in contemporary media. For example, I conducted experiments and surveys to better understand how people respond to sex in advertising and what it means to them. I interviewed over fifty creative directors, art directors, and copywriters to get their perspectives on sex in advertising. I reviewed and wrote about the current state of academic research in this area.

More recently, I traveled to the best collections of American advertising and commerce to analyze past uses of sexual appeal. I visited Duke University and its J. Walter Thompson advertising archive, the Library of Congress, and most recently, the collections and archives at the Smithsonian National History Museum in Washington, D.C. In my opinion, one can only hope to tackle the complex issues that surround the use of sex in advertising by examining it from multiple perspectives.

One of my many discoveries—at least for me—is that sex in advertising is not new. Advertisers and marketers have used sex in their promotional efforts since the early days of modern advertising. Although contemporary use has expanded to more product categories and to more brands, many of the earlier ads rival those of today. People are often surprised to see that ads from the 1880s and early 1900s are just as sexually suggestive and scintillating as present-day advertising.

Another discovery is that there are risks to writing a book like *The*

Erotic History of Advertising. I've found that people question the motives of someone writing about sex. Even William Masters and Virginia Johnson, two pioneers in the area of sex research, were advised not to pursue sex research until they were fully tenured. Just a few days ago, a colleague whom I respect and regard as a close friend, asked me if I had considered my reasons for pursuing this topic. "Have you examined the reasons that caused you to study sex in advertising?" was the gist of his question. The fact that he even asked the question caught me by surprise. I had never even thought to question his motives for his research.

My response to questions like this is that there is a good story not being told. Because of real or perceived aspersions on authors, some of the best writers decidedly pursue more socially acceptable topics. As a result, there is much about consumer responses to sex in advertising that we don't fully understand, and the age-old response, "sex sells," is much too simplistic to provide any meaningful answers. My hope is that this book will tear down some walls about sex in advertising so that the story can finally be told.

With that said, there are many examples in this book that emphasize women's breasts. You may even think the author has a breast fetish. Like most North American men, I wouldn't doubt it. In my defense, however, I would argue that any attention to women's breasts in this book is more a reflection of the subject matter and a breast-crazed culture than any fetish of the author. Fascination with women's breasts and their presence in advertising may have more to do with a biological predilection than any other factor.[1] As men control the means to production, especially in advertising, the emphasis on women's bodies in advertising also may simply be the expression of male collective desire.

In addition, this book is not meant to be a volume on women's portrayal in the media but it does illustrate how female beauty ideals are transmitted within our culture. Since perhaps 90 percent of sexual content in advertising involves women, this history does provide information on women's portrayal in the media. The content in this book serves as an additional resource, detailing how women are publicly held up for inspection. It provides many examples of how women are used to sell products to themselves and to men. Ads illustrate, subtly and not so subtly, how women can get a man, usually by primping, cleaning, dressing, and emphasizing aspects of themselves men find appealing—notice I didn't mention breasts. At the same time, men are shown what they should value in women and direct their attention thusly.

Overall, this book provides both perspective and background regarding the use of sex in advertising. My goal is to cover the most sexually provocative campaigns, and to describe many individual sexual ads that have appeared in the last century and a half. Obviously, many single ads or minor campaigns could not be covered. I attempted to include those that are representative of their times. I selected ads that are clearly sexual, though sexual content comes in many sizes and shapes. It's probable that examples I selected may not be considered sexual by everyone.

If you're interested in advertising, marketing, popular culture, and American studies, this book may be right for you. If you're interested in sexuality and its expression throughout modern history, I hope that you find this book an interesting resource. I only hope it is as enjoyable to read as it has been to write.

Introduction

Many people consider sex in advertising, the use of sexy words and images in selling messages, a recent phenomenon—that Calvin Klein, Guess, and Victoria's Secret set the bar for provocative nudity and sexual fire.

These people might be surprised to discover that Rockford Varnish Company, an industrial manufacturer based in Rockford, Illinois, ran ads in the 1930s that would make Calvin's models blush. Similarly, James Buchanan Duke stuck images of scintillatingly posed, busty starlets in cigarette packs almost one hundred years before a Guess model struck a pose. Think that Victoria's Secret and Wonderbra were the first to extol the virtues of breast shaping? The Kabo Bust Perfector was advertised in magazines as far back as the 1890s.

We will explore here how American marketers and advertisers have used sex to sell their brands since the early days of advertising. The book will catalog some of the most sexual and controversial advertising campaigns of all time, quarter century by quarter century. We will begin by describing how images of naked women adorned ads for tobacco in the 1800s. We will describe how the need for admiration and intimacy was emphasized to sell soap and lotions to ladies in the 1920s. And we will detail how romance and titillation were used in campaigns of the 1950s and 1960s for brands such as Noxzema, De Beers, Maidenform, and Miss Clairol.

Lest contemporary readers feel slighted, I allocate over half of the book to descriptions of sex in recent campaigns for soft drinks, alcohol, intimates, designer clothing, fragrances, and, most recently, condoms. If you want to find out more about Cindy Crawford and Britney Spears starring in Pepsi ads, the Taster's Choice romantic serial, and Lucky Vanous in Diet Coke ads, it's to be found here as well as details about campaigns for Stroh's, Gucci, Vassarette, Candie's, Durex, Christian Dior, Abercrombie & Fitch, Tommy Hilfiger, and many more.

To illustrate these campaigns, we reveal interesting stories and little-known details. For example, advertisers debated whether models in corsets should be shown covered or uncovered in 1897. Ninety years later a live woman clad only in a bra from the waist up (as opposed to a mannequin) aired for the first time in a Playtex commercial. In another instance, Elliot Springs, president of a textile manufacturer, couldn't convince a Madison Avenue agency to handle his account in the late 1940s. As a result, he developed his own style of sex-tinged ads that were more popular and better remembered than ads produced by the powerful New York agencies. Last, a recent study revealed that ads for Polo/Ralph Lauren, once know for its country-club images of upscale patricians, have taken a decidedly sexual turn since 1991.

The book also reveals facts about the people behind the scenes. For example, some of the same photographers and art directors have worked on a wide variety of sex in advertising campaigns. The famous photographer Richard Avedon was not only involved in the Calvin Klein jeans commercials featuring Brooke Shields, but his work also appeared in Maidenform's "Dream" campaign. In addition, few people are aware that one of the masterminds behind the recent Abercrombie & Fitch makeover, Sam Shahid, also was a creative director on provocative advertising campaigns for Calvin Klein, Banana Republic, Perry Ellis, and The Gap.

ROUSING ISSUES

The book goes beyond discussion of advertising campaigns to touch on the important issues surrounding sex in advertising. One question raised throughout the book is, "Does sex sell?" It's clear not all ads that utilize busty blondes and innuendo are successful, but the book contains a wealth of examples of successful campaigns featuring scantily clad models in romantic escapades. Some of these ads fell flat, but many more resonated with the intended consumers, and, ultimately, made their companies a lot of money. The book also addresses a related question, "How does sex sell?" Throughout the book, I describe many examples demonstrating that sex does much more than simply attract attention to the ad.

Issues of gender images in sexy ads are also discussed. Whereas women represent the vast majority of sexual content in advertising, advertisers are beginning to insert beefcake images—svelte, unclothed men with six-packs—into their campaigns. We see that some of these images are meant to be appealing to women, but many of these images are appearing in men's magazines. For example, fragrance ads in the 1980s and 1990s for colognes such as Davidoff, Paco Rabanne, and Joseph Abboud showcased muscular males in feminine poses. Are these images meant to titillate male consumers or to serve as aspirational models or both?

Another contemporary trend is the use of *lesbian chic* imagery in advertising. Titillating images of female homoeroticism are showing up in fragrance, fashion, and designer-brand advertising. I discuss why designer brands use these images, and why the lesbian chic imagery is targeted to women instead of those who might find it more sexually appealing—men.

In addition to sexy images, the book addresses audience issues. Advertisers always use sex to appeal to men, but a different style of sensual appeal is directed toward women. Recently, teens have been targeted as contemporary advertisers tap new markets. For example, a 2000 commercial for Chup Chups "Oral Pleasure" campaign featured an attractive blonde arousing men by the manner in which she licked her lollipop. Similarly, fragrance marketers such as Candie's and Lucky You are attempting to grab a chunk of the $1 billion teen fragrance market with provocative images of popular teen celebrities Carmen Electra, Dennis Rodman, Jamie Pressley, Alyssa Milano, and Mark McGrath.

These issues and many others are discussed in the context of modern-day advertising. As such, the book describes the development of advertising and media from early print media such as posters and newspapers, to television, to the Internet—and the affect of these developments on the look and nature of sensual advertising appeals.

FROM INNOCENCE TO MATURITY

The first half of the book describes the use of sensuality in advertising from the 1850s to 1975. We begin by looking at how images of nude or nearly nude women were used to "brand" products such as corsets, tobacco, and beverages. As illustrated in chapter 2, many of these ads featured women in low-cut bodices and hiked-up skirts. For example, a woman in a 1885 Excelsior Ginger Ale sips her soda as the entangled hem of her dress is pulled up by a rising hot air balloon.

Chapter 3 describes the passion plays used by advertisers to sell beautifying soaps and lotions. Ads for Andrew Jergens and Pond's emphasized the love and adornment that were the outcomes for women who used their products. These ads often contained images of handsome men in tuxedos who were enraptured by the smoothness of the women's skin. Many of the ads developed for Woodbury's soap were the result of early consumer research designed by women in the J. Walter Thompson advertising agency. The sex appeals that were developed out of that research were deliberate attempts to appeal to the romance women desired.

The period from 1925 to 1950 witnessed a continuance of romantic appeals for brands such as Palmolive and Lux soaps. Chapter 4 also describes how advertisers during the 1930s differentiated their sexual messages based on the audience (men or women). Whereas advertisers used romance to woo women, trade ads targeting men utilized titillating shots of fully nude women, or playful peek-a-boo images on calendars and direct mail pieces. Other ads during this period included those for Listerine that played on the fear of lost love as a result of chronic halitosis.

If the previous sex appeals were image oriented, the quarter century from 1950 to 1975—discussed in chapter 5—is characterized as one of blatant sexual allusion. In the 1960s, Noxzema's infamous "Take it off. Take it a-l-l off" shaving cream commercial illustrated the not-so-subtle double meaning inherent in many commercial appeals. Other innuendos included English Leather's "All my men wear English Leather, or they wear nothing at all," and Miss Clairol's "Does she or doesn't she? Only her hairdresser knows for sure," campaign. Other long-running campaigns during this period included campaigns for Maidenform and De Beers.

The second half of the book describes contemporary sex in advertising campaigns from 1975 to the present. Each chapter describes the development of sex appeal within product classes: intimates and underwear, designer jeans, fashion, fragrance, beverages, and sex-related products and social health. For example, chapter 6 discusses the sexualization of men's underwear and women's intimates in the 1980s. Brands that pushed the envelope included Jockey, Fruit of the Loom, Berlei, and Playtex. Brands that carried the torch—Victoria's Secret, Wonderbra, and Vassarette—are discussed as well. Despite the importance of these advertisers, none had a larger influence on contemporary undergarment advertising than Calvin Klein's campaigns in the 1980s and 1990s.

Calvin Klein's advertising campaigns for designer jeans also influenced the look of denim marketing in the late 1970s and 1980s. Chapter 7 describes the success of advertising campaigns for Jordache, Calvin Klein, Guess, and, more recently, Levi's "opt for the original" campaign. Sensual marketing efforts for aspirational fashion brands such as Polo/Ralph Lauren, Tommy Hilfiger, and Abercrombie & Fitch are described in chapter 8. These brands weave together images of sexy models with lifestyle images of affluence, fun, and popularity. The chapter also includes advertising for high fashion brands such as Gucci, Versace, and Christian Dior. Recent ads for these brands have been described by critics as pornographic—and even rejected by some publishers—but the ads contribute to sexy brand images that consumers continue to pay for.

If sex was used to solicit only one product, that product would be a fragrance. Ads for cologne and perfume not only contain images of beautiful bodies and rapturous couples, but they emphasize the ability of fragrances to stimulate the libidos of desired others. Groundbreaking ads for Aviance, Chanel, Jovan, and Charlie are described in chapter 9, as are the influential Obsession, Escape, and Eternity campaigns of Calvin Klein. Other recent campaigns described in the chapter include Davidoff, Polo Sport, Romance, Michael, Curve, Bernini, and Candie's.

Chapter 10 describes how sex sells a range of contemporary beverage brands. The chapter begins by telling the story of the evolution of beer advertising and its use of bimbos in bikinis until the Old Milwaukee Swedish Bikini Team debacle. Recently, titillating shots of women are once again in ads for Coors Light, Miller Lite, and Smirnoff Ice. Advertising for spirits is described as well, including: Revelstoke, Disaronno, Bacardi,

Absolut, and Johnnie Walker Red's *"And* he drinks Johnnie Walker Red" campaign. The chapter wouldn't be complete without the tale of Pepsi ads featuring Cindy Crawford and Britney Spears, and Diet Coke's Lucky Vanous, as well as the Taster's Choice romantic serial.

In chapter 11 we see that sex is used to sell sex-related products and issues such as condoms and sex-ed videos. We begin by tracing the history surrounding the first condom commercial in the 1970s, to issues surrounding condom advertising in general, to recent Trojan and Durex ads that emphasize the pleasurable benefits of prophylactics. But ads with sexual themes also successfully promote awareness of social causes such as child molestation, breast cancer, safe-sex practices, and teen pregnancy. Americans will see more of these sex-tinged public service announcements for a variety of causes because they work; as sexual themes they capture the interest of those most at risk.

Last, chapter 12 discusses the use of sex appeals for mainstream online advertisers. Pop-up windows and banner ads are programmed to find the surfers most interested in and open to sex appeals. In addition, homepages—another form of online advertising—for marketers such as Baywatch.com, Beer.com, and Playboy.com, as well as sites for men's magazines, contain a wealth of titillating imagery designed to draw in young male viewers. The chapter concludes with observations about the future of sex in advertising, such as advertisers pushing the bar too far, and recycling of sexual ad content.

English writer Norman Douglas once said, "You can tell the ideals of a nation by its advertisements."[1] After reading this book, you will have a much clearer concept of where the ideals of many Americans reside. From the titillating shots of the 1800s to the recent renaissance of bikini-clad babes in Coors Light commercials, this book provides the best (and worst) sex in advertising marketers have to offer. At the very least, you'll be informed about uses of sex in advertising in the American marketing landscape and its power to influence consumers.

1
Sex and Money

O
n a Sunday in January 2002, CNN abruptly pulled an in-house promotional ad that had started running only the day before. The ad promoted the newly signed Paula Zahn and her morning news program. As clips of the attractive Zahn flashed on the screen, the voice-over commented, "Where can you find a morning news anchor who is provocative, super smart.... Oh yeah, and just a little sexy?"[1]

The promo was pulled because Zahn was offended. She said it denigrated her journalistic reputation. It was obvious that CNN was promoting Zahn's sex appeal to increase viewership, most likely among men. But the promo caused a flap because it explicitly used the word "sexy" to promote news programming. Attractive newscasters are the norm, but until the CNN promo, sex appeal had never been explicitly touted to sell the news. Whereas CNN's product is programming content, increased viewership is the commodity sold to advertisers. Fox News Channel's Bill O'Reilly may have offered the most honest appraisal of the situation. He said Zahn was only being politically correct when she objected to the ad, and that: "If Paula Zahn doesn't think she's there partially because she's a good-looking babe, then she's in never-never land."[2]

The use of sex to sell products, and the occasional controversy it causes, is as American as apple pie. As far back as the 1850s and the birth of modern advertising, sexual imagery and promises of sexual fulfillment have been integrated into ads to attract attention, to build carefully crafted brand identities, and to sell products—even the news. Here we will examine some of the ways advertisers successfully, and sometimes unsuccessfully, use sex to boost revenues.

ADVERTISERS TURN UP THE HEAT

As everyone's favorite whipping boy, advertising is often blamed for societal ills ranging from sharp increases in the incidence of anorexia and breast implants to the perpetuation of economic and social inequality. Am I simply overstating the case when I say advertisers use sex to sell products? In a word, "No." Many advertising professionals I've spoken with readily admit that sex is used to sell products. Advertisers often associate sexual information with particular brands to increase sales. Sexual information can be represented in a variety of ways for different purposes, but its ultimate goal is to nudge consumers closer to buying the brand.

Throughout the book, we address the question, "Does sex sell?" A more pertinent question is, how can it not sell? Sex *and* advertising is a powerful combination. First, you have sex, a potent instinctual drive. A drive that ranks high among essential survivalist drives and motivations such as the need for safety, shelter, appetite, thirst, and companionship. There's truth in the old saying, "Every species on Earth does two things well—eat and fuck."

Sex, as evolutionary psychologist David Buss refers to it, is a drive to procreate that is represented by millions of years of psychobiological evolution.[3] It's the drive to have offspring and to further one's own kind. A person's sexuality shapes his/her approach to the world, his interactions with others, and his conceptions of himself. Needless to say for most people, sex is fundamental to human existence—a fundamental need, as are intimacy and the desire to be attractive and valued by others.

Sex is powerful, but advertising is no slouch when it comes to influencing people's lives. It's one of the most prolific and all-encompassing forms of communication in the world. It bombards us in our homes through magazines, television, online surfing, radio, and direct mail. One

Figure 1.1: Victoria's Secret.

can hardly escape it even outside the home in our automobiles through radio ads and splashy billboards. Projections are that $250 billion will be invested in American advertising in 2003.[4] With that amount of capital continually pushing, urging, and prodding us, it's tough to deny advertising's influence.

If you link sex and advertising, you have a powerful one-two punch. Companies deliberately link their products with sexual information: because of our biology we can't help but be drawn to it. Advertising is about getting one's message noticed among the thousands of promotional messages and other data people are flooded with every day. Companies also associate their products with sexual needs and desires. You want more romance and intimacy? You want to attract beautiful people and have great sex, or even better sex? No problem, just pull out your pocketbook. Advertisers position their brands as sexual conduits, as magnets, that help us better desire and be desired. After all, advertising is about communicating the utility of products and services to satisfy wants and needs. Rare are those of us who are completely sexually—or materially—satisfied.

Needless to say, advertising is a prolific marketing tool designed to stimulate, facilitate, and reinforce purchases. At its simplest level, advertising is about informing likely prospects about the availability and terms for obtaining the product. But advertising is also about creating impressions and positioning brands—constructing identities for branded products—in consumers' minds.

In today's advertising environment, creating impressions and positioning brands are not easy tasks. Most consumers consider commercials, print ads, and Internet ads intrusive. They passively attend to ads while engaging in other activities (e.g., talking on the phone, getting dressed, eating a meal). They speed by billboards, quickly flip through magazines, and push the mute button during commercials breaks. As a result, advertising creators must construct ads that swiftly grab the viewer. To do this, advertisers use readily identifiable symbols, story lines, and cultural signifiers—people and things that evoke a common meaning for many people. Stereotypes are one tool advertisers depend on to enable viewers to quickly recognize categories of people and situations. Advertisers use these tools to cut through the clutter and ensure that their story is understood.

Sex in advertising is one device often used for the same purposes as

Figure 1.2: In the 1800s illustrations of topless women, like this one for David Dunlop's Columbia tobacco, were often featured for tobacco products. Duke University. Columbia Tobacco ad (n.d.), "David Dunlop." Domestic Advertising Collection, J. Walter Thompson Company Archives, Hartman Center for Sales, Advertising & Marketing History, Rare Book, Manuscript, & Special Collections Library, Duke University, Durham, North Carolina.

Figure 1.3: Billboards appeared throughout the country in 1937 and 1938 to promote the "positive" effects of White Owl cigar smoking on men's breath. General Cigar ad (n.d.), "Easier on Your Breath." Domestic Advertising Collection, J. Walter Thompson Company Archives, Hartman Center for Sales, Advertising & Marketing History, Rare Book, Manuscript, & Special Collections Library, Duke University, Durham, North Carolina. White Owl is a registered trademark of Pinkerton Tobacco Co. LP.

stereotypes. It's used to get the ad noticed and to tell a story. It's used to associate branded products with sexual thoughts and feelings, and to position the brands as cutting-edge, avant-garde, and even alluringly taboo. And it's also used to convince consumers that certain brands are sexual panaceas that enhance sexual attractiveness, sexual performance, and sexual opportunity. When advertisers use sexual information in their messages such as people, objects, and situations associated with sexual meaning, they introduce erotic properties to their brands.

SUCCESS WITH SEX IN ADVERTISING

Over the past 150 years several brands have sold products with a heavy dependence on sexual appeal. For many people, today's brands such as Victoria's Secret and Calvin Klein may seem like they are pushing the envelope, but advertisers, as noted, have used sexual imagery and promises for many years. Sexy ads at the turn of the century probably evoked responses similar to those evoked by contemporary sexy ads.

Figure 1.4: Rockford Varnish Company. "Individuality," (1939), Warshaw Collection of Business Americana, Archives Center, National Museum of American History, Smithsonian Institution, 02040405.

A LESSON IN *Kissing Technique*

LISTERINE TELLS YOU WHAT THE MASTERS SAY ABOUT KISSING

The anatomical juxtaposition of two orbicularis oris muscles in a state of contraction.
DR. HENRY GIBBONS

*What is a kiss? Why this, as some approve:
The sure sweet cement, glue, and lime of love.*
ROBERT HERRICK

*A kiss, when all is said, what is it?
. . . a rosy dot
Placed on the "i" in loving; 'tis a secret
Told to the mouth instead of to the ear.*
EDMOND ROSTAND

The sound of a kiss is not so loud as that of a cannon, but its echo lasts a great deal longer.
O. W. HOLMES

Kissing don't last: cookery do. GEORGE MEREDITH

Lord! I wonder what fool it was that first invented kissing. SWIFT

*And when my lips meet thine,
Thy very soul is welded unto mine.* H. H. BOYESEN

*Say I'm weary, say I'm sad,
Say that health and wealth have missed me;
Say I'm growing old, but add
Jenny kissed me.* LEIGH HUNT

*A man had given all other bliss,
And all his worldly worth for this,
To waste his whole heart in one kiss
Upon her perfect lips.* TENNYSON

Excerpts taken from "The Home Book of Quotations"
by Burton Stevenson; Dodd, Mead & Co., Publishers.

WHETHER it's the kiss given in the first fine rapture of love's discovery, the kiss you give your husband of twenty years as he rushes out in the morning, or the kiss of mother and son—don't be careless. Remember . . . nothing is so intimate or so revealing as a kiss.

FOR LOVE'S SAKE

So—for love's sake!—don't ever be guilty of offending HIM with halitosis (bad breath). It freezes love . . . yet anyone may have it at some time or other.

Wouldn't any woman be foolish to chance losing this regard unnecessarily when it's often so easy to make breath sweeter, purer, with Listerine Antiseptic?

Halitosis is sometimes due to systemic conditions. Usually, however, say some authorities, it is caused by the fermentation of tiny food particles in the mouth. For that condition, a good rinsing of the mouth with refreshing Listerine Antiseptic morning and night works sweet wonders!

Listerine Antiseptic halts such fermentation, then overcomes the odors it causes. Your breath becomes sweeter, less likely to offend. Use Listerine Antiseptic as a mouth rinse night and morning.

"P.S." TO MEN: *Don't imagine you're immune from halitosis! (Who is?) Keep Listerine Antiseptic on hand—make it a morning and nightly ritual! Always remember to rinse your mouth with this delightful, breath-sweetening antiseptic deodorant before any important business engagement—or your date with Her. It pays. Lambert Pharmacal Co., St. Louis, Mo.*

LET LISTERINE LOOK AFTER YOUR BREATH

Figure 1.5: Listerine's "Lesson in Kissing Technique" (1941), Domestic Advertising Collection, J. Walter Thompson Company Archives, Hartman Center for Sales, Advertising & Marketing History, Rare Book, Manuscript, & Special Collections Library, Duke University, Durham, North Carolina. Courtesy of Pfizer Pharmaceutical Group, Pfizer Inc.

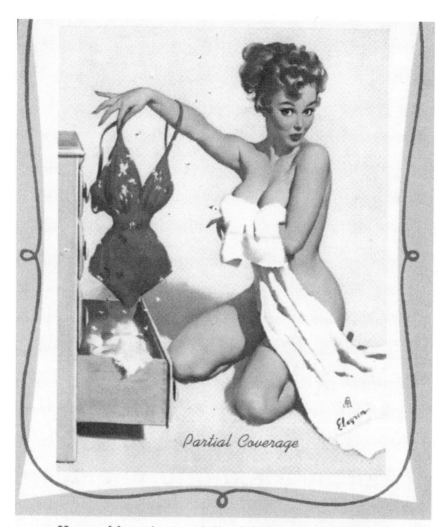

Partial Coverage

No problem is too full of holes for our personal and efficient attention. Our experts are
as close as your phone. Call us today.

Figure 1.6: Calendar Art. © Brown and Bigelow, Inc.; "Partial Coverage,"
(1958), Warshaw Collection of Business Americana, Archives Center,
National Museum of American History, Smithsonian Institution, 02040406.

Figure 1.7: Model Sara Dolley was "wanted" in this 1960 Western-style *Wanted* poster shot by photographer Richard Avedon. Maidenform, Inc. All Rights Reserved.

As far back as 1850, advertisers used illustrations and photographs of buxom women to attract attention. Although some advertising historians argue that images of women's bare ankles were considered racy in 1900,[5] images of women with exposed bosoms and deep cleavage were certainly present at the time. Ads with photographs of women in corsets date to the 1890s, as do images of women holding up their skirts in tobacco posters throughout the Northeastern United States. The image of a gust of wind blowing up a women's full-length skirt to reveal her ankle may have been considered scandalous, but full-color posters of a beautiful woman with fully exposed breasts advertised a brewing company in 1904.

In the 1880s, for example, the heir of the Duke cigarette fortune used sexual images of women to sell packs of a new-fangled product, machine-rolled cigarettes. Small paper cards were placed in cigarette packs as incentives to smokers to buy packs until they completed the set. The tactic was one reason Duke's company became the leading cigarette maker by 1890.

In the early years of the twentieth century, sexual themes were used to sell beauty products such as soap, lotions, fragrances, and hygienic products to women.[6] For example, sales of Woodbury's Facial Soap had been lagging for some time until the account was awarded to a new agency in 1910. The agency promptly took the soap from being outsold 20-to-1 to the leader in its field in fifteen years. New ads featured images of romantic situations and conveyed the message that if women used the soap, their skin would be so "flawless" men would find them irresistible.

In the 1930s, sex was used to sell another tobacco product. This time it was cigars. Within the five-cent-cigar market, White Owl cigars were lagging behind other competitive brands. All of this changed when lab tests revealed that White Owl's caused less noxious smoker's breath than other leading brands. What followed was a series of ads constructed to relieve smokers' fears that cigar smoke would decrease their attractiveness to women. The ads on conspicuous billboards featured men kissing attractive blondes, resulting in a bump in sales.

Similarly, ads for Listerine, the multipurpose hygienic, featured images of couples kissing, or of people either being attracted to each other or repelled by each other, because of "halitosis" or other socially undesirable odors. An ad in 1941 offered "A lesson in kissing technique." What was the lesson? Use Listerine. And in 1953, the headline from the infamous

Figure 1.8: Close-Up Toothpaste (1987). Close-Up ad, "Tartar Isn't Sexy." Domestic Advertising Collection, J. Walter Thompson Company Archives, Hartman Center for Sales, Advertising & Marketing History, Rare Book, Manuscript, & Special Collections Library, Duke University, Durham, North Carolina. Close-Up ad reproduced courtesy of Unilever PLC and Unilever N.V. or their subsidiaries, copyright holders.

campaign read, "Often a bridesmaid. . . . Never a bride." Thanks to the benefits of Listerine antiseptic, intimacy, marriage, or at least a kiss, is something everyone could aspire to.

Aside from mouthwash, tobacco, and soap, sex was used to sell linens and intimates. For example, Elliot Springs created a stir with his sexual ad appeals in the 1940s and 1950s. Springs personally oversaw his company's advertising campaigns, which featured nudity, erotic situations, "peekaboo" shots (up-blown skirts), and sexual innuendo. Despite disapproving letters from female consumers, Springs continued to run the ads for many years with great success. During the same time period, Maidenform's long-running "Dream" campaign featured playful, yet tantalizing, images of women clad only in their bras from the waist up. The twenty-year campaign not only tripled sales of Maidenform bras, but established the bras as a top brand.

Not to be outdone by advertisers' blatant allusions for intimates, shaving cream, and cologne, the state of Virginia adopted a sexy tourism slogan to counter a drop in tourism. In 1969, the slogan "Virginia is for Lovers" first appeared in promotional material. Almost immediately, tourism in the state turned the corner, and within two years, Virginia was ranked as the top vacation destination spot in the country.

During the sexual revolution, the fragrance marketer Jovan introduced its line of musk-based scents with double entendres and promises of sexual attraction. As a result, Jovan's revenue rocketed from $1.5 million in 1971 to $77 million seven years later. In 1975, a campaign for Aviance perfume promised stay-at-home women a sensual transformation and the ability to arouse their husbands when they came home from work. Despite the perfume's "strong, slightly musky scent," the spot resonated with women, resulting in over $7 million in sales the first year and a "best commercial" award.

Fast forwarding to the 1990s, a clothing company successfully transformed its image from that of a fishing gear retailer to that of an apparel retailer featuring sexy and hip clothing for young people. The company, Abercrombie & Fitch, did this with provocative catalogs, advertising, and in-store displays. The makeover fueled growth from 36 stores in 1993 to over 491 in 2002, as revenue jumped from $85 million to over $1.35 billion. During the same period, sexy ads, as part of a new branding campaign, helped Tom Ford and Domenico De Sole turn around an ailing Gucci brand. Their trend-setting ads with slinky models in surrealistic settings boosted sales from $264 million in 1994 to over $1.5 billion in 2002.

But sex isn't used to sell just fragrances and fashion. Since 1991, Sinclair Intimacy Institute, a leading sex-education company, has educated (and titillated) millions of consumers with its sex-ed videos. The privately owned company grosses $8 million annually thanks to its scintillating full-page ads that appear in mainstream magazines such as *Cosmopolitan, Redbook, Esquire,* the *Nation, Harpers, USA Today,* and the *New York Times Book Review.* According to Kathy Brummitt, Sinclair's marketing director, the spicier the ad, the better the response.

Sex also boosted sales of an instant coffee drink. Initiated in 1990, the Taster's Choice romantic serial campaign propelled the brand to the top of the instant coffee segment in 1992. Many of the campaign's thirteen commercials were ranked by viewers as some of the most memorable on television during the seven-year campaign. Sales of diamonds also benefited from appeals to love and romance. The diamond conglomerate De Beers scored a major marketing success in the 1990s with a campaign based on romantic silhouettes. The company generated $50 billion in global sales on a $55-million ad budget.

Even a subtle reference to sex can bring success. By sexing up its online advertising, Internet marketer X10 increased sales of its small video camera by driving people to the company's Web site. The company added to its ad an image of an attractive woman and a reference to "bedroom" as a place where the camera could be used. The result was a huge jump in traffic that propelled the company's Web site to one of the five most visited sites in May 2001.

Of today's most recognizable and profitable brands, two, Victoria's Secret and Calvin Klein, stand out as having built long-term brand identities virtually indistinguishable from sex. For example, the Victoria's Secret catalog—one of the most anticipated and read pieces of direct mail in America—features tantalizing shots of supermodels in the company's lingerie, bras, and panties. Because of its catalog, sexy ads, Web presence, store displays, and a $110 million annual marketing budget, Victoria's Secret now ranks ninth among "most recognized brands." The company's sexual positioning has also paid off: currently it commands a 15 percent share of the $12 billion intimate apparel segment.

Similarly, Calvin Klein produces some of the most recognizable and memorable ads each year, resulting in annual retail sales of over $5 billion. Since the beginning these ads have evolved and varied, but almost always featured entangled limbs, nudity, and flirtation with the taboo: from a 1978 billboard with model Patti Hansen on her hands and knees, to Brooke Shields's commercials in which she spoke lovingly about her *Calvins*, to Klein changing the meaning of men's underwear when he sexualized it with a Bruce Weber shot of briefs-clad Olympic pole-vaulter Tom Hintinaus.

Today, Calvin Klein and Victoria's Secret may be the most successful marketers of sexualized brand identities, but they are not alone. I recently asked more than two hundred college students to identify ads they thought were particularly sexy.[7] They mentioned ads for over sixty-seven different brands. The brands mentioned most frequently included (in order), Victoria's Secret, Levi's, Calvin Klein, Candie's, Clairol, Uncle Ben's, Doritos, Trojan, Miller Lite, and The Gap. Their responses demonstrate that sex in contemporary advertising is common and that an increasingly wide range of contemporary brands use sexual information in their ads to sell products.

WHAT IS SEX IN ADVERTISING?

As the previous examples illustrate, sex can sell. But as the examples also suggest, sexy ads come in a variety of forms. For example, sex in advertising is often characterized as attractive models in stages of undress, models displayed or posing decoratively, or models engaged in suggestive behavior, either alone or with others.[8] In addition, advertising also employs sexual double entendre, innuendo, subliminal sexual imagery, and sex-related promises. These forms of sexual content and imagery serve to provoke consumers' sexual interest, as well as to fuel romantic feelings.

By far the most discussed and clearest examples of sex in advertising revolve around clothing—what models are wearing or not wearing. Sexy clothing and revealing displays of the human body represent a fundamental type of sexual information. Most of the ads discussed and illustrated in this book contain models that are either suggestively dressed or partially nude. Female models wear open or low-cut blouses that expose cleavage as well as mini-skirts and tight-fitting clothing that display the body. Sexualized male models often wear shirts or shorts that showcase chiseled chests, six-pack abdomens, and well-defined biceps and quadriceps.

More revealing attire is often in the form of underwear, intimates, lingerie, swimwear, and bikinis. One need only to recall recent ads for intimates' marketers such as Victoria's Secret, Vassarette, Donna Karan, Polo/Ralph Lauren, and Calvin Klein to know what I'm referring to. Taking revealing body displays a step further, shots of topless women (although full frontal nudity is extremely rare, even in European advertising) do appear sporadically in contemporary magazine ads. Typically, viewers must infer that models are nude when covered with towels, under the sheets, or in the shower.

In a recent study, a young man described what he found sexy in an ad, "[A woman in] tight Guess jeans that hugged her nicely. She also had on a halter top that showed a lot of cleavage."[9] A similar response from a young woman described the physical features of models in ads as sexual, "When women or men are showing a lot of skin. I relate nakedness to sexy. Also, when people are wearing provocative clothing." These responses were representative of many of those surveyed in the study.

It's not all about clothing, however. It's also about what's under the clothing, even the underwear. Beauty and good looks turn people on, and advertisers have known that for a long time and that attractive models draw attention. Ads containing good-looking models get hung up in cubicles, offices, and bedrooms across the country. Advertisers also know that attractive models serve as an implicit argument to buy the brand: Good-looking people use the brand, so the brand will make you good looking.

Often what models *do* is sexy. Models can pose seductively. They can communicate sexual interest by flirting with the viewer or with someone else in the ad. Often models appear to make eye contact with the viewer as they assume a sexually receptive posture. Models can sit with their legs spread, flex their muscles, and move seductively to music. Models can speak in seductive tones making references to the brand with sexual inferences, much like the recent "Totally Organic" Herbal Essences campaign featuring women excitedly exclaiming "Yes! Yes! Yes!" as they wash their hair in public restrooms.

Images of closeness between a couple are commonly found in advertising. These images can include touching, kissing, or the simulation of

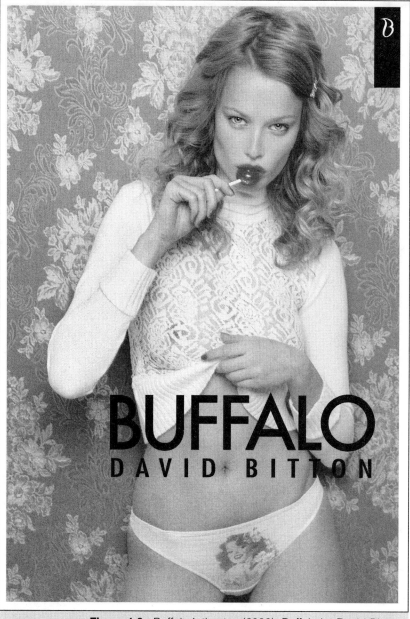

Figure 1.9: Buffalo Intimates (2002). Buffalo by David Bitton.

Figure 1.10: Guess? Inc., Creative Director: Paul Marciano, Photographer: Pablo Alfaro.

sexual behavior. For example, some contemporary ads display striptease, fondling, group sex, oral sex, and intercourse. One woman described a subtle sexual ad characteristic as, "The closeness of the man and woman. The way he caresses her face and looks at her." Another said, "The people [man and woman] are lying on the beach holding each other in their arms," and that was sexy.[10] Ads for Sinclair Intimacy Institute feature couples engaged in foreplay and steamy embraces. Although the action in the ads is staged, viewers are treated to a voyeuristic spectacle of a couple's lovemaking.

Production elements such as an ad's execution—the way the commercial is constructed—can contribute to its sexiness. These elements can include suggestive photography, edits and pacing in commercials, sexy music, lighting effects, and romantic locales. A young woman said that, "Black and white ads; also ones that take place by the ocean or the tropics," are what she finds sexy in advertising. Another person offered the following description, "[The ad] has vague sensuous photography and concepts. I don't want to see anything or get the picture too much because then it's just trashy. Soft music, soft light, soft voices, hard bodies."[11]

Although most sexual content is visual in ads, sexual language and words also constitute examples of sex in advertising. I'm reminded of signage for an unfinished wood furniture retailer that boldly proclaims "Nude Furniture." Sometimes phrases have innocent meanings until they are accompanied by sexual images. Another furniture company, this one in the Dallas area, runs ads with the headline "Cheap Ass Prices." The image in the ad isn't furniture but a woman's bikini-clad backside. Sex in advertising? Yes. Sexist? Unquestionably.

Paradoxically, sometimes what's *not* shown in an ad is considered sexual. A Haagen-Dazs ad from the 1990s shows an empty ice cream container and spoon on satin sheets with the headline "Who needs mistletoe?" The advertiser leaves it for the viewer to infer that a couple hedonistically consumed ice cream—and ended up consuming each other. Similarly, a recent Levi's ad employed blue-screen technology to render its models invisible. All viewers saw was a woman's figure outlined in her tight-fitting Levi's. Imaginations were left to fill in the blanks, especially as she stripped out of her clothes.

SEXUAL PROMISES

Sex in advertising isn't just skin and erotic behavior. Advertisers place sex in their ads as a tacitly promised result of buying and using the brand. These sex appeals can be thought of as sexual promises that either implicitly or explicitly offer sexual benefits to consumers. Research Jacque Lambiase and I conducted revealed three promises common in sexual ads: (a) sexual attractiveness for the consumer, (b) likely engagement in sexual behavior (and more enjoyment from these encounters), and (c) feelings of being sexy or sensual.[12]

Consider ads for Listerine that made subtle promises about using the brand. If you didn't use Listerine, some ads said you risked social ostracism and loss of love. If you did use Listerine, the world of romance, love, and a thousand kisses were yours to savor. Smokers of White Owl cigars were cajoled into thinking that their cigar breath would not prevent them from being kissed by attractive women.

Consider a Godiva Liqueur ad that ran in a recent *Sports Illustrated* swimsuit edition. The ad features a young attractive couple at home after a black-tie affair. The copy offers men an unmistakable sexual promise, "When you give someone chocolate be prepared to get back more than the obligatory, 'Oh, thanks.'" The image of the couple, combined with the headline, offers male readers a powerful benefit that says essentially, "Want sex? Buy Godiva Liqueur for your woman."

Sex in advertising doesn't always promise to make consumers sexual magnets or reapers of sexual pleasures; it can offer consumers the opportunity to feel better about themselves. If you're a woman and you want to feel sexier, buy Hanes Sensuale underwear. According to the ad, Sensuale underwear "lets you be comfortable enough to feel confidently sexy." To fully grasp how sexual appeals motivate purchases, one must truly consider the promises and pledges made by advertisers for their brands.

HIDDEN SEXUAL PERSUADERS

Another type of sexual information, subliminal sexual imagery, deserves mention, because for many people, sex in advertising is about hidden per-

During lovemaking,

sexual stimuli

travel to the brain at

170 miles per hour.

Fly first class.

Set yourself free. In a new Durex® condom.

Feel what you've been missing. With the most exciting condoms ever made.
New **Durex** condoms for ultimate pleasure. Now safe sex doesn't have
to feel that way. Free sample at www.durex.com.

Figure 1.11: Durex condoms. "Durex" ad,
Photography © Michele Clement Studios, Inc.

suaders. When I mention my research, many people I speak with say, "Oh, yeah. You're researching naked people in ice cubes." Undoubtedly, these people and many others have been influenced by the subliminal craze spawned most recently by Wilson Bryan Key. In the 1970s and 1980s subliminal advertising was popularized by Key's best-selling books *Subliminal Seduction* and *The Clam-Plate Orgy*.[13] In his writings, Key described the use of sexual words and images airbrushed into a glass of Seagram's whiskey, among other objects.

Although we are primarily exploring here the type of sexual content you can see—provocative models in seductive poses—I'll provide a brief overview of sexual "embeds" and subliminal fascination.

Sexual embeds are small forms of sexual information—naked body parts and words like *sex* hidden in ice cubes—that are meant to be perceived only at a preconscious level so that they go undetected by viewers. A second type of hidden sexual content is more symbolic: representations of normal objects that connote genitalia or sexual acts to the subconscious. For example, the image of a key inserted into a lock might represent intercourse in the receiver's subconscious. In a recent Seagram's ad, a woman is holding a huge swizzle stick so that it angles up and away from her waist. Given the shape and position of the woman's stick, believers in sexual embeds might argue that viewers unconsciously interpret the swizzle stick as a penis.

Both types of hidden sexual persuaders supposedly work by motivating viewers toward the product associated with the imagery. So if someone is exposed to a vodka ad containing embeds, he/she will be more likely to purchase that vodka. According to experts who believe in the use and effects of subliminal imagery, the power of sexual embeds diminishes in relation to their conscious perceptibility because viewers are better able to resist their appeal.[14]

Needless to say, few topics evoke as much controversy as subliminal advertising. Many researchers and advertising professionals consider embeds a hoax because very little published research proves it can actually motivate consumers to make purchases. Wilson Key argues, however, that advertisers' proprietary consumer research, unavailable for scholarly examination, proves that subliminal ads do work.

Ad professionals also argue that at no point in the creation or production process does anyone say, "I need the ad for the vodka account by five o'clock. And oh, by the way, airbrush some boobs into those ice cubes, will you?" Ad folks argue that you can hardly get a person's attention with perceptible messages, so why hide it? Key dismisses these claims: "Advertisers use the technique, which they deny using, because it sells products. People are scared to even consider the plausibility of its existence because it threatens their sense of free will."[15]

Finally, one must consider the media's fascination with subliminal advertising. James Twitchell, author of *Adcult USA*, provides a frank description of James Vicary, a Madison Avenue charlatan who initiated America's obsession with subliminal effects.[16] Vicary's tool, the Tachistoscope, could flash images so fast that viewers wouldn't realize that they had seen anything, but the image would still be imprinted in their minds. In 1958, a test of Vicary's method proved to have negligible effects. The test, ordered by the Federal Communications Commission, was conducted in Washington, D.C., for an audience of congressmen, reporters, and government officials. The subliminal message flashed for the audience was "Eat Popcorn." The test dispelled any chance of a federal investigation, but Vicary quickly lost his ability to charm the advertising community, and later that year skipped town with millions of dollars in retainer fees.[17]

Given subliminal seduction's past, it's easy to see why the ad community is skeptical of its existence and supposed effects. I encourage readers to consult what's been written about sexual content on subliminal advertising and reach their own conclusions.[18]

CONCLUSION

It's obvious that sex in advertising is manifested in various forms. Whereas the network promo described at the beginning of this chapter makes a subtle allusion to Paula Zahn's physical attractiveness and sex appeal, sex in advertising often features more graphic content and quid-pro-quo promises. Many ads feature models in revealing attire, but other variations include suggestive behavior, interaction between models, and contextual factors such as lighting, editing, and location. These sexual elements rarely appear in isolation but are woven together to evoke sexual responses and sexual interest in viewers. Unfortunately for the producers of Zahn's CNN spot, their intent was made explicit, which was wrong for that particular purpose.

Sex appeals, whether romantic or overtly sexual, have appeared in many ads and promotional materials over the decades. Whereas standards may have changed, images with sex appeal have been designed with the same goal: to manipulate feelings through sexual interest. They serve to attract attention and to imbue products with sexual meaning—meaning that resonates with consumers in a way that will make the cash register ring.

Sex has been used throughout the history of modern American advertising to sell products and position brands. Here we provided a lens for identifying the content and forms of sex used to sell those brands. We will next describe in detail advertisers' use of sexual content in ads from the 1800s to the beginning of the twentieth century. As modern advertising blossomed and reached critical mass, as specialists have formed agencies, and media, markets, and technology have progressed to a point where advertisers could reach regional, national, and international markets, sex—one of the most powerful human drives—has been used to help companies increase their visibility and profits.

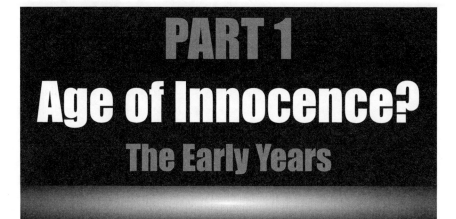

PART 1
Age of Innocence?
The Early Years

2
Smoke and Leers
1850–1900

Tobacco advertising was a significant force in the latter half of the nineteenth century. During that period, manufacturers used all available promotional means—like today—to stimulate sales: posters, billboards, packaging, and premiums. Often, tobacco manufacturers differentiated their brands through images of beautiful women in revealing poses. Consider the Pearl tobacco label that appeared in 1871 (see fig. 2.1). The image is of a lightly draped, voluptuous young woman rising from the waves. The colored lithograph accentuates the woman's rosy cheeks and long flowing locks, not to mention the plumes of smoke billowing from somewhere behind her feet.

The woman in this poster, like many other women in ads during this period, is a nude in the classical style with breasts exposed and pubic area barely covered. The image is similar to representations of beauty produced by Greek sculptors and Renaissance painters, but it also represents the use of nudity to sell products to men who may not appreciate the finer distinctions between high art and titillation. In addition, these images in ads were viewed out of context. Whereas classical-style nudes in gilded frames were meant to be viewed in great mansions and museums, the mass production of bodies through commercial outlets compromises their dignity, even if well drawn.

Figure 2.1: This Pearl brand tobacco label appearing in 1871 features a full-color illustration of a woman rising from the waves. "Pearl," Library of Congress, LC-USZC4-3215.

Nonetheless, nude images like the Pearl girl certainly attracted buyer attention and interest. Men were the primary, if not sole, consumers of cigars, plug tobacco, and new-fangled machine-rolled cigarettes. The purpose of the illustration was to associate beauty and sensuality with the Pearl brand of tobacco in an effort to create distinction among often indistinguishable brands. Tobacco wasn't alone, however. Manufacturers also used images of woman to create identities for a variety of beverages. But the nature of women's images stimulated debate about how to advertise women's corsets before the turn of the century—a period that supplied the underpinnings of modern advertising.

ADVERTISING AND AMERICA'S INDUSTRIAL AGE

To fully understand advertising in the latter half of the nineteenth century, it's important to provide a brief sketch of what was taking place at that time in America. It was an era when world fairs were spectacular and citizens were in awe of inventions, gadgets, and the promise of industrial science. It was a period of massive growth and economic expansion. It was a time of war, both domestic and foreign, and political and social upheaval and healing. It also was a time of unprecedented American artistic and literary endeavors. According to advertising author and educator Bill Arens, these events provided the essential ingredients—mass-produced goods, mass distribution, mass communication, and mass education—for the development of modern advertising.[1]

Innovations in packaging helped to solve the problem of spoilage since packaged goods did not spoil as quickly as fresh produce. Canned and boxed goods could be distributed and warehoused in growing markets across the country. Some of these brands sold in the early days were so successful they remain household names today, including: Arm & Hammer, Fleischmann's Yeast, Campbell's Soup, Vaseline, Ivory Soap, Coca-Cola, Quaker Oats, Planter's Peanuts, and Listerine.

Railroads and steamships provided improved transportation that moved goods and people around the country and the world at an unprecedented rate. In 1853 railroad lines reached just beyond the Mississippi, but by 1869 the first transcontinental railroad was completed at Promontory Point, Utah Territory. For the first time, citrus grown in the fertile valleys of the West could be shipped to markets in the Eastern states. The expansion in transportation also contributed to westward migration. As new markets opened up, the established communities in the East grew at an accelerated pace. America's population tripled to 76 million from 1850 to 1900. As areas become more densely populated, it was profitable for advertisers and marketers to concentrate their efforts.

The industrial era also was an age of inventions, many of which contributed to mass communication. The advent of the telephone, phonograph, motion picture camera, and telegraph resulted in changes in communication, commerce, and perspectives on how people viewed their world.[2] For example, publishing technology such as web and rotary presses, as well as the Linotype, contributed significantly to faster printing. Media sources benefited because newspapers, magazines, and posters could be produced more efficiently and cheaply than in the past. Advances in image technology made photographs and illustrations easy to produce and, as a result, more widespread. For the first time, Americans were awash in images of far-off places, both the familiar and the exotic.

During the industrial era, mass communication, especially in the form of newspapers, but also magazines, reached larger and larger audiences. For example, overall newspaper circulation increased from 758,000 in 1850 to over 15.1 million in 1900.[3] Newspapers reached their zenith as the dominant medium in the latter half of the nineteenth century. The penny press, begun by Benjamin Day and his *New York Sun* in the 1830s, was perfected by Joseph Pulitzer and William Randolph Hearst in the 1890s in their monumental circulation battles. They jockeyed for more readers—and profits—by offering their papers at low prices and feeding readers a steady diet of sex, scandal, corruption, intrigue, disaster, crime, and news of exploration from around the world.

Subsidization through advertising revenue enabled newspapers to offer prices low enough so they were available to masses of newly arrived immigrants and workers. Advertisers, local as well as national brands, were interested in reaching the large concentrated markets that newspapers delivered. Volney Palmer of Philadelphia is credited with becoming the first advertising *agent* in 1841. He would buy large volumes of newspaper space at a discount then sell it at a higher rate to advertisers. N. W. Ayer, another businessman in Philadelphia, began specializing in the placement of ads in newspapers for clients. His agency would plan, create, and produce the advertisements.

Early newspaper ads resembled modern-day classified ads.[4] The ads, primarily all text in the early days, notified readers of new items that were for sale. Advancements in printing technology soon resulted in a profusion of ad illustrations. In the 1880s, illustrated ads for soaps, lotions, medicinal tonics, cigarettes, matches, breakfast cereals, and canned goods were common.

Magazines also were flourishing as a national medium by the end of the nineteenth century. Some of the more successful titles included *Atlantic Monthly, Harper's Bazaar, Good Housekeeping, McClure's, Life Magazine, The Saturday Evening Post, Ladies' Home Journal,* and *Scribners.*[5] Whereas newspapers were effective for reaching large concentrated local markets, magazines were able to reach thousands if not millions of readers regionally and nationally. Cyrus Curtis, publisher of several successful magazines, initiated the agency commission system (agencies received a 10 percent discount while charging the client full price for media placement).[6] The commission system, still in use by some agencies today, provided an earnest incentive for advertising agencies to direct their advertising toward magazines.

Other forms of advertising and promotion were expanded during this period as well; they included outdoor ads, signs, packaging, and promotional material. As advertising grew, so did the opportunity for the expression of sexual themes and sexual content. Advances in photography and printing techniques contributed to the use of images in promotional messages among the array of communication avenues now available to advertisers.

TOBACCO

Sex was evident in advertising and promotional materials for tobacco products in the second half of the nineteenth century. Images of buxom young women—sometimes topless, sometimes with a low-cut neckline—adorned posters, flyers, and newspaper ads touting various brands and types of tobacco.

Tobacco, similar to other staples, was not a branded product until the 1850s. According to advertising historians Charles Goodrum and Helen Dalrymple, tobacco was literally "branded" for the first time when growers and producers took a branding iron and burned identifying labels into wood crates containing a particular tobacco.[7] Until then, tobacco was a simple commodity much like flour or sugar.

As branding progressed, images of women on promotional material became a point of distinction. Manufacturers associated their products with illustrations, and later mainly photographs, of attractive maidens. More often than not, the images featured illustrations of women with partially exposed breasts or the alluring draping of clothing that compelled the viewer's mind to complete the disrobing.

If not nude, images of women were designed to suggest the process of disrobing. Consider the label for Gentlemen's Delight tobacco which appeared in the 1870s (see fig. 2.2). Manufactured by B. H. Watson of Lynchburg, Virginia, the brand's image featured a beautiful dark-haired woman with a broken string of pearls. The woman is collecting her pearls in what appears to be either a seashell or a tobacco leaf. Much to any gentleman's delight, the attractive young woman is illustrated with her covering draped down off her shoulders, exposing her neck, shoulders, and upper arms.

The images typified by Pearl and Gentlemen's Delight certainly attracted attention. If you consider that smokers or users of tobacco were almost entirely men at the time, the images functioned to speak a language common among men. The images carried implicit messages about the tobacco brand. They said, we're associating ourselves with beauty, with attractive women, and with classical, yet subtle, allusions to sexuality as exemplified by the female figure.

Pipe tobacco, popular before the Civil War, gradually lost favor among

Figure 2.2: B. H. Watson's Gentlemen's Delight (1870s). "Gentlemen's Delight," Library of Congress, LC-USZ62-79320.

smokers and was replaced in popularity by cigars and chewing tobacco.[8] By the late 1870s, technology advanced to such a point that production of rolled cigarettes was possible. Methods of cigarette mass production increased so that a single machine could produce thousands of cigarettes a day. Someone who foresaw the potential of cigarettes and tapped the marketing with sexualized images was James Buchanan Duke.

W. DUKE, SONS & COMPANY

One of the first to recognize the market potential of cigarettes was James Buchanan Duke, president of what was to become a large American cigarette producer, W. Duke, Sons & Company. Duke discovered early that promotion was the key to growth and profits.

With advertising to increase awareness and price incentives to encourage purchases, Duke went from selling 30 million cigarettes in 1883 to 100 million cigarettes one year later.[9] By 1890, his company was the leading producer of cigarettes in the country. In the same year, Duke merged with four other companies to form the ruthless American Tobacco Company that dominated the tobacco industry until 1911, when it was broken up by government regulators.

As alluded to earlier, Duke placed small paper cards, or premiums, in cigarette packs. According to Patrick Porter, a Harvard University business historian, the cards featured "photographs or lithographs of buxom young ladies in what must have seemed very daring, if not shocking, costumes."[10] The women on the cards were identified as actresses or "women of the stage," and a common theme was sex appeal.

For example, card 346 featured the image of Leonda Jarcaw in an unladylike pose—considering the times (see fig. 2.3). Ms. Jarcaw's legs are crossed but she's reclining in a relaxed position. Her hands are resting behind her head and she's wearing a sleeveless top. More revealing, the photograph emphasizes the back and side of a hosed thigh for men's viewing pleasure, especially men who buy Duke's Cameo brand cigarettes.

Catching a glimpse of women posed like Ms. Jarcaw served as a purchase incentive since men were almost exclusively the buyers and consumers of tobacco products. For them, obtaining "girlie" images often served as enough inducement to buy a particular brand of cigarettes. Porter speculated that few of the actresses were recognizable to buyers.[11] For that reason, the aim of the incentives was to provide a small but pleasurable bonus to the purchaser.

In addition, purchasers were encouraged to buy packs until they completed a set, which often contained hundreds of cards. Some of the successful tobacco marketers encouraged consumers to complete a set of trading cards, which they could then mail to the company for another

Figure 2.3: Ms. Leonda Jarcaw. This card and many others were inserted into cigarette packs in the 1880s and 1890s as a sales induce-ment. W. Duke, Sons & Com-pany card (n.d.), "Ms. Leonda Jarcaw." Rare Book, Manu-script, & Spe-cial Collections Library, Duke University, Durham, North Carolina.

prize. The strategy was considered very successful and one of the reasons Duke's company became the leading cigarette maker by 1890.

Another card found in a pack of Kinney Brothers' Sweet Caporal cigarettes featured an enticing image of Mademoiselle Demongey (see fig. 2.4). The actress was photographed from the hips up standing between two curtains. She is smiling as she looks at the camera/viewer. She is positioned in such a way that her profile is accentuated, highlighting her breasts and small waist. Mlle. Demongey is clothed, but her dress is cut very low in front to reveal her bosom and deep cleavage. The image of the actress provides a few moments of "free" pleasure for any man purchasing a pack of Sweet Caporals.

A Duke card, numbered 334 in the set, features Eva Barrington. Ms. Barrington is photographed full-length so the viewer sees her back and right side. She is looking up and out of the frame, but viewers are treated to a shot of the backs of her legs. Ms. Barrington is wearing hose and a waistcoat that ends at her hips. The emphasis of the shot is clearly on her legs and derrière. So buyers will not forget who supplied the card, "Duke Cigarettes are the best. W. Duke, Sons & Co" is printed at the bottom of the card.

Other images feature women smoking, dancing, and posed in various positions. A collection at Duke University has over 1,770 premium cards displaying images of actresses as well as images of a series of famous landmarks and inventions.[12] According to Porter, "Advertising devices such as Duke's card sets removed the average citizen from his familiar surroundings and transported him to distant lands, or else they served to amuse, instruct, and divert him."[13] Aside from "Actresses," other sets of premium cards that featured women were labeled "Stars of the Stage," "American Stars," and "Gems of Beauty."

Not all men approved of the premium cards. James Duke's father, Washington Duke—the W. Duke in the company name—wrote a letter to his son protesting the use of trading cards that featured provocative starlets. In a the following letter dated October 17, 1894, W. Duke wrote:

My dear Son: I have received the enclosed letter from the Rev. John C. Hocutt, and am very much impressed with the wisdom of his argument against circulating lascivious photographs with cigarettes, and have made up my mind to bring the matter to your attention in the interest of

Figure 2.4: Mlle. Demongey for Sweet Caporal cigarettes (*front/back*). W. Duke & Sons card (n.d.), "Mlle. Demongey." Rare Book, Manuscript, & Special Collections Library, Duke University, Durham, North Carolina.

morallity [*sic*], and in the hope that you can invent a proper substitute for these pictures which will answer your requirements as an advertisement as well as an inducement to purchase. His views are so thoroughly and plainly stated that I do not know that I can add anything except to state that they accord with my own, and that I have always looked upon the distribution of this character of advertisement as wrong in its pernicious effects upon young man and womanhood, and therefore has not jingled with my religious impulses. Outside of the fact that we owe christianity all the assistance we can lend it in any form, which is paramount to any other consideration, I am fully convinced that this mode of advertising will be used and greatly strengthen the arguments against cigarettes in the legislative halls of the States. I hope you will consider this carefully and appreciate my side of the question. It would please me very much to know that a change had been made. Affectionately, your father, W. Duke[14]

Consider it a gentle fatherly scolding. At first it seems as if the elder Duke was concerned about the effects of sexualized trading cards on America's youth, as well as their eroding effects on religious fortitude. His last argument, however, may have contained his, or what he considered his son's biggest fear: that the premiums would cause such an uproar that members of Congress would be forced to take action, possibly by restricting the sale of cigarettes. W. Duke's protest nevertheless failed to dissuade James Duke or other tobacco marketers from using sexual images to sell their brands.

BUFFOS

Outdoor advertising featuring provocative images of women were also used to sell tobacco products like cigarettes and cigars. Consider the illustration in the poster for Columbia tobacco (see fig. 1.2). The poster featured an illustration of a woman sitting on top of the world with her breasts revealed—one completely—as she holds a tobacco plug. She served to grab attention and to differentiate David Dunlop's brand of tobacco from other brands.

Outdoor billboards were often very successful in 1898. One billboard in particular featured an image of what a magazine at the time described as a "very catchy picture of a dancing girl."[15] The image displayed an attractive woman lifting up her dress with both hands while she danced. Smiling, she appeared to be enjoying herself.

In an interview with *Display Advertising* in 1898, Mr. B. Keit, in charge of promotions and publicity for Buffos, described the Buffos girl campaign as very successful.[16] Buffos was an all-tobacco cigarette marketed by E. Seidenberg Stiefel & Company. Mr. Keit noted that the billboards were very effective in the "Far West," which included Colorado and California. The campaign also achieved great success in the Northeast. Mr. Keit described how the company contracted to have six hundred sixteen-sheets posted in

New York and Brooklyn. The campaign was so popular that it was repeated and copied by competitors. The observation was made that "men are always liberal spenders when their desires are to be appeased."[17] At the time of the interview, Mr. Keit was considering other poster designs, but since the Buffos girl had been used extensively producing great results, he was somewhat reluctant to change the design. He recounted how his company had recently posted billboards in Providence, Rhode Island, two or three days before his salesman was to arrive. The result was that Buffos was the talk of the town and sales were better than expected.

CORSET ADVERTISING

Tobacco was not the only product to contain sexual imagery in its marketing communications. Advertising for underwear was initiated during this time as well. As can be expected, advertising about underwear stirred some controversy. One of the earliest disagreements was whether an image of a person clothed only in underwear should be shown at all. This debate surrounded the precursor to contemporary women's underwear advertising—the corset.

Corsets, an early form of undergarment designed to provide support for the bust and compression of the waist, were de rigueur for women in the late 1800s. According to Valerie Steele, author of *Fashion and Eroticism*, corsets were widely used between 1840 and 1910. "Almost every woman, of all classes wore corsets in those times. Fashion was formed by the upper class, so they were the primary users of the 'fashion devices' like corsets and the crinoline, but even the working classes obeyed the trends of fashion to as high a degree as possible," writes Steele.[18] An 1897 magazine article called corsets an "indispensable article of women's wear."[19]

In the mid-nineteenth century, fashion styles, including corset-wear, were introduced in the royal courts of Paris and London. In 1842 corsets with lacing in the back were first produced. In the 1860s, hygienic corsets of rubber material were introduced. By the 1880s the corset style of a tinier waist and full, protruding bustline and rounded hips became the rage.[20] More innovations occurred in the 1890s because of changes in women's roles in society. Women were taking part in sports like tennis and bicycling, so manufacturers were clamoring to produce corsets that could accommodate women's active lifestyles. Despite changes in fabric engineering and the increase in corset manufacturers, women's figures still had to conform within a prescribed norm. According to M. Crawford and Elizabeth Guernsey in their book, *The History of Corsets,* the "pattern of the '90s shows the ideal figure had a 36-inch bust, 22-inch waist and 40-inch hip."[21]

By some accounts, Dr. Lucien C. Warner opened the door for advertising the corset with his lectures on the health preserving qualities—easier on the stomach and bowels—of his company's "Coraline" corset brand.[22] Warner's company, Warner Brothers (not to be confused with the Warner Brothers Studio), was to survive many years. Their first ad appeared in 1874 with the headline, "Dr. Warner's Sanitary Corset."[23] Manufacturers and marketers of corsets traditionally resorted to distributing information about their wares to store clerks in women's wear departments. The clerks would then distribute the information cards to women as they shopped for underwear. At the time, the subject of the corset was not mentioned in public amid so-called polite society by gentlemen and ladies.[24]

Corset cards were often quite colorful. The front would contain an image of the corset or a woman wearing a corset. Sometimes the front image contained only the manufacturer's name superimposed over an idyllic setting. The back of the card was printed in one ink and described the features and benefits of the particular corset. Similar to contemporary intimates ads, the cards touted benefits of increased attractiveness for the wearer as well as value and comfort. Corset ads eventually became a mainstay in fashion and women's oriented magazines, but not in general interest magazines. Large posters were introduced in the early to mid-1890s, whereas smaller posters had been used earlier.

Most corsets came in white, gray, or black and were priced at one dollar.[25] A variety of colors were available at a higher cost. Again, ads emphasized some of the same reasons to buy corsets as those for purchasing contemporary intimates. For example, ads for the Kabo Bust Perfector, a garment designed to be worn over a corset, touted its ability to enhance one's figure. The headline, "For smart dressers," appealed to women interested in being stylish. The copy in the ad attracted women concerned with bodily flaws: "Indispensable to ladies who lack perfect proportions, as it supplies every deficiency, conceals every imperfection." The garment's manufacturer, the Chicago Corset company, even boldly guaranteed the Kabo Bust Perfector would provide the wearer with a perfect bust or her money back.

Several manufacturers emphasized heath and thrift when advertising corsets. The back of a hand card featuring Ball's Health Preserving Corsets listed several reasons why women should buy Ball's: "They need no breaking in; Invalids can wear them with ease and comfort; They do not compress vital parts of the wearer; They have had the unqualified endorsement of every Physician who has examined them; They last twice as long as an ordinary Corset." The front of the card contained a colored illustration of a woman riding sidesaddle on a horse. A drawing of the corset was featured in the corner of the card. The card even listed the corset supplier, P. A. Brugh, Dry Goods & Notions, of Hagerstown, Maryland.

A principal debate among corset advertisers and manufacturers was about the way the corset was advertised.[26] The more liberalized view argued from the standpoint that ads were more effective if the image was of the woman clothed only in a corset. It held that displaying the corset allowed it to be shown in final form after it had been adjusted. For example, R & G Corset company of New York ran a half-page ad featuring a photograph of a model clad only in a corset (and a slip from the waist down; see fig. 2.5). The woman's arms are raised to demonstrate the effect of the corset on her form. The ad ran in the October 1898 issue of the *Delineator*, a fashion and fine arts journal aimed at women. The ad clearly demonstrates the use of real models clad in their intimate wear to sell corsets.

Similarly, Birdsey, Somers & Co. in New York City was one of the first firms to use coordinated billboard advertising for corsets.[27] One of the sheets for F. P. Corsets displays an image of a woman standing between two curtains clothed in a corset. She's pale, wearing a light-colored corset against a black background that highlights her form. Her breasts and the curve of her waist are directly in the center of the ad. On either side of her waist are the initials "F." and "P." The only other verbiage reads, "Create Handsome Forms."

On the other hand, some corset advertisers preferred to show the woman wearing clothing over the corset. The idea was that women could see the end result—the ultimate benefit of what a dress looked like over the

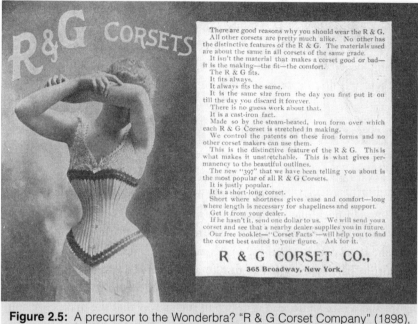

Figure 2.5: A precursor to the Wonderbra? "R & G Corset Company" (1898), Warshaw Collection of Business Americana, Archives Center, National Museum of American History, Smithsonian Institution, 0206062.

corset. According to an article in *Display Advertising*, "A neat, well-moulded, stylishly dressed form is believed to attract more attention than one in corset undress" (p. 6).

Mr. Miller, the advertising manager for the New York corset firm Langdon, Batcheller, and Company, est. 1856, contended that the female form in a dress is the most effective form of corset advertising. "I believe in the full-dressed figure every time, as it shows what a woman wants to know—how the corset will make her look." Miller continued, "There is nothing about a corset to show; it is not intended to show or to be shown, consequently but a few women, if any, would be interested in a picture of it" (p. 6).

Miller described one of the ads his firm developed: "It shows the effect of our 'glove-fitting' corset. A catchy, attractive figure, you see; just the effect a woman desires" (p. 7). The poster was dominated by an image of a woman fully dressed with a duster, possibly to allude to the mobility and ability to do housework allowed by "Glove-Fitting" Corsets. The dress, however, featured a low neckline accentuating the woman's bosom and displaying deep cleavage. The poster also contained a small image of the same woman clothed from the waist up only in a corset, despite Miller's saying that there was no purpose in showing it.

BEVERAGE ADVERTISING

Even ads for a wide array of beverages contained subtle instances of sexual content. Many times the promotional materials featured attractive women with low-cut necklines and curvaceous figures. For example, table top displays from 1892 for Moxie soda featured an attractive woman describing why she loves Moxie (see fig. 2.6). Moxie was a leader in soda sales around the turn of the century partly due to an aggressive advertising campaign and claims of medicinal powers. The illustrated women has an attractive figure and a nice smile, and is drawn in such a way that she makes eye contact with the viewer. The woman is sure to attract attention and add strength to Moxie sales.

Similarly, a slight tease was used in an ad for Excelsior Ginger Ale. The ad featured two young women preparing for a hot air balloon ride (see fig. 2.7). One maiden is in the capsule with the pilot, while the other woman gulps down the remnants of her ginger ale. The woman drinking soda appears to have the hem of her dress tangled on the ladder, which reveals her leg, a subtle tease for the year 1885. Both women are the centerpiece of the ad. Whereas the other prominent figures in the ad are wearing dark coats, the women are wearing light-colored dresses. Aside from the exposed leg, the bodices are low cut, revealing cleavage. Needless to say, the balloon's pilot was looking forward to his trip as he appears to wink at the viewer. What does the Excelsior ad say to consumers? Probably that people who drink its brand of ginger ale are fun, lively, and carefree. And that sensual women either drink Excelsior, or that a man can attract fun-loving young women with a bottle of the nonalcoholic beverage.

Promotional material for coffee contained instances of subtle sexuality as well. Consider the woman in the 1876 ad for Granulated 7 O'clock Breakfast Coffee (see fig. 2.8). She is presented as a somewhat suggestive

Figure 2.6: Moxie soda. "Moxie" (1892), Warshaw Collection of Business Americana, Archives Center, National Museum of American History, Smithsonian Institution, 02006058.

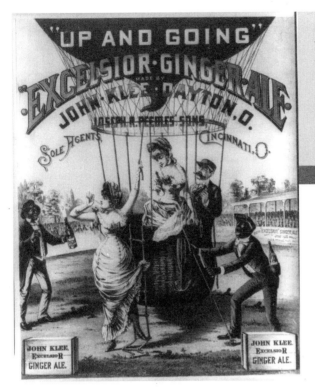

Figure 2.7: Two women prepare for a hot air balloon ride by drinking Excelsior Ginger Ale (1885). "Ginger Ale," Library of Congress, LC-USZ62-2588.

ornamental figure. At first glance she is covered in a drape, holding a cup of steaming coffee in one hand and a clock in the other. If one looks closely, the drape barely reveals the nipple of her left breast. The image provides a subtle taste of eye candy for those who are interested. It also continues the tradition of using images of women's breasts in early forms of promotional material. Since she presents a classical Grecian appearance, she resists viewers considering her risqué or uncouth.

Despite most of the examples in this chapter, sexual content isn't always centered on women's breasts. The situation depicted in the 1889 Bock's beer image is subtle but evokes sexual innuendo—sans the mountain goat (see fig. 2.9). The dapper gentleman is feeding his giddy and apparently light-headed fraulein with a pint of Bock's best. She's laughing as she sits on his lap, or rather, between his legs. At one level it's an image of a couple simply having a good time. This interpretation would suggest that Bock contributes to fun times. On the other hand, if it's assumed the couple is drinking beer, it's quite obvious that they are experiencing a nice

Figure 2.8: Granulated 7 O'clock Breakfast Coffee (1876). "Granulated Breakfast Coffee," Library of Congress, LCUSZ62-16777.

buzz and one thing will likely lead to another. He does have his left arm around her waist as he holds her close.

The Bock ad illustrates a theme carried through to contemporary alcohol advertising: that alcohol contributes to fun times, and if you want to be in a situation like the one in shown in the ad, pick up a few bottles of Bock. Whereas the image is subtle and viewers are responsible for piecing together the details, it is an instance of a lightly suggestive sexual ad.

LONDON GAIETY GIRLS OPERA

Not everyone was in favor of sexually suggestive images on public posters and outdoor displays. In 1897, the mayor and council in the little town of Mt. Vernon, New York enacted a form of censorship with regard to billboard content, primarily in response to posters exposing too much skin. The ad displays in question were theatrical posters for the London Gaiety Girls Opera Company featuring women kicking their legs high as they danced. According to a report of the incident in *Display Advertising*, an outdoor-advertising trade journal, "The brevity of attire in which these poster girls appeared and the abandon with which they kicked the cap off the board was too much."[28] All future displays had to be submitted to the mayor for

Figure 2.9: Bock beer (1889). "Bock," Library of Congress, LC-USZ62-59586.

approval. Those who flouted the new ordinance were fined ten dollars, enough in 1897 to be a deterrent.

PATTERSON COAL

Coal and sex? Coal and romance? S. J. Patterson's coal ad in the late nineteenth century was arguably able to make the connection between the warmth of an energy source and a romantic moment (see fig. 2.10). The ad features images of S. J. Patterson coal operations across the nation: stocking sheds in Cincinnati, and mining and shipping operations in the West. The ad also features images of miners, such as the one in the bottom right hand corner and one whom we may presume to be S. J. Patterson himself in the portrait centered in the upper center of the ad. More important, the corporate boasting is literally torn away to reveal an important benefit of Patterson coal—igniting courtship. The poster is split and rolled back to show a young man wooing a young lady in the warmth of a coal fire. Unfortunately for them, their amorous activities have drawn the attention of what is undoubtedly the young woman's father.

The Patterson ad demonstrates the array of Patterson coal operations, but the centerpiece is the romantic image of a couple, a man trying to wedge his way into a woman's heart. The image serves to pique the reader's interest as well as demonstrate one of the benefits of Patterson coal. It says

Figure 2.10: A romantic image is at the heart of this S. J. Patterson Wholesale Coal ad (n.d.). "S. J. Patterson," Library of Congress, LC-USZ62-4848

that you too may be able to warm yourself by the fire as you ignite the sparks of romance, hopefully without a parental intrusion.

CONCLUSION

The expansion and modernization of American advertising and printing technology contributed to the opportunity for sexual themes and content to surface. Enhancement of printing techniques, as well as color techniques and photographs, enabled the mass production of pages in print publications; this provided an important tool for communicating sexual imagery in conjunction with branded products.

What type of sexual content was present in ads? Practically without exception, it was the female form. Images of women adorned brands in all manner of promotional material. Sexualized images appeared in boxes (cigarette cards), on packaging (tobacco labels), posters, billboards, handbills, and print ads. Occasionally the images were of topless women. Sometimes the women were clothed but their busts and curvaceous figures were emphasized. Often, ads included images of fully clothed but young, smiling, and physically attractive women.

Before these ads, images of female busts appeared in art, on the bows of ships, and painted signs for many years. For many products, sexual images served only to adorn the brand. Mass production of images was available and inexpensive, so why not borrow the allure of a beautiful woman for the product? At the very least, sexual imagery served to direct the attention of a burgeoning consumer mass market toward one's brand. It also helped that men were the target audience for many of these products, especially tobacco and beverages. For corset advertising it is simple. Images of attractive women served to demonstrate the performance of the corset.

Change continued, and so did the evolution of American society as one century ended and another one began. Women became more active in roles inside and outside the home, engaging in sports, activism for women's suffrage, and the workforce. How these changes are reflected in the first twenty-five years of the twentieth century are discussed in the next chapter.

3
Passion Plays
1900–1925

"Askin you love to touch," cooed a 1915 magazine advertisement for Woodbury's Facial Soap. The full-page ad, similar to the Pond's ad in figure 3.1, contained a beautiful illustration and an instructive block of copy. Working together, both elements provided reasons why women should consider buying Woodbury's soap. For one, the illustration features an attractive upper-class couple in a affectionate embrace. The handsome beau, dressed in formal eveningwear, tenderly places his face next to that of his female companion as he holds her close. Exuding a cool confidence, the woman looks at the viewer as if to say, "See what I have."

The copy informed women that they too could have beautiful skin, even if their skin was colorless, sallow, coarse textured, or excessively oily. The copy outlined a regimen of treatment with Woodbury's soap that included rubbing an ice cube on one's face for a minute-and-a-half after every wash—to rejuvenate skin and provide women with the benefits of "a skin you love to touch." Although this benefit was explicitly stated, the illustration and copy worked together to allow readers to piece together the intended meaning. For those so moved, they could send ten cents to the Andrew Jergens Company (Woodbury's parent company) for a reproduction of the illustrated image.

Radiance

The hostess who breathes charm, happiness and hospitality upon her guests, who radiates the spirit of well being and contentment, must be sure of herself and her appearance.

No matter how perfect her surroundings or how delightful her manner, if her complexion is not as perfect as she can make it, she loses one of her chief powers of attraction and is conscious of a lack of something vital. The consistent use of

POND'S Extract Company's

VANISHING CREAM

will aid substantially in making your skin soft and velvety. It has a soothing and refreshing influence on the skin and should be applied to your face, arms and neck at least once or twice a day.

No matter how dry and tight the skin may be as a result of strain and fatigue, sun or wind burn, Pond's Vanishing Cream will afford relief.

Prepare for entertaining by applying Pond's Vanishing Cream lightly, and give to your skin the lovely finish that makes it a delight to look upon.

Free sample tube on request or send 4c for large trial tube—enough for two weeks. Pond's Extract Company, 159 Hudson St., New York.

Pond's Extract

A splendid lotion for cuts, bruises and burns—an absolute necessity in every home—keep a bottle on hand for safety's sake. Trial bottle for 4c to cover postage. *Also Talcum, Cold Cream, Tooth Paste, Soap.*

Figure 3.1: This Pond's Vanishing Cream ad titled "Radiance" extolled the virtues of a clear complexion (1914). Chesebrough-Ponds ad, "Radiance." Domestic Advertising Collection, J. Walter Thompson Company Archives, Hartman Center for Sales, Advertising & Marketing History, Rare Book, Manuscript, & Special Collections Library, Duke University, Durham, North Carolina. Pond's Vanishing Cream ad reproduced courtesy of Unilever PLC and Unilever N.V. or their subsidiaries, copyright holders.

The ad is remarkable because it exemplifies a sensual appeal that is still employed in contemporary advertising. It is a pitch that says, "You too can obtain love, intimacy, and all the wonderful accoutrements of a grand romance if you simply buy and use our brand." More notable, it was an appeal written and developed by women for women and based on a new concept—consumer research. Female agency employees not only went door-to-door asking women about soap preferences, they posed as shop girls in boutiques to observe women's soap purchases. The goal of this newfangled research was to discover who needed what products and the benefits consumers were seeking. The results of this research were then used to construct compelling ad appeals. One of these women included Helen Lansdowne Resor, a copywriter for J. Walter Thompson, the agency that developed the Woodbury appeal, "A Skin you love to touch."

AMERICA AT THE TURN OF THE CENTURY

Often referred to as the beginning of America's modern era, the commencement of the twentieth century was a time of continued growth and progress. As America entered its modern era, change was constant and the use of imagination was limitless. The first twenty-five years were particularly remarkable. America began the century without flight, but within twenty-five years commercial airline service was available. In 1899 the combustion engine was finding its way onto a contraption with wheels, but by 1925 American car makers had produced over 15 million automobiles. Women were unable to vote in 1900, but in 1917 the first woman was elected to Congress, and in 1920 the Nineteenth Amendment was ratified granting women the right to vote. These were a few of truly sweeping changes that marked the first few years of the twentieth century.

Socially and culturally, these years were ones of contradiction. Prohibition of alcohol was instituted in 1919, yet the Ziegfeld Follies first hit the stage in 1907, as did the Charleston in 1923.[1] While prohibition reflected a return to "morality," the Follies and Charleston represented its unraveling. In the same quarter century, e.e. cummings's first collection of poems was published, and W. C. Handy in 1912 introduced the blues to mainstream culture with his recording, *Memphis Blues*. America was flexing muscle abroad as it entered and helped the Allies win the First World War and workers completed construction of the Panama Canal in 1914.

At home business was booming. In 1900, the United States became the world leader in overall productivity.[2] The U.S. was first in iron and steel production, and soon produced up to one-third of goods in the world. As commerce grew, limits were beginning to be placed on business and its excesses. Several trusts, including Standard Oil and American Tobacco, were forced to restructure. The precursor to the Food and Drug Administration was established in 1906, and the Federal Trade Commission was established in 1914. Upton Sinclair's *The Jungle*, published in 1906, served to expose unsanitary practices and working conditions in the meat packing industry, and ultimately led to important reforms. Although America's economy was expanding at an ever accelerating pace, working conditions, wages, and competitive opportunities struggled to catch up.

MEDIA AND ADVERTISING

On the media front, several new innovations (e.g., silent movies and radio) worked alongside established media. Newspapers continued their competitive struggle for readers though they enjoyed higher and higher numbers of readers as cities continued to grow through immigration and urbanization. In 1910, for example, almost 9 million immigrants entered the U.S., mainly from Europe.[3] They amassed in cities already teeming with newly arrived immigrants. The Great Migration began in 1914, marking the beginning of the African-American movement from Southern rural areas to Northern cities in search of employment. These events created ever larger concentrated markets that made advertising in cities more profitable.

Magazines began the century as a luxury item but soon lowered their subscription costs to ten cents, making them available to the masses. As a result, magazine circulations could be counted in the hundreds of thousands and millions. Magazines benefited national advertisers by bringing attention to their products across the country. Two successful magazines launched during these years include *Time* and the *New Yorker*.

New media converged on the American scene. In 1905, the first movie house was built in Pittsburgh; admission was a nickel. Radio was also emerging as a communication source. The Radio Corporation of America, RCA, was founded in 1919, and the first commercial radio station, KDKA, began broadcasting in 1920. Advertisers made use of these new media. For example, Warner Brothers Company, the corset manufacturer, distributed short films to movie theaters about its corsets, and advertisers sponsored radio programs.

Advertising evolved as well. As new products spilled into the market, many of them competing with existing products, consumers had to be provided with compelling reasons to buy particular brands. As such, advertising evolved from an information orientation (just the facts) to one of creating value for brands—a persuasion-based orientation. Brands that utilized the value approach during this period are household names today: Hoover Vacuum Cleaners, Morton Salt, Kellogg's, Formica, and Kleenex. Others included Gillette, Coca-Cola, Eastman Kodak, and Kotex.

A few of the pioneer advertising professionals who created this transformation include John E. Kennedy, Claude Hopkins, Elmo Elkins, and Albert Lasker.[4] Hopkins and Kennedy were writers who believed consumers should be provided with "reasons why" they should buy products. This involved going one step further than merely describing product attributes. Consumers would be more compelled to buy a product over its competition only if they knew how that product bettered their lives more than its competitors. Advertisers therefore wrote rich copy describing brand benefits, but something was needed to draw in the viewer, and Elkins provided that piece to the puzzle. Elkins believed that advertising should be more visually enticing than it had been, so he increased the use of appealing illustrations, color, and tasteful layouts. Manufacturers were going to large agencies, many of them based in Chicago and New York, to perform these services in order to better sell their products.

PERFECTION AND ROMANCE

Advertising is about communicating ideals: what we want to be like, whom we want to be with, and what we want to have. Advertising paints a picture of our dreams and aspirations, and positions brands as a means to those ends. One dream that advertisers tried to appeal to during this era was to women's success. Not career success mind you, but marrying successfully and building a family. To achieve this dream, women were told they first had to appear lovely and youthful so they could attract a man—or an array of men to choose from. Naturally, brands that could claim to help women accomplish these goals did so. Advertisers used images and copy, emphasizing courtship, romance, and adoration.

During this period, the importance of courtship was viewed as a necessary means for marriage and family. Consider the following explanation provided to women by Havelock Ellis, a recognized authority on sex in the early half of the twentieth century: "Every act of sexual union is preceded by a process of courtship. There is sound physiological reason for this courtship, for in the act of wooing and being wooed the psychic excitement gradually generated in the brains of the two partners acts as a stimulant to arouse into full activity the mechanism which ensures sexual union and aids ultimate impregnation. Such courtship is thus a fundamental natural fact."[5] Ellis's exposition, *The Love Rights of Women*, meant to educate women about sexual issues, but it also served to reinforce notions of the era's gender roles.

Advertisers addressed related needs as well. One involved maintaining a youthful appearance. Those who did so would be admired for their beauty by men and women alike. Though very subtly alluded to, sex was also addressed. Women, once married, would desire sexual intimacy, as well as the need to be touched, caressed, and stimulated. Any ad that showed a man sensitively attending to, and enamored with a woman, played to that desire.

Advertising championed a host of products to help women achieve their desired relationship goals. Needs for family, beauty, and sexual intimacy were foremost. What better way to help women realize their aspirations than with beautification? Soaps, lotions, and other toiletries were sold as conduits to help women achieve these dreams.

WOODBURY'S FACIAL SOAP

The story of Woodbury's Facial Soap is important because it exemplifies the changes that were taking place at the turn of the century, especially in regard to advertising. It's a story in which sagging sales were reversed when all else had failed. Through research, empathy, positioning, and an emphasis on romance and intimacy, the J. Walter Thompson agency of Chicago reestablished Woodbury's as a superbrand.

Woodbury's Facial Soap had enjoyed success since its introduction in 1885. The product was peddled as a premium soap that could be used to cleanse the entire body, even the scalp. It also touted itself as a complexion enhancer. Demand for the product grew until 1897, when sales became static and eventually declined. In 1900 Woodbury's was sold to Andrew Jergens Company for $250,000.[6] Executives at Jergens initially thought they had gotten a steal.

By the turn of the century, Andrew Jergens Company was one of the leading manufacturers and marketers of soap and associated toiletries.[7] Jergens was on the move, aggressively seeking opportunities to increase profits and take advantage of its elaborate distribution network. Jergens had its eye on Woodbury's and purchased it after Woodbury's sales began to fall. Brand recognition was still strong, but Woodbury's market niche had become saturated. It was priced at twenty-five cents per bar, much more than comparable soaps selling in the nickel and dime range. A year later, in 1901, Jergens purchased the lotion manufacturer Robert Eastman Company. The new acquisition provided a smooth white lotion that would later be known as Jergens Lotion. Sales of the lotion quickly took off, but Woodbury soap sales continued to languish. Something was amiss, and sales of the brand with so much promise disappointed managers at Jergens.

Despite a series of efforts, sales of Woodbury's continued to decline for fourteen consecutive years. Jergens was exasperated, since all means of reversing the negative sales trend had been attempted to little avail. First, an advertising agency was hired. The agency repositioned Woodbury's as an inexpensive medicinal skin cure.[8] Ad images featured "neckless heads" and ad copy describing litanies of awful symptoms. When it was clear that this approach wasn't working, the agency reversed its approach. Instead of emphasizing maladies and bodiless heads, ads were constructed to be beautiful and pleasing. New ads featured images of attractive women, intricate hand-styled lettering, and other artistic elements. The result? Sales continued to decline.

The agency was eventually fired and the business was given to a media-owned organization. The media company, Street Railways Advertising

Company, figured it had the answer. The first year it had the account, in 1906, all advertising expenditures were placed where? You guessed it—ads were placed on street cars. The result was another sales decline.

Burned by the street car move, Jergens decided to go it alone. It hired an advertising manager and primed the advertising pump. He invested hundreds of thousands of dollars in advertising over a three-year period. A range of advertising maneuvers and sales promotion activities were inaugurated, but nothing seemed to work. Even the commission paid to salesmen was increased to 10 percent, a sizable portion at the time, but that didn't work either. In 1909 alone, approximately $253,000 was invested to advertise Woodbury's soap.[9] This was more than had been paid for the Woodbury name nine years earlier. The results were not good. The sales curve continued south. It seemed the more Jergens tried to turn the tide, the worse the result.

By 1910, Cuticura, the only similarly priced competitor, was outselling Woodbury's more than twenty to one. According to agency records, "Woodbury's became known to the trade as dead."[10] This meant that wholesalers and distributors, as well as buyers for drugstores and markets, considered Woodbury's a lost cause.

Faced with the steady decline, Jergens executives came close to believing what was said in the trade. In what it may have considered a futile effort, Jergens awarded the J. Walter Thompson (JWT) agency the Woodbury's business in 1910. It wasn't much of an opportunity, however. Jergens allocated only $25,000 for advertising that year, less than 10 percent of its allocation the year before. With scrappy persistence and a few tricks up its sleeve, those working at JWT did the unimaginable—they stopped the Woodbury bloodletting.

What did they do? JWT followed an advertising method similar to that used today. One of the first things they did was commit six months to researching all facets of the brand. They interviewed "modern authorities on the skin and its needs."[11] These specialists included a skin cancer physician and a range of healthcare professionals which probably included dermatologists and cosmetologists. As a result, writers at JWT came to understand the leading methods and procedures at the time for caring for one's skin. After researching the cleansing method, JWT initiated intensive consumer research. Some of the female employees went to shops, pretending to be sales clerks so they could observe which skin care products women were buying and why. In addition, door-to-door interviews were conducted to discover how women cared for their skin and what they wanted in a facial soap.[12]

What JWT discovered was that skincare for the masses was still a relatively new concept. Women practiced a wide range of cleansing procedures, and apparently most women didn't know how to care for their skin.[13] Armed with its research findings, those at JWT had a good idea who would constitute Woodbury's target audience: middle- and upper-class women ages sixteen to sixty. It also discovered how best to reach them, and most important, what they needed to see and hear to get their attention and compel them to action.

The advertising strategy culminated in a two-pronged approach. The copy strategy was designed to instruct women how to wash and care for their faces. This provided value to women and helped to position Woodbury's against its competitors. The campaign provided a series of cleansing treatments meant to alleviate common skin problems identified in the research. Each ad contained a prescription for clearing up some form of skin condition, whether it be blackheads, sallowness, or oily skin. The following passage from internal agency documents describes the copy strategy: "Woodbury advertising...present[ed] to women throughout the country, the important facts, based on the best scientific authority, as to the nature and working of their skin; the vital necessity, to a healthy skin, of proper cleansing; the cause of common skin defects...; and the way in which these defects can be overcome, by the right cleansing methods."[14]

The second approach entailed embedding the instructions within a strong emotional appeal.[15] Appeals revolved around the desire to be beautiful and to enjoy beauty's amorous outcomes. As such—and the female writers understood this point well—the appeal emphasized the benefits of beauty: what beautiful women have and what beautiful women are able to possess. As always, beauty and its effects were just out of the average women's reach. That is, unless they used Woodbury's. Furthermore, everyone knows that beautiful women attract men with means. Women in this period thought so, and the ad played up this belief with images of fashionable men and women in luxurious settings and stylish clothes.

The emotional appeal was described in agency files as one that "graphically depicted the ultimate benefit resulting from the use of Woodbury's, an appeal selling masculine admiration and feminine envy as much as the product."[16] It went on to say that it was really selling "beauty, and the love, envy and admiration which beauty engenders." In a letter to Stanley Resor written in 1929, Howard Henderson, the manager of JWT's Cincinnati office, described past Woodbury's ads as follows: "An analysis of Woodbury advertising since 1911 reveals three essential elements. (a) A romantic man and woman situation with sex appeal dominant, focused on 'the skin you love to touch.' (b) Woodbury's Facial Soap as the key to this more desirable charm. (c) The famous Woodbury treatments as specific methods of over-coming skin defects which shut the door of love and romance against a woman."[17]

After tremendous success, Woodbury's sales began to drop off by 1929. Based on his review, Henderson advocated continuing the emphasis on these elements, except perhaps in a more modern way. He firmly believed that, as in the past, Woodbury's ads should "rouse a feeling of romance in the reader, by dramatizing largely through the illustration, a man and woman in ardent pose."[18]

Another Woodbury's ad that appeared in March 1928 contains the elements of JWT's creative approach. The headline proclaims, "Youth and Love. Keep them by keeping a beautiful skin." It also contains some of the results of research JWT conducted in 1923. The agency conducted a very extensive study, asking some of the most admired women in America what facial soap they used.[19] Those most "admired" and socially "valued" women included college girls at Vassar, Brown, Bryn Mawr, and the University of California, among others. Debutantes across the country were interviewed, as well as women of the New York City Junior League and other exclusive women's clubs. They even got the lists of women who had stayed at exclusive resorts. The research revealed that most of these women used Woodbury's, and JWT emphasized it for all it was worth. Campaigns emphasized the fact that young debutantes used Woodbury's: the "loveliest girls in America" at some of the most prestigious women's colleges use Woodbury's. If you want to be more like them, and have what they have, use Woodbury's.

What were the results of JWT's campaigns? For one, the research and execution paid off. With $25,000 the agency was able to stabilize Woodbury's sales the first year. In a little over fifteen years, the advertising approach developed by JWT, which included continuous research, not only expanded the market for facial soaps but had made Woodbury's a leader in its price category.[20] Female consumers rewarded the brand for its expertise and helpfulness. Woodbury's began to enjoy an enviable market position that spawned several imitators. The appeal and approach initiated by JWT for Woodbury's was copied many times, especially for other women's products.

National campaigns for Woodbury's were centralized in women's magazines, while local campaigns relied on newspapers. For example, ads in 1914 ran in twenty-one magazines and twenty-one newspapers.[21] In 1919, JWT ran over 105 full-page Woodbury's ads, including fifty color ads and eighteen back covers. Thirteen color ads and two back covers were run in the *Saturday Evening Post* alone. Ads also appeared in over 183 newspapers that year. The previous year, 231 newspapers were used with a total combined circulation of 217 million. With this much exposure, it's clear women were certain to be familiar with Woodbury's and its benefits.

The campaigns and the appeals embodied in Woodbury's ads exemplified the new use of consumer research to understand the product, the market, and the consumer. It also exemplified the value of conducting product research so that the agency could fully familiarize itself with the marketing situation and possibilities. Most important, however, the Woodbury's story shows how consumer research could be used to build compelling copy appeals that were well-written and persuasive. Advertisers were beginning to see the purpose of emotional benefits articulated in a combination of words and images, saying in essence: "We know what you want. If you use our product, we'll help you get it."

JERGENS LOTION

Sales of Jergens Lotion had been brisk since the beginning. To further the lotion's success, Jergens, in 1922, placed its first national ad in *Ladies Home Journal*.[22] Response to the first ad proved positive and Jergens Lotion appeared in more magazines. By the next year, $84,000 was invested in magazine advertising for Jergens Lotion. These ads featured attractive women in nightgowns and eveningwear pitching the lotion that softens and moistens their skin.

True to form for ads of this period, a Jergens Lotion ad featured a dominant image of an attractive couple in a tender pose. He's resting his mouth against her temple and his fingers on her cheek. She displays her well-lotioned left hand against her fiancée's face. Similar to the Woodbury's ad described earlier, she too looks confidently at the camera. The romantic image is framed with the intriguing headline, "Hands can be so thrilling!"

Hmmm. Thrilling for whom, I wonder. Thrilling for him when he's touched with her soft and youthful hands? Or is he simply thrilled because he's being touched? I hate to imagine what runs through his mind when his fiancée touches him with chapped hands. Is it thrilling for *her* because she wants to touch him only when she feels comfortable with the condition of her hands? One can only imagine what thrills are in store for this couple after readers flip the page.

At the risk of carrying their message too far, Jergens positioned itself in this ad as a vital element in the intimacy equation. Its lotion is offered as the spark, the grease, or what have you, that facilitates romance and the thrill it engenders. It eliminates old-looking hands, hands that for any number of reasons can keep people from experiencing the love and closeness they need and truly desire.

Jergens soon extended its love pitch to radio. Beginning in the 1930s, Jergens Lotion became a sponsor for the popular Walter Winchell radio program.[23] For sixteen years Winchell's signature sign-off at the end of his program began, "With lotions of love…" As a result, Jergens maintained its strong dominance in the lotion and cream category—a dominance that remained unchallenged for many years.

POND'S

Pond's, a leading manufacturer and marketer of skin creams and tonics, also used the romance and adoration formula that had been developed for Woodbury's. In a quarter-page ad that appeared in November 1914 (see fig. 3.1), Pond's touted its Vanishing Cream as a means to attractiveness and male attention. The black-and-white ad featured a dinner party scene in which two well-heeled men gaze approvingly at the hostess. Her smile attests to the fact that she's enjoying the attention she is receiving.

The ad's copy serves to couple the illustration and the intended benefit of regular use of Pond's cream. The simple one-word headline, "Radiance," describes the cream's effect. Regular applications on the face, arms, and neck gives women a "lovely finish that makes your skin a delight to look upon." Women are delicately told that despite their sparkling personalities, superior intellects, and comfortable manner, they aren't going to get the right kind of man. The ad's writer tells women the essential element that draws men's attraction is the appearance of their skin. "No matter how perfect her surroundings or how delightful her manner, if her complexion is not as perfect as she can make it, she loses one of her chief powers of attraction." Women were sure to get this message over and over again. This particular ad ran in *Ladies World, Etude,* and *Women's Home Companion.* It likely ran elsewhere and with much repetition. At the very least, this ad exemplifies other appeals used to sell Pond's Vanishing Cream.

The "Radiance" ad was a sharp departure from some of Pond's earliest ads. A small ad that ran thirty-nine years before was totally devoid of any romantic element. The bold headline contained only four words: "HORSE EPIDEMIC AND INFLUENZA." The ad looked like other tonic and patent medicine ads of its era. It was devoid of any attractive illustrations and mentioned several undesirable health conditions. "Pond's Extract cures coughs, colds, sore lungs, [etc]. . . . It is *invaluable* in *livery stables.* No *Railroad men, Breeders, Trainers,* or any one having the care of horses can afford to be without it. *All* have tried it, and successfully recommend it."[24]

Pond's Extract was the company's original product. In 1846, Theron T. Pond, a chemist, found a way to extract elements from bark of the witch hazel scrub.[25] He combined it with alcohol and marketed it as a dressing for minor cuts and abrasions, analogous to modern-day Bactine. It relieved pain, cleaned the wound, and promoted healing. Similar to other remedies at the time, Pond's Extract claimed to cure a number of ailments. For example, an ad from 1881 proclaimed that Pond's controlled all forms of hemorrhages, whether of blood or mucous origin. Soon, the Extract line was diversified with toilet cream, ointments, and salves.[26]

Early advertising efforts consisted of placing printed advertising cards in drugstores and distributing booklets containing product testimonials. In 1886, JWT began handling the account, and it initiated Pond's first national campaign.[27] JWT won an award for its Pond's Girl advertising

After the Bath
Pond's Extract
Company's
Vanishing Cream

should be gently applied with the tips of the fingers. Some kinds of cream require violent massage, which temporarily seems to benefit — but ultimately injures the tissues. Vanishing Cream immediately sinks into the skin—vanishes—and nourishes it.

Vanishing Cream is the purest, most efficacious and most delightfully fragrant cream made. It conforms to the same peerless standard of quality which characterizes all the Pond's Extract Company's Products.

In order that you may

Test these Products
at Our Expense

we will be very glad to send upon receipt of your name and address, and the name and address of your dealer, a sample of the Vanishing Cream or Pond's Extract. If you wish an extra large sample of Vanishing Cream, it will be sent upon receipt of 4 cents in stamps.

Why not try the other Pond's Extract Company Products—Tooth Paste, Talcum Powder, Cold Cream, Soap, etc.?

Pond's Extract
"The Standard for 60 Years"

The oldest product of the Pond's Extract Company, first produced in 1846, should be in every household for use in emergency, particularly for those everyday injuries, such as cuts, bruises, burns, etc.

The Pond's Extract Company
Dept. A, 131 Hudson St., New York

Figure 3.2: "Pardon me as I reach for my Pond's." This ad, appearing in 1910, featured an unclothed, but covered, model. Chesebrough-Ponds ad, "After the Bath." Domestic Advertising Collection, J. Walter Thompson Company Archives, Hartman Center for Sales, Advertising & Marketing History, Rare Book, Manuscript, & Special Collections Library, Duke University, Durham, North Carolina. Pond's Extract ad reproduced courtesy of Unilever PLC and Unilever N.V. or their subsidiaries, copyright holders.

Figure 3.3: Pond's Extract (1911). Chesebrough-Ponds ad, "Toilet Necessity." Domestic Advertising Collection, J. Walter Thompson Company Archives, Hartman Center for Sales, Advertising & Marketing History, Rare Book, Manuscript, & Special Collections Library, Duke University, Durham, North Carolina. Pond's Extract ad reproduced courtesy of Unilever PLC and Unilever N.V. or their subsidiaries, copyright holders.

campaign in 1904. The ads featured images of attractive young women. The illustrations were held up as examples of smooth, clear skin.

Sometimes, women in Pond's ads were present only to attract attention or to demonstrate a usage context for the product. For example, an ad running in 1910 featured an unclothed, though covered, woman in her bathroom (see fig. 3.2). The ad is suggesting another use for Pond's Vanishing Cream, that it be used immediately after bathing. The woman is reaching for her bottle of cream as she covers herself with a towel. Interestingly, she's illustrated so that she's making eye contact with the viewer. It's almost as if the viewer has walked in on her, but she isn't protesting. On another note, similar to other Pond's cream ads at the time, a pitch for Pond's Extract is included.

Far from "Horse Influenza," the 1911 ad for Pond's Extract displays a photograph of a smiling woman coddling a bottle of Extract (see fig. 3.3). The model is sitting at her vanity in her underwear. Yes, that's what underwear looked like in 1911. What's the appeal in the ad? Just to have a bottle handy for guests. They can wash up with it or use it to relieve their sunburns, mosquito bites, and irritation caused by chafing.

These ads supplemented Pond's appeals that featured attraction and romance. A 1916 Pond's cream ad appearing in *Vogue* minced no words about the benefits of being attractive. The ad depicted an illustration of a woman sitting in the middle of four male suitors. The headline hammered home the message, "What a man looks for in a girl." Like all good advertising, it provided a description of a treatment regimen—very similar to those in Woodbury's ads—and the line, "How you can acquire a charm that has universal appeal." The key to love was simple: cultivate a clear complexion—with Pond's of course.

Pond's ran a variety of ads over many years. The ones I've highlighted are representative of its marketing approach at the time. The company has been very successful throughout the years, especially during the first few decades of the twentieth century. Like Woodbury's and many other toilet and beauty brands at the time, appeals targeted to women about perfection resonated with full effect.

Innovations in manufacturing, technology, and consumer chemistry resulted in a plethora of new skincare and cleansing products. To market these products advertisers unearthed a need they exploited as best they knew how—the need to be attractive and to be loved. Then, as now, tremendous value is placed on women's outward appearance. Products were simply positioned as a mechanism for enhancing a woman's perceived value. Once she had it in her grasp, she too could experience the intimacy, romance, and adoration every girl dreams of.

ADVERTISING WOMEN'S INNERWEAR

Hosiery

Changes in fashion and style are reflected in advertising. An area relevant to sex in advertising is the development of promotional material for hosiery and silk stockings. Showing women's stockinged legs in advertising proved to be something of a challenge because women's legs were seldom seen in public until hemlines began to rise in the 1920s. Despite the dictates of polite society, advertisers presented the product as it was meant to be worn.

At the turn of the century, many hosiery and stocking producers existed. A directory of hosiery manufacturers published in 1883 listed over 560 in the United States.[28] These manufacturers were heavily concentrated in the Northeast. For example, over 200 were located in New York, and 150 were based in Philadelphia.

According to ad historians Charles Goodrum and Helen Dalrymple, by the 1920s silk stockings were available to the masses. Actually, mainstream advertising for silk hose appeared much earlier. In 1903 a full-page ad for Onyx Hosiery graced the pages of the April 25 issue of *Town & Country* magazine (see fig. 3.4). Even then, images of women lifting their hems to show off their stockings were available to the public. A full-page ad for McCallum Hosiery Company of Northampton, Massachusetts appeared in 1911. The ad featured the image of the "madam" of the house sitting cross-legged in her petticoat. The maid was readying the madam's hair for the day. According to the ad, the most expensive pair of McCallum's silk hose was priced at two dollars. Basic styles were available for half that amount. The appeal in these ads was that women could have well-made hose at low prices.

Figure 3.4: In 1903, women raised their hems to display the wide selection of Onyx silk hose. "Onyx Hose," Warshaw Collection of Business Americana, Archives Center, National Museum of American History, Smithsonian Institution, 02006060.

Although they weren't just selling hose, Holeproof Hosiery Company ran a massive campaign during the 1910 Christmas shopping season. It ran full-page color newspaper ads in the twenty-six largest metropolitan areas.[29] In addition, it placed a full-page and in many consumer magazines, among them the *Saturday Evening Post* with a circulation close to two million. Holeproof's ad campaign wasn't its first, and it's likely that other hosiers were advertising prodigiously in the first decade of the twentieth century.

Also according to Goodrum and Dalrymple, the first ad to show the back of a woman's knee was published in 1925. Up until then, the back of the knee was said to be as taboo in advertising as pubic hair is today.[30] A Holeproof Hosiery ad published in 1922 comes rather close (see fig. 3.5). The ad depicts a young woman clothed in a sheer slip bending over to admire her hose. The back of her knee is certainly visible, as is the middle of her thigh. The full-page color ad appearing in *Scribner's* is beautiful as it

Figure 3.5: Holeproof Hosiery (1922).
"Holeproof," Warshaw Collection of Business Americana, Archives Center,
National Museum of American History, Smithsonian Institution, 02006061.

displays the peacock's plume. There may be an even earlier image of the back of a woman's knee, but it has yet to be unearthed.

Manufacturers even advised retailers to use sexy clerks to promote business. In 1910 Holeproof encouraged retailers to contact women's civic organizations to set up a one-day fundraising event. An arrangement was to be made so that a chunk of a day's sales proceeds would go to charity if the organization provided "popular young women" to work as sales clerks. "The men will also be attracted, on account of the clerks. If you can secure the most beautiful young women for the day, so much the better."[31] Such was the belief in the early days of the commercial power of attractive women.

Corsets

Corset styles were continually changing in the first two decades of the twentieth century, and advertising reflected these variations. The century began with women wearing heavy corsets supported by whalebone and steel. A dominant ad appeal at this time was that "our brand is rustproof." One need only imagine wearing rusty underwear to gauge the power of *that* advertised benefit.

Conformity to style contributed to the need to maintain an "appropriate" figure. But corset styles continued to change as each season brought a new look. The top of the corset moved up or down, as did the waistline. Technological improvements and new innovations also resulted in style preference changes, sometime overnight. According to one account of the fluctuating corset trade, "millions of dollars worth of corsets on merchants' shelves and in manufacturers' stocks, were rendered obsolete in a few month's time."[32] The testimonial ad in figure 3.6 illustrates the change in corset styles from rear-laced to front-laced corsets. Olga Petroby, perhaps a well-known celebrity at the time, wrote the H. W. Gossard Company to state that she was against front-laced corsets until she wore one made by Gossard. The ad is dominated by a photograph of Miss Petroby, presumably wearing her new-style corset under her stylish dress.

By 1912, Warner, the largest American corset and brassiere manufacturer in the world, demonstrated its belief in advertising. The company ran large-scale campaigns to sell its innerwear. According to company docu-

Figure 3.6: An endorsement for H. W. Gossard Company's new front-laced corset (1916). H. W. Gossard "Olga Petroby." Domestic Advertising Collection, J. Walter Thompson Company Archives, Hartman Center for Sales, Advertising & Marketing History, Rare Book, Manuscript, & Special Collections Library, Duke University, Durham, North Carolina.

To The H. W. Gossard Co.
Flushing, L. I.,
March 1st, 1916.
Dear Sirs:
Yes! I do wear the Gossard Corset, although I must admit I was very
much against a front laced corset until I was converted to yours.
Yours very truly,

ments, "newspapers carried large advertisements announcing that the new styles could first be obtained in leading stores."[33] Warner's ad budget grew substantially during this era. For example, it invested $50,000 in 1900. By 1914, the company's annual advertising outlay was $300,000. The company also pioneered cooperative advertising in 1902, a concept still in practice: Retailers ran ads in their local newspapers featuring Warner products and Warner would split the cost of the ad fifty-fifty.[34] This way women were able to easily distinguish the stores that carried the manufacturer's brand.

In 1914 Warner's "Redfern Corset Lady" made her first appearance in advertising. She was an illustration that, according to Warner documents, displayed a woman's complete form, including her legs.[35] Until 1914, images of women in corsets were not shown with legs. This changed, of course, when corsets were styled to fit over the hips. Some media outlets initially refused to run ads featuring the Redfern Corset Lady, but they soon changed their minds when their competition ran the ads and pocketed the extra revenue.

By the 1920s corsets had run their course and were deemed outmoded. According to Warner documents, corsets were abandoned in the 1920s. By 1925, women wore low corsets (girdles) and brassieres, or bound their breasts to appear more "boyish." Brassiere advertising in the next quarter century (to be discussed in the next chapter) takes corset advertising to a much higher level.

WATER, TONIC, AND ALE

What showed almost no evolution was the use of women in ads for beverages. As a vestige of the past, advertisers continued to associate their beverages with provocative images of women. Many ads simply featured nudes in reclining poses. Others contained images of classic beauties with big smiles, low-cut necklines, and deep cleavage. It's too simplistic to say that advertisers were only trying to attract attention to their posters and promotional materials. The attention-getting properties of sexually dressed women was one reason they were used, but other factors played roles as well.

For one, advertisers wanted to associate their beverages with vitality. During this period, drinks were made with sugar, caffeine, coca derivatives, and other "energizing" elements. A central attribute of these beverages was that they promised to give drinkers a "kick," more "pep," and make them feel "refreshed." In essence, consumers were promised a physiological boost. Interestingly enough, reactions to sexual imagery provide a similar physiological response: dilated pupils, slight perspiration, and heartbeats that are ratcheted up a notch. Pairing the two, sex and beverages, served to provide a subtle link between the reactions to the image and the drink's effect on us. Physiological responses to sexual images may have been attributed to the drink, which is not too different from the results of the conditioning process of Pavlov's dogs.

Second, how advertisers want consumers to perceive their products may also play a role. Consider an example for tonic water. A turn-of-the-century poster for Celery-Fo-Mo tonic boldly features a reclining woman—nearly nude—pondering her thoughts.[36] The woman in the illustration is unclothed except for dark, knee-high stockings held tight with garters. It's clear the manufacturer's intention is to attract attention to the

Figure 3.7: The topless White Rock sprite graced the back cover of *Town & Country* magazine in 1909. "White Rock," Warshaw Collection of Business Americana, Archives Center, National Museum of American History, Smithsonian Institution, 02006063.

sign, as few things are better able to attract attention than a nude. But the illustration serves another purpose: The manufacturer wanted to associate the product with a pleasant and provocative image. Aside from claims that the drink was "harmless, pleasant, magical," the woman serves as a source of meaning in the ad. What little we know about the product is influenced by the symbols and signs associated with it. ·

Despite complex explanations, maybe advertisers used nudes because it was in vogue. Reproductive technology made it possible to reproduce works of art inexpensively. Since paintings of nudes were a long-standing staple in fine art, once they were available for low-cultured purposes, advertisers put them to work. We don't see nudes in posters and packaging for today's soft drinks, but we do see them in promotional work for beer and spirits.

The topless White Rock sprite was a mainstay in turn-of-the-century advertising. The image of the nymph looking into the water appeared as a full-color ad on the back cover of *Town & Country* magazine in August 1909 (see fig. 3.7). The image appeared as early as 1893 in the World's Columbian Exposition. White Rock Corporation, based in New York City, touted its product as "The World's Best Table Water." The bottled spring water was noted for its purity and medicinal qualities.

The winged fairy, wearing only a white covering gathered at her waist, is leaning over the edge of jutting rock as she peers into the water. The fact that she's topless is interesting. She's not sexy per se, but her exposed breasts do draw attention, at least initially. Despite the assumption the sprite represents purity, it's doubtful men failed to give her a quick once-over, perhaps experience a smidgen of shame or embarrassment, and move on.

Images of women appeared in other ads for table waters. A 1903 magazine ad for Schweppes displays a peculiar image. A large circle visually dominated the ad. Within the circle is a photograph of a smiling women in a low-cut bodice. She has a bottle in one hand and a glass of Schweppes in the other. The image is odd because the woman seems to be peering out of a jagged-edged hole in a metallic wall. Aside from the attention she evokes, the image is also likely to arouse curiosity.

An early ad for Rosbach table water also features a tantalizing image of a woman (see fig. 3.8). Rosbach billed itself as the "Empress of Table

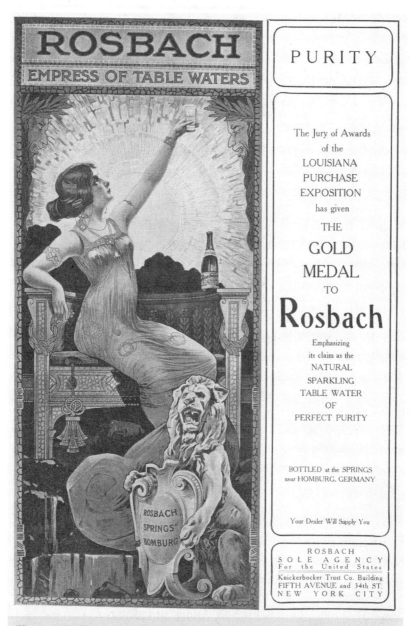

Figure 3.8: Rosbach, "The Empress of Table Waters" (1904). "Rosbach,"
Warshaw Collection of Business Americana, Archives Center, National
Museum of American History, Smithsonian Institution, 02006059.

Waters." Its "perfectly pure" sparkling water came all the way from a spring near Homburg, Germany. To illustrate its moniker, a 1904 ad featured an illustration of a young empress lifting her glass of Rosbach. Her dress fits tightly over her bosom so viewers can see she that her nipples are erect. The empress's dress is also illustrated in such as way that it shows she's sitting with her legs spread. No wonder the image of a lion at her feet is roaring.

Sexualized images of women didn't appear just in ads for bottled water, sodas, and tonics. Posters for Robert Portner Brewing Company of Alexandria, Virginia, contained nothing but images of attractive women. At the turn of the century, Portner advertised with at least three large posters that became progressively risqué. One appearing in 1900 was simply titled "Betrothed." It features a mid-shot of a fully dressed woman who is beautiful but obviously off-limits. These posters were simple, full-color lithographic reproductions of what appear to be oil paintings. The women in the portraits occupy a position front and center. Above them, in a stylish font, is the name and location of the brewing company. The women in the posters are attractive, young, and in one instance—topless.

"La Debutante" appears in 1903, and *she* may be available. She's wearing a strapless dress and her necklace stretches across her shoulder and bosom, with the pendant dipping deep into the crease of her breasts. Her fair brown hair is pulled back so that it fully exposes her pale face, neck, and upper torso.

The third poster, dated 1904, is untitled (see fig. 3.9). It features the image of a young woman who could be the Mona Lisa's daughter. She's topless, of course, and her green dress is draped over her legs and lap. She has a vacant, languid stare—directed not at the viewer, but at something off the canvas, or perhaps nothing at all. The shadows and light play in such a way that the model's breasts are fully illuminated. There's no mistaking where the artist intended viewers' eyes to fall.

The posters may have been displayed around town or in neighborhoods or saloons where Portner ale was served.[37] "Compliments of" was printed in small letters on one poster. This suggests that the posters were distributed to places where Portner was available, much like today's Coors and Budweiser posters of bikini-clad women adorning bar and tavern walls.

Figure 3.9: This poster for Robert Portner Brewing Company of Alexandria, Virginia, is dated 1904. It's likely the poster was hung in establishments where Portner ale was served. "Portner Brewing," Warshaw Collection of Business Americana, Archives Center, National Museum of American History, Smithsonian Institution, 2002-2217.

ADVERTISING CARDS

An interesting bit of promotional material was produced for the Pond's Bitters Company of Chicago (unrelated to the tonic and lotion manufacturer previously discussed). The promotion was an advertising card (undated) that touted the benefits of the tonic on one side and contained a light-hearted sexual cartoon on the other. Typical advertising cards were about the size of a modern-day postcard. The cards were distributed in stores, handed out by street vendors, and placed in areas where people would be likely to pick them up.

This particular card was designed so the cartoon was what people were likely to see first. The cartoon featured red and blue colors that were bold and patriotic. The scene was a long table set for a meal. On either side sat white-haired generals in long coats, smoking and sipping wine. Banners meant to look like the American flag decorate the edge of the card. On one of the banners it says, "Grand Army Re-Union." It's obviously a gathering of Federal generals who fought in the Civil War. Two people are standing at the head of the table. One is a well-decorated general. The other is an attractive young woman holding a server's tray and wearing an apron decorated like a flag. The old general has hold of the woman's apron and says, "Many a battle have I fought under that flag." The young woman pushes the old man's arm away as she says, "No Sir, not under this flag."

Although subtle, the cartoon was placed on the card to grab attention. People would pick the card up, chuckle at the humor, and flip it to see what was on the other side. What did they find? A simple appeal for Pond's Bitters, a tonic that cures constipation, biliousness, and malaria.

Sexual imagery often had nothing to do with the business that was promoted. Consider an advertising card with sexual imagery used to promote a Boston merchant. The card, printed on only one side, featured the image of a naked and obviously pubescent young woman. She is standing in what appears to be a garden pond with water just covering her pubic area. Although the water is see-through, several strands of strategically placed foliage help to cover her groin. The viewer is meant to be treated to the image of the young woman. Given that the card is a full-color reproduction of a painting, it may have been intended to serve as a reminder to visit the merchant when displayed on the wall at home or at the office. The merchant's business, "J. H. Getchell & Co., Gent's Fine Clothing," was printed in the upper right hand corner of the card.

CONCLUSION

As America entered the age of modernity, so did advertising. Ever increasing transportation lines created extensive distribution networks that linked manufacturers with new markets. Existing markets were burgeoning with increased urbanization and immigration. Technology and industrialization created more product and newer products, and the means to communicate the benefits of those products to the masses of new consumers. As these changes were occurring, advertising blossomed into a profession, a well-respected trade that brought the promise of prosperity to everyone.

Specifically, advertising specialists worked within agencies to develop writing and graphics to promote products. This approach came to dominate much of what advertising would look and sound like for the much of the twentieth century. Ad writers emphasized benefits as well as product features, and illustrated the benefits through images of beautiful people.

Women continued to adorn ads and men were inserted into ads, usually as handsome, adoring lovers. The brand was held up as the key, the one essential ingredient in the love formula. This formula translated into results, especially when measured at the cash register. Woodbury's soap, for example, was one such brand rescued from the brink of obscurity by advertising's new approach. It was saved by emphasizing beauty and the admiration beauty engenders. More important, as images of well-dressed men were inserted into the illustrations, advertisers advanced the subtle argument that women, if they bought the product, could become the object of the right kind of men's desire. And with that desire came the romance, intimacy, and fulfillment a woman yearned for.

Woodbury's ads and others like them were successful because they were conceived and written by women. Armed with research and their own insights, women working in advertising constructed sensual appeals that expressed women's needs for affection and intimacy. This formula was copied by other brands to create similar appeals and to stimulate sales. Did women learn to better care for their skin? Definitely. Did they get the romance they were promised? Who knows? That didn't stop advertisers. Appeals to perfection and its romantic and sexual outcomes have continued to be employed in contemporary advertising. The work and ingenuity of Helen Lansdowne Resor and her work for Woodbury's left a lasting impression on advertising in the understanding of the essential needs of consumers.

Ads targeted to men changed little during this period. Aside from enhanced printing and reproduction technology that made images of models appear more life-like, busty women adorned labels, packaging, posters, and print ads for male-oriented products such as tobacco and beverages. Sexual images of women continued to be used to attract men's attention and position brands favorably with male consumers.

4
Show and Sell
1925–1950

To most Americans, "Show and Tell" is a familiar activity in which people describe objects of interest. Show and *sell*, on the other hand, involves *revealing* objects of interest, principally to promote sales. The objects are not products, however, but sexualized images of women's bodies.

Depending on the audience, show and sell serves two purposes. If women are the target, skin is shown to reveal the brand's beauty-enhancing benefits. If ads are targeted to men, skin serves to titillate and arouse sexual interest, and to associate those responses with the brand. In advertising, the sexual show is designed—one way or another—to sell. Nowhere is this more evident than in ads appearing in the 1930s and 1940s, when classically painted nudes evolved into nude photographs.

Woodbury's Facial Soap was one of the first advertisers to feature nude female images in mainstream publications. The brand broke the nudity boundary in the 1930s with what were considered tasteful nude images shot by highly respected artistic photographers such as Edward Steichen. A 1936 Woodbury's ad is often credited as the first full-length photograph of an obviously fully nude woman sitting with her back to the camera.[1] Although women in these Woodbury ads were photographed nude, their breasts were covered by a prop of another part of the model's body. Nipples were never shown, nor was the pubic region.

Just as shapliness of limb and grace of contour draw the eye to the human figure, so does a distinctive eye-appealing finish on your product compel attention. It makes an impression that carries on to consumate a sale.

Perhaps your product needs boldness, color, dash . . . perhaps a modest richness with personality and character.

Our studio can be of service in creating a finish best suited to your product. Write for details.

ROCKFORD VARNISH COMPANY
Manufacturers of Finishing Materials
R O C K F O R D • I L L I N O I S

NO TAMPERING
WITH QUALITY

Kindly mention WOOD PRODUCTS when writing advertisers

Figure 4.1: Rockford Varnish Company ran ads like this in trade magazines from at least the 1930s to the 1950s. This nude appeared in 1939. "Rockford-Eye Appeal," Warshaw Collection of Business Americana, Archives Center, National Museum of American History, Smithsonian Institution, 02040409.

Whereas Woodbury's nudes were designed to communicate aesthetic qualities of a beauty brand, images of women in direct mail, trade ads, and promotional products had a more prurient purpose. These titillating images were used to get attention, arouse, and entertain. More important, many of these images were doled out to male clients to be hung up on walls, thus maintaining awareness of the sponsor's business. Promotional calendars that featured revealing shots provided eye candy for each month of the year.

Nudity was taken a step further in specialized business publications targeted to men. A 1939 ad for Rockford Varnish Company featured a nude photograph of a woman (see fig. 4.1). The woman's pubic region is covered by her leg, but her breasts are fully exposed. Rockford Varnish ads were not alone. Promotional material for many other companies featured exposed breasts, peek-a-boo images, and scintillating tease shots designed for male consumption.

Despite the presence of skin, romance continued to be foremost in ads designed to appeal to women—and occasionally to men. Ads for Lux and other products taught women how to enhance their attractiveness by touting romance, intimacy, feelings of worthiness, admiration, and desire. Ads for White Owl cigars demonstrated to men the tangible benefits of smoking the product. And Listerine used a "lost love" approach to convince both woman and men that halitosis could result in social failure. Many ads, especially those targeted to women, contained these love lessons.

AMERICA FROM 1925 TO 1950

The period in American history from 1925 to 1950 was marked by maturation and great fluctuation. The quarter century began with rising stock markets, but soon dropped into a deep economic depression that lasted over a decade. From 1929 to 1941, more than a quarter of America's workforce, over 12.8 million people, were unemployed.[2] Advertising spending dropped from $3.4 billion in 1929 to $1.3 billion four years later. Entry into world war in 1941 helped to bring the nation out of depression, and ultimately resulted in America's emergence as a world power.

Involvement in Korea and the beginning of the Cold War coincided with a sizable economic postwar boom—and the baby boom. This quarter century was notable for the significant entry of women into the workforce.

Over 5 million women went to work from 1941 to 1943.[3] It is difficult to imagine that all these changes occurred in the span of one generation. Consider that Charles Lindbergh completed his monumental transatlantic nonstop flight in 1927. Twenty years later, Chuck Yeager made the first supersonic flight in a jet. Prop planes, like those used by Lindbergh, were replaced by jet propulsion in 1950.

With regard to sexual matters, the infamous Hays Code was established in 1930. Among other things, it imposed strict censorship on sexual depictions in motion pictures. But its strictures, while not directly applicable to advertising, were evident in mainstream ads of that period. Eighteen years later Alfred Kinsey published the results of his comprehensive survey, *Sexual Behavior in the Human Male*. Kinsey's groundbreaking report revealed that certain patterns of sexual behavior considered deviant, were, in fact, normative. For instance, the report detailed incidences of masturbation, premarital sex, oral sex, extramarital affairs, and homosexual experiences. As Americans faced the reality of their sexual habits and predilections, sexual mores eventually relaxed—contributing to the sexual revolution—and advertising followed suit.

MEDIA AND ADVERTISING

During the 1930s and 1940s, a media revolution was taking place with the introduction of television. In the early 1930s, radio was a powerhouse. Jack Benny and Fred Allen were among the most popular entertainers, hosting well-liked radio programs. In 1932, Americans owned over fifteen million radios, and over ten million people tuned in nightly.[4] Advertisers sponsored many popular programs to reach captive audiences and to associate their brands with the well-known personalities and celebrities.

The emergence of commercial television in the 1940s had a devastating effect on radio and other media. In 1939, the first regularly scheduled television broadcasts began, and by 1948—the same year Ed Sullivan's popular variety show began to air—over 1 million sets were in America's homes. Television had a similar effect on motion pictures. In 1927 successful "talking" feature films replaced silent pictures, only to be struck a near-fatal blow when talking pictures were introduced into the home—for free. Large circulation general interest magazines were just beginning to feel the competitive effects of television as the twentieth century neared its midpoint. Magazines survived by aggressively positioning themselves to narrowly defined audiences, something this *broad*-cast medium, television, didn't do in the early days.

Even the advertising profession itself couldn't escape volatility. Advertising was an admired profession in the 1920s, but by the late 1930s and early '40s, advertising's reputation was diminished.[5] Celebrity endorsements were challenged and a wave of consumerism accused the industry of deceptiveness and waste. But advertising kept going. The industry sought to increase professionalism through training and the development of professional organizations. Ads continued to become more creative and artistic, but more appeals were based on market research. For example, surveys conducted by George Gallup established that men responded to ads based on quality and sex, whereas women responded to sexuality, vanity, and quality (in that order).[6] These themes were evident in advertising messages at the time when one considers the trade ads during this period.

TRADE ADS

Rockford Varnish Company

What do varnish and nude women have in common? Both "glorify a smooth velvety complexion," as readers were told in January 1939. Month after month images of sexualized women appeared in trade ads for Rockford Varnish Company of Rockford, Illinois. At least as far back as 1939, pictures featuring naked or partially clad women adorned Rockford ads in *Products Finishing, Industrial Finishing*, and *Wood Products* magazines.

Each month a different black-and-white image of a woman dominated the ad. Headlines made reference to the woman and the theme of the message. For example, a May 1939 ad in *Wood Products* contained the headline, "Eye Appeal..." (see fig. 4.1). The ad featured the image of a reclining nude. "Just as shapeliness of limb and grace of contour draw the eye to the human figure, so does a distinctive eye-appealing finish on your product compel attention. It makes an impression that carries on to consummate a sale."

Rockford ads had similar themes and a similar formula: (1) a singular woman in either a revealing pose or without clothing, (2) a headline and appeal making reference to the woman while emphasizing the outward finish of the varnish, (3) a description of the company's commitment to quality, and (4) a call to action. For example, a 1939 ad in *Industrial Finishing* led with the headline, "A Cast Without the Correct Finish." The visual in the ad is a photograph of a woman surprised to find her cast hooked on the back of her skirt (see fig. 4.2). Her efforts have pulled the skirt up to reveal the backs of her thighs and her derrière. "When you cast your product into the sea of sales be sure of a good finish," reads the first line of copy. "Without the correct finish your product will never reach the best spots . . . never lure the best buyers." Readers need not imagine long to figure out where the "best spot" can be found. Needless to say, Rockford Varnish Company considered their provocative approach as reasonable—reasonable enough to attract prestigious firms. The last line of copy reads, "We invite reputable manufacturers to use this service without cost or obligation."

What purpose did sexy women serve in Rockford ads? They served to illustrate an unspoken dialogue among men: "Hey, look at this gal. We know that you, like all real men, like looking at sexy women. Keep us in mind when it comes time to purchase, okay?" It's highly likely the target audience consisted primarily, if not exclusively, of men in trades. Presumably, men were also principals at Rockford Varnish. The publishers, also likely to be men, agreed to run the ads because there was little probability of their being seen by women, thereby minimizing any potential objections. At this time, the use of provocative images of women was acceptable to, and enjoyed by, the "Boy's Club" of industrial business communication.

The ads also served to attract attention. It's doubtful that good-looking nude women would fail to attract attention in a magazine about wood products. The images also drew readers to the copy since buyers may have asked themselves, "How are they going to link the woman to the product *this time?*" In this sense, the use of sex serves not only to attract initial attention, but to maintain interest exposure after exposure. By attracting attention and creating interest, the nudes provided an increased likelihood for getting the intended message across to customers. Rockford's use of nude women in its ads is only one example of a company that used sex in the dialogue of business trade advertising during this period.

A Cast Without the Correct Finish

When you cast your product into the sea of sales be sure of a good finish.

Without the correct finish your product will never reach the best spots .... never lure the best buyers.

In order that manufacturers may give their commercial products the benefit of sales-stimulating finishes we maintain a creative studio where products are analyzed and new, original finishing schemes are worked out. We invite reputable manufacturers to use this service without cost or obligation.

ROCKFORD VARNISH COMPANY
Manufacturers of Finishing Materials
R O C K F O R D • I L L I N O I S

NO TAMPERING
WITH QUALITY

Kindly mention INDUSTRIAL FINISHING when writing advertisers

Figure 4.2: "Oops." Peek-a-boo images offered men a snapshot of the forbidden (1939). "Rockford-Cast," Warshaw Collection of Business Americana, Archives Center, National Museum of American History, Smithsonian Institution, 02040408.

The Ohio Pattern Works & Foundry Company

The Ohio Pattern Works & Foundry Company of Cincinnati, Ohio, produced several advertising cards in 1939 that were either mailed to customers or used as leave-behinds. Each four-by-six-inch card is printed on both sides. One side, presumably the front, displays black-and-white photographs of fully nude women. Pubic regions are covered by a leg, window shade, or shadow, but breasts are fully exposed. At times women were classically posed, other times women were posed in action shots. For example, one image features a brunette kneeling with both legs under her as she rests on her ankle and supports herself with an outstretched arm. The model is looking off camera and over her shoulder. The studio setting is devoid of objects except the nude woman. Another card, dated August 1939, features the image of a young blonde looking for someone from behind a window blind that partially covers her naked body.

Perhaps it's not surprising that these women bear no obvious link to the information on the other side of the cards. "Lighter—Faster—Convenient—Abuse Proof," began one card, "that was the order so-o-o OPW [Ohio Pattern Works] created a light Heat Treated alloy." The copy describes technological advances in industrial metallurgical products supplied by the company. Analysis of several cards reveals no obvious reference to the women, such as tongue-in-cheek double entendres present in many sexual promotions.

If sexual references are intended, they are subtle. At the bottom of one card describing the features and advantages of the company's Opalumin fuel nozzles, it reads, "P.S.—There's also a complete Bronze selection if you prefer them." Standard nozzles may be cast in bronze, but the remark could be interpreted as a hair color preference.

Another card's copy, describing the company's armored tubing, reads like sales copy for a dildo: "Designed for full pipe flow. Two speed control, plus notched heelguard. Ribbed three point skid protectors." Another card reads, "This armored tube has more lives than the proverbial cat." The last line on the card states, "A sagless, flexible tube, that won't crimp, break or unravel—with all parts renewable." Without a doubt, these references can easily be defended as being absent of sexual meaning. I can hear the copywriter now, "For god's sake, I was only describing *pipe*." Whether intentional or not, when those words are coupled with nude images there is an inevitable sexual implication.

If you consider the psychological theory of "priming," sexual interpretations of copy are likely to occur, whether intentional or not, when copy is packaged with sexual images. Priming theory describes how information (nude images of women) can influence the interpretation of subsequently viewed information (pipe characteristics), especially when viewed within a short time span. The provocative image stimulates thoughts that influence the meaning of unrelated information. When customers received the card in the mail, they inevitably looked at the provocative image. Flipping the card over, descriptions of "tubing" and "tight fitting ribbed" outercasting would have stood out to the reader as subtle references to sex. In this way, the naked women on the front of the card can influence the perception of the brand and its products.

More likely, however, the women were used because of their appeal to male buyers of pipe fitting. Given that these cards were mailed out each month, perhaps for several years, the images may have created an expectancy. Male buyers were eager to see what this month's card from OPW looked like, thereby increasing readership of the company's direct mail solicitation.

MY CALENDAR GIRL

Aside from traditional advertising, sexual imagery—always of women—adorned men's offices and work areas in the form of calendars, magnets, and pins. These images were especially prevalent in the 1930s, and continued to be produced for many years.

An entire industry is devoted to getting businesses' logos and phone numbers in front of consumers, especially in frequently trafficked areas. Common promotional products include pens, mugs, ball caps, and shirts. The calendar is a special item because, if used, it guarantees a year of exposure—of having the business name and phone number right in the consumer's face. What better way to ensure the adoption of a calendar than with provocative images of women—as long as wives and female coworkers don't see it.

Figure 4.3: Calendar images like this one introduced each new month to millions of men. JII Promotions, Coshocton, OH.

Promotional product representatives sold businesses these calendars to distribute to customers. The calendars came in many forms. Two popular calendars were the desk calendar and the hanging calendar. Those intended for desk display consist of pressed cardboard with die cuts that can be folded so the calendar sits upright on the desk, much like a picture frame. Printed on the front of the calendar is the name, phone number, and address of the sponsoring business. The front also contained sheets of stacked paper, with each page containing an image of a woman and a monthly calendar. The paper might be stapled or glued to the cardboard so that each month a page could be removed to reveal another sensual beauty. These complimentary calendars were given to customers as a pleasing reminder and a way to maintain awareness.

Many images featured salacious illustrations of women dressed in scant clothing, raised hems, underwear, swimwear, or nothing at all. The women were leggy and voluptuous. The illustrations emphasized the women's deep cleavage that often was barely covered by towels, furs, or shower curtains. Many of these peek-a-boo shots captured women in compromising positions. For example, towels would be falling off or dresses were flying up. A woman in a short skirt might be bending over, unaware that her bottom is exposed when her skirt catches on a doorknob.

Many images featured puns. For example, one representative image displays a woman bending down to unplug her vacuum cleaner (see fig. 4.4). In so doing, she's surprised to find the end of the suction hose lifting the hem of her dress to reveal her upper thighs and derrière. "Caught in the Draft," is the title for that month's image. Below the image is the promotional copy, "Let us untangle your problems . . . customer satisfaction is our aim . . . call us now." The sponsoring company was a stainless steel distributor in Thorndale, Pennsylvania.

Another image, referred to as "A number to remember," features an enticing woman in her underwear, talking on the phone. Smiling, she's lying on her back with her legs, crossed at the ankles, raised in the air. "Modern methods and efficient service stand ready for your call. If you want action as well as satisfaction, ours is a good number to remember." The "number" is an obvious double entendre referring to the woman and the business's telephone.

In many of these images, the women are illustrated so that they are making eye contact with the viewer. With mischievous smiles, it's as if they are communicating their sexual interest and availability. In one peek-a-boo shot, a woman is in the midst of pulling off her top. The woman's arm is covering her mouth but her eyes communicate that she knows she's being

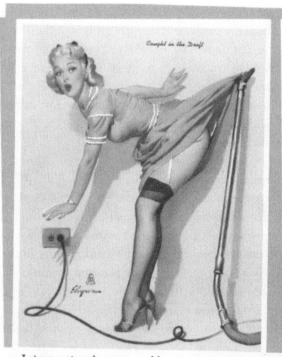

Figure 4.4: "Caught in the Draft" calendar image. © Brown and Bigelow, Inc.; "Caught in the Draft" (n.d.), Warshaw Collection of Business Americana, Archives Center, National Museum of American History, Smithsonian Institution, 02040407.

Let us untangle your problems . . . customer satisfaction is our aim . . . call us now.

watched by the viewer, and that she's enjoying it. Many of these "tease" images take disrobing to the edge of nudity, leaving viewers to imagine the revealed body.

What needs no imagination is how women are illustrated. Their breasts are accentuated and barely covered. In another representative image, a bare-breasted woman is wearing alpine-style short-shorts with the suspenders covering her nipples. Tight-fitting undergarments with straps hold up hose on her long, well-defined legs. Typically, these women are sitting or standing, or crouching in poses that showcase their legs, rear end, hips, and inner thighs. Many of the women wear enticing smiles designed to inflame a spark of sexual interest in viewers.

Similar to today's sexy calendars that feature *Sports Illustrated* swimsuit

Figure 4.5: Calendar image. JII Promotions, Coshocton, OH.

models and female celebrities, hanging calendars were distributed as promotional material. One example is "The MacPherson Sketch Book" calendar from 1949. The calendar, featuring sexy images of suntanned babes, was supplied to customers courtesy of The Queen City Barrel Company of Cincinnati. According to the cover: "Glorifying those lithe and languorous lovelies who linger in the path of the sun, these choice treasures captured by MacPherson have been selected for your entertainment throughout 1949."[7]

The only difference between desk and wall calendars might be size, since images on wall calendars have the potential to be larger and contain more detail. Images in the MacPherson calendar featured pinups of topless women with nipples barely hidden from view. Interestingly, the actual calendar on each page represented only a fraction of the space. As the calendar's description discloses, the purpose of these sexy calendars often lay in their entertainment value, not their masquerade as helpful time-keeping devices.

UNDERWEAR TRADE ADS

Today Victoria's Secret, Calvin Klein, and Jockey are often credited with pushing the boundaries of underwear advertising. Little do people know about intimates advertising in the late 1930s. For example, a very interesting trade ad for B. F. Goodrich appeared in November 1938. The ad touted the benefits of rubber panties produced by B. F. Goodrich Company. It features a fully naked woman—she is wearing high-heeled slippers—sitting in front of her vanity holding a pair of Latex panties. The model's legs are crossed and her arms cover her breasts from the camera as she holds up the underwear. Still, she is unmistakably unclothed.

Only lately has underwear advertising, even for the most provocative contemporary advertisers, been this explicit. The B. F. Goodrich ad appeared in issues of the trade publications *Purchasing* and *Factory Management & Maintenance*. *Purchasing* was a national journal read by industry and government executives. The purpose of the ad was not to sell underwear but to treat execs to an alluring shot while making the point that Goodrich makes a wide range of industrial and consumer rubber products. The headline read, "Another Goodrich 'Belt' that Flexes Longer." In the second block of copy, readers see the connection between the image and the manufacturer: "The same engineers who developed a transmission belt which flexes five times longer now developed a new rubber yarn for girdles which lasts longer, helps female America 'keep in shape.'"

Another trade ad, this one for a manufacturer, contained a photograph of an underwear-clad model. The ad for Union Special Machine Company in 1939 featured a head-to-toe photograph of a woman clad only in a bra, panties, and mid-thigh hose. The panties were more generously cut than in today's ads, but it was 1939.

The woman is standing in a classic pose with one hand lightly touching her chest and the other hand behind her. Her head is lowered and her eyes are closed. The only copy reads, "The neat panties this young lady is wearing were produced by The Well-Made Bloomer Company, Brooklyn, N. Y., on Union Special machines."

The ad, a promotional piece, ran in the trade publication, *The Needle's Eye*. The magazine's readership consisted of buyers for industrial sewing machines as well as machine-sewn merchandise. The ad demonstrates the product while undoubtedly catching a lot of attention. Even in 1939, many buyers of sewing machines and sown fabric were men. And for those who were not, the model's eyes were modestly downcast.

TRUCK AND BOLT CARDS

A card for The Service Caster and Truck Company, based in Boston, Massachusetts, and Albion, Michigan, provides another example of sexy images and double entendre headlines. The image, not dated but assumed to be distributed in the 1930s, features an illustration of a naked blonde wearing pumps and bending over to pick up her slip as it floats close to the shore. She is pictured from behind and the side, so a full-length view of her legs, rear, and breasts are visible. She's smiling as she looks at the viewer.

The only line of copy, aside from the company's identification, is printed beneath her; it reads, "Waiting *for* her slip *to* come in." It's an obvious reference to the wait for a shipment or sales invoice as well as the obvious sexual meaning. The name and address of the sponsoring business is printed at the top of the card. Most likely, the printer had images printed on cards

Figure 4.6: Customers who flipped over this eye-catching 1938 direct-mail piece only saw illustrations of nuts, bolts, and "specialty" fasteners. "Fasteners," Warshaw Collection of Business Americana, Archives Center, National Museum of American History, Smithsonian Institution, 02040402.

that pertained to various industries. The printer simply printed the name of the sponsor at the top of the image. The sponsoring company then distributed the promotional pieces to customers to serve as reminders.

Another promotional piece from 1938 appears to be an underwear or hosiery ad, but it's not. On the front of a five-by-seven-inch brochure is a photograph of a woman fastening her hose to her girdle strap (see fig. 4.6). The only copy line reads, "Special Fastenings." The viewer is privy to a shot under the woman's dress and between her legs as she lifts her left leg to "fasten" her hose. In fact, the camera angle is crotch-level, which makes the relevance to fastenings all that more intriguing.

When the promotional card is flipped, the other side contains pictures of screws, nuts, and fasteners—actual hardware materials that have no relevance to hosiery. The sole purpose of the woman is to draw the consumer to the piece. The image on the direct mail piece also serves to give the male viewer a quick peek at forbidden fruit. At the very least, it's an example from the 1930s of subtle nudity and wink-wink pictures in advertising that contain images as risqué as those in many contemporary ads.

APRIL SHOWERS TALC

Ads with implied nudity weren't always targeted to men. A 1943 ad for April Showers Talc advised women to use its fragranced powder to be more attractive to men.[8] "Its luxurious perfume speaks a language men understand..." was the written appeal. Eyes were more apt to be drawn to the photograph, however. The image was an unmistakably nude woman cropped from the bottom of her breasts up. A copy box just happened to cover the woman's nipples, but there could be little doubt for viewers that the model was photographed nude.

Because this 1943 ad was targeted to women, one can only speculate as to the use of the nude female. Combined with the copy appeal, it's likely that the meaning of the image was that sex was a result of using the powder. It could be argued that the nude simply served to demonstrate where the talc was to be used on the body. However, the hint of salaciousness in the image suggests the former reason is more appropriate—not to mention the intention of attracting attention to the ad.

LOVE LESSONS

Consumers may have needed to be schooled in sex appeal, according to a shampoo ad in 1940. Halo Shampoo, a Colgate-Palmolive-Peet Company brand, boldly proclaimed, "Learn a Lesson in Sex Appeal." The ad literally plays on the promise of sex appeal; that women need only use a ten-cent hair preparation to possess sexual attractiveness. "Halo Shampoo brightens your hair with seductive luster." The image in the ad is an illustration highlighting a woman's blond hair and attractive face. Discernable, though not fully visible, is a man. "Many a heart has been won by a thrilling head of hair. For when a man looks at you, remember his eyes start with your head." (Based on ads from the turn of the century, I thought men were influenced by a woman's hands, complexion, or the condition of her underthings.)

Promises of sensuality and romance were common in advertising during this era as well. Product benefits developed for beauty products became a mainstay in advertising. At the risk of being repetitive, ads with love appeals served to position the brand as an element in the sexual-attraction formula. The psychological benefit of the brand is that it allows the consumer to experience romance, love, and intimacy—and all the wonderful benefits of courtship and mate selection. Those who fail to heed the ad's lesson risk loss of love and unhappiness.

McCall's

During the 1930s and 1940s, brands were consistently positioned as avenues to love. For example, casual perusal of a May 1947 issue of *McCall's* magazine reveals the plethora of love and attraction appeals at the time. The woman's magazine contained sixteen ads that positioned the brand as a latchkey to romance and sexual intimacy. These ads contained illustrations of couples kissing or embracing as a result of one of the models receiving or using the brand.

Not surprisingly, half of *McCall's* sixteen ads were for toilet lotions and beauty soaps. Without exception, these ads contained the classic appeal of brand-induced attraction as the means to loveliness. A full-page ad for Woodbury's beauty-blended lotion features a photograph of a necking couple, and the headline, "Now! Keep your hands as kissable as your lips…" Female readers were told that Cashmere Bouquet soap, "Adorns your skin with the fragrance men love." The image, a tuxedoed lothario kissing his sweetheart's temple, is accompanied by the question, "Would you care to have the fragrant appeal of so many popular girls?"

Palmolive used medical authorities to characterize its soap's beauty properties. "Doctors prove 2 out of 3 women can have lovelier skin in 14 days." As if newlyweds need any help, an ad for Hinds lotion features a couple in their wedding attire kissing as they are locked in a tight embrace. The headline reads, "He's helpless in your hands with the *New* Hinds!"

Romance wasn't always associated with toilet products. Five ads in the magazine featured images of intimacy as a result of men or women giving the other a gift. For example, one ad depicts a man dressed as Santa being kissed by his wife. The happy smirk on his face seems to say, "I need to do this more often." He is giving his wife a National Presto "Pressure" Cooker. Similarly, an ad for Oneida's Community silver-plated flatware contains a close-up image, practically covering the entire ad, of a couple kissing. "Make it for keeps," reads the headline. How does one do that? Give her the flatware "she'll treasure."

In a very interesting ad, Aunt Jenny tells readers, "Mrs. Santa Claus couldn't make a better tasting cake." She advises women to use Spry vegetable shortening, and even supplies a scrumptious cake recipe. In the upper left-hand corner of the ad, a man is standing behind his wife indicating that he wants another slice of cake. He says, "I don't need mistletoe for inspiration after a delicious Christmas cake like this!" Maybe it's not a piece of cake he's after.

Another ad presents a subtle, but unmistakable, romantic image. The full-page ad features an illustration of a couple dressed as if they are at a masquerade party. The woman, leaning back slightly, is in the forefront of the ad. She's dressed in a white, short strapless dress that accentuates her figure. The man, mostly covered from view by the woman, is supporting her with one arm behind her back as he lifts off her mask. Her eyes are closed and she's positioned for a kiss. Who's sponsoring the ad? Kotex sanitary napkins. According to the copy, "*You answer* appraising eyes with a smile. With complete composure, always one of your charms, and very personally yours wherever you are… whatever the time of month."

The appeal is that women can more confidently and comfortably deal with more situations, thanks to Kotex. The visual in the ad is essentially saying that readers don't have to miss out on tender moments. "Yes, with Kotex for your ally you can meet all trying moments, assured. As gaily as you don your mask, you can laugh off care with a special peace-of-mind…"

A brassiere ad contained the visual argument that male attraction is a benefit of the shaping characteristics of the brand. The quarter-page ad displays a photograph of two men checking out a busty young woman. Her smile accentuates her satisfaction with the bra's effect. "The secret's in the circle!" states the headline. The "secret" is a circular-style cup that "transforms a small bust into alluring feminine curves." An obvious precursor to the push-up bra.

LUX

Lux is another brand that used promises of romance and attraction in its appeals to women. Interestingly, these sensual assurances were used to sell suds for two Lux soap products that had very different purposes. Both Lux soap brands were intended for cleaning: laundry and dishwashing flakes for clothing, and later, perfumed bar soap for personal use.

Lux, a laundry soap developed and marketed by Lever Brothers, was very popular in its home country of Great Britain as early as 1888.[9] When Lux was introduced in the United States in 1906, it was unique because it consisted of boxed soap flakes instead of the bar soaps and washing powder available at the time. The laundry soap enjoyed muted success until the early teens when women began wearing more silks and lacier articles of innerwear. As Lever Brothers placed more promotional emphasis behind Lux, sales steadily increased. People were now using Lux flakes to wash their clothes, their dishes, and increasingly, themselves.

Pledges of adoration and attraction helped to sell the flakes. Consider an ad with the headline, "Adoration is the tribute men pay to *femininity*" (see fig. 4.7). In this 1930 ad, women were advised to buy and wear colorful lacy lingerie because wearing it makes women feel, well, more feminine. "A clever woman knows that one of the surest ways of feeling feminine is to wear feminine underthings." Lest the message be unclear, the ad contained the classic vignette of a tuxedoed man admiring his attractive sweetheart. The message was reinforced with an image of a woman in her silky slip.

"ADORATION is the tribute men pay to *femininity*"

says

DOROTHY
DIX

"I HAVE never known a man yet who didn't adore the quality we call femininity.

"It makes a woman seem precious and mysterious to men—yet it's not mysterious, really. If you yourself *feel* feminine and charming, men find you so.

"One of the clever ways of feeling feminine is to wear feminine underthings. The charming colors, the soft touch of the fragile silks and laces, all give you a sense of femininity that is magically contagious.

"I often repeat these 2 simple rules:

1. Wear colorful, lacy lingerie.
2. Keep it exquisitely new with Lux.

"I say Lux because it's made especially to preserve color and charm. Ordinary soaps, even the 'good' ones, too often dim colors, spoil lustre and finish. But with Lux, lovely things stay new, retain their enchantment, for months and even years!

"AND REMEMBER, TOO, that your *surroundings* can also cast a glamorous spell about your personality. So cherish the daintiness of draperies, slip covers, sofa cushions, table linens—keep them all color-fresh and new with Lux."

Dorothy Dix

The Secret of Dainty Femininity

Peach satin lingerie washed 12 times in Lux—all its exquisite beauty of color and texture retained. Just as colorful and charming as new!

Duplicate lingerie washed 12 times in ordinary 'good' soap—the charming color faded and drab, lustre gone, lace and satin damaged. Unattractive!

The magic promise . . . if it's safe in water alone, it's just as safe in LUX

Figure 4.7: To attract men, women were advised to buy lacey "under-things" and keep them looking new with Lux laundry and dishwashing soap flakes (1930). Lux Flakes ad, "Adoration is the Tribute.' Domestic Advertising Collection, J. Walter Thompson Company Archives, Hartman Center for Sales, Advertising & Marketing History, Rare Book, Manuscript, & Special Collections Library, Duke University, Durham, North Carolina. Lux ad reproduced courtesy of Unilever PLC and Unilever N.V. or their subsidiaries, copyright holders.

How were women to preserve the key to their femininity? By washing their underthings in Lux.

Many of these ads contained advice from columnists such as Dorothy Dix and Elinor Glyn. Their advice would be integrated within the copy and accompanied by a photograph of a romantic vignette. Lux was positioned as a key to a romantic outcome by one of several reasons. For example, an ad from 1930 emphasized the importance of choosing and maintaining clothing with colors that accentuate a woman's beauty. The headline reads, "Choose Colors that make your Hair gleam with Beauty." The image features a young couple in an intimate position. What follows is Dix's advice: "So many letters from girls—all longing for the loveliness that will awaken romance! Dear, eager girls—nowadays no girl needs to be plain. Any girl who wears the right COLORS can seem so radiantly charming that the men simply flock around her—for men love color."

Women were advised to wear color and to wash their clothes in Lux to preserve its color. One can hardly imagine men's reaction to drab, faded clothing. Although sex was not used in early ads, sales of Lux flakes began climbing in the early teens. As the result of its first full-scale ad campaign, sales of Lux flakes jumped from 10,000 cases in 1915 to over 1 million cases by 1918.[10]

To capitalize on the quality perceptions consumers had for Lux flakes, the company introduced Lux Toilet Form in 1923. The product was a perfumed bar soap intended for personal use. It was positioned as similar to fine French toilet soaps but at a much more reasonable price.[11] Lux bar soap was priced at ten cents, compared to popular French soaps that cost anywhere from fifty cents to two dollars. But even at a dime, executives were worried that American women would consider the soap too expensive, according to a 1925 letter from the Lever Brothers president, Mr. Countway, to agency executives: "I feel that we must throw more glamour around our new product to justify the price in the consumer's mind of 9¢ to 10¢ per cake which she will have to pay."[12]

Early campaigns emphasized the soap's French influence. For example, the headline of a 1927 ad read, "France's cherished secret...Smooth Skin in this new toilet soap at 10¢." A photograph of a beautiful woman posing in her bathroom was the ad's focal point. The photograph's caption read, "Beauty-wise France knowing well the skin itself must be smooth, exquisite, for loveliness, developed the method by which Lux Toilet Soap is made." (The soap's name had been changed to Lux Toilet Soap earlier that year.) The full-page ad ran in women's magazines such as *Modern Priscilla*, *Ladies' Home Journal*, and *Women's Home Companion*.

The next year, JWT put Mr. Countway's directive into literal form. In 1928, Lux Toilet Soap began an association with glamorous Hollywood stars that lasted, in one form or another, for many years. The 1928 campaign sought to associate the beauty and physical attractiveness of Hollywood's biggest stars with the soap. One headline of the campaign was "9 of 10 screen stars use it." By some means, perhaps by salesmen, it was discovered that the vast majority of movie stars did indeed use Lux Toilet Soap.[13] Given that stars could afford any brand of soap, especially expensive imported brands, that they preferred Lux was not lost to the company or its agency.

What followed were ads featuring popular female movie stars endorsing Lux Toilet Soap. Notable celebrity endorsers included Clara Bow, Marion Davies, Lupe Velez, Joan Crawford, and Mae Murray. For example, an ad in 1930 featured the names and faces of Clara Bow, Betty Bronson, and Janet Gaynor. And even these movie stars had their skin scrutinized: "Every woman must face the Close-up Test." According to the ad's copy, "A girl's lovely skin is an instant attraction, say 45 Hollywood directors. A whole audience is swept by enthusiasm when the close-up brings a star's loveliness near."

In the ad, women were reminded that they, too, were subject to the "close-up test." "And every woman must meet the scrutiny of close appraising eyes. Does *your* skin quicken the heart like the alluring stars'? It can." In addition to the image of the three movie stars, a vignette shows a man and woman embracing, but the man appears to be looking critically at the woman's face. The implication is that as men swoop close to embrace, they judge a woman's skin. If it doesn't pass the test, it's likely a man will be disappointed and pull away. The approach was that female celebrities knew first-hand about beauty and loveliness and its effects. If they used and recommended Lux, all women should use it as well.

The use of glamorous movie star endorsers continued for many years. In 1946 a campaign was initiated using stars that promised female con-sumers that they, too, could "be lovelier tonight."[14] From 1948 to 1950, leading couples in feature films were pictured in positions designed to sig-nify romantic interest. Some couplings included Ruth Hussey and Ronald

ELIZABETH TAYLOR as she plays opposite DON TAYLOR in Metro-Goldwyn-Mayer's *"FATHER OF THE BRIDE"*

"I'm a Lux Girl"

says ELIZABETH TAYLOR

A bride of dreamlike loveliness—that's Elizabeth Taylor in her latest picture. Notice the radiant beauty of her complexion—it's a *Lux* Complexion, given the gentlest, most cherishing care with Hollywood's own beauty soap.

"Lux Soap facials with ACTIVE lather give my skin new loveliness—so quickly!" says Elizabeth. In recent tests by skin specialists, actually 3 out of 4 complexions improved in a short time. Try this beautifying care Elizabeth Taylor recommends! You'll love the generous *bath* size Lux Toilet Soap, too—so fragrant—so luxurious!

FOR ALL-OVER
LUX LOVELINESS
TRY THE NEW
BATH SIZE

ANOTHER FINE PRODUCT OF
EVER BROTHERS COMPANY

HOLLYWOOD'S ACTIVE-LATHER FACIAL:

1. Here's the beauty facial screen stars never neglect: Smooth the creamy Lux Soap lather in well—

2. It's such rich, *abundant* lather, even in the hardest water . . . Just rinse with warm water, then cold—

3. Pat gently with a soft towel to dry. Marvelous—how soft and smooth your skin feels now—how fresh it *looks!*

9 out of 10 Screen Stars use Lux Toilet Soap

Figure 4.8: Lux Toilet Soap (1950). Lux Toilet Soap ad, "Elizabeth Taylor." Domestic Advertising Collection, J. Walter Thompson Company Archives, Hartman Center for Sales, Advertising & Marketing History, Rare Book, Manuscript, & Special Collections Library, Duke University, Durham, North Carolina. Lux ad reproduced courtesy of Unilever PLC and Unilever N.V. or their subsidiaries, copyright holders.

Reagan in "Louisa," Joan Caulfield and William Holden in "Dear Wife," and Hedy Lamarr and Ray Milland in "Copper Canyon."

A 1950 Lux ad featured Don Taylor nuzzling Elizabeth Taylor (see fig. 4.8). Both starred in Metro-Goldwyn-Mayer's "Father of the Bride." The headline was "You're adorable." Elizabeth Taylor confided, "I'm a Lux Girl." Sales of Lux soap amounted to 135,000 cases in 1925, increasing to one million cases in 1928, and 1.7 million by 1929. Sales of Lux continued to surge and it ultimately became the leading soap in its category by 1949. The Lux story is yet another example of the attraction and associated benefits of sensuality used to sell products.

LISTERINE

A company known for making "halitosis" a household word and selling mouthwash to prevent social ostracism, often used love—and loss-of-love —themes in its advertising. Lambert Pharmacal Company, later known as Warner-Lambert, was aggressive in its marketing of Listerine. The antiseptic was promoted through use of fear and claims to cure several undesirable odors and conditions. According to one source, "Early [Listerine] ads heralded a new age of shame-based advertising that urged consumers to be ever mindful of their bodily odors and secretions"[15] (see fig. 4.9).

Dr. Joshua Lawrence invented the antiseptic in 1879, naming his concoction Listerine after similar products called Listerols promoted by a traveling English physician.[16] Lawrence's Listerine was made of thymol, eucalyptol, methyl salicylate, and menthol. Without time to devote to marketing, Lawrence entered into an agreement with businessman Jordan Lambert. Lambert formed the Lambert Pharmacal Company and began selling Listerine as a surgical antiseptic in 1881. Fourteen years later it was sold to dentists as an oral antiseptic. And in 1914 Listerine was sold directly to consumers as the first mouthwash.[17]

To improve lackluster sales in 1926, Lambert's sons asked the company chemist to list some of the properties of Listerine. One item that caught their eye was that Listerine eliminated "halitosis." Even the term sounds horrifying. The company enlisted the help of New York-based advertising agency Lambert and Feasley to promote that fact.[18] Ad campaigns soon fol-

Often a bridesmaid but never a bride

EDNA'S case was really a pathetic one. Like every woman, her primary ambition was to marry. Most of the girls of her set were married—or about to be. Yet not one possessed more grace or charm or loveliness than she.

And as her birthdays crept gradually toward that tragic thirty-mark, marriage seemed farther from her life than ever.

She was often a bridesmaid but never a bride.

* * *

That's the insidious thing about halitosis (unpleasant breath). You, yourself, rarely know when you have it. And even your closest friends won't tell you.

Sometimes, of course, halitosis comes from some deep-seated organic disorder that requires professional advice. But usually—and fortunately—halitosis is only a local condition that yields to the regular use of Listerine as a mouth wash and gargle. It is an interesting thing that this well-known antiseptic that has been in use for years for surgical dressings, possesses these unusual properties as a breath deodorant.

It halts food fermentation in the mouth and leaves the breath sweet, fresh and clean. *Not* by substituting some other odor but by really removing the old one. The Listerine odor itself quickly disappears. So the systematic use of Listerine puts you on the safe and polite side. Lambert Pharmacal Company, St. Louis, Mo.

Figure 4.9: This Listerine ad described how a woman's desire to marry could easily be thwarted by halitosis (n.d.). Listerine ad, "Often a Bridesmaid." Domestic Advertising Collection, J. Walter Thompson Company Archives, Hartman Center for Sales, Advertising & Marketing History, Rare Book, Manuscript, & Special Collections Library, Duke University, Durham, North Carolina. Courtesy of Pfizer Pharmaceutical Group, Pfizer Inc.

lowed that hailed Listerine's ability to prevent social ostracism by doing away with bad breath.

Many of these ads contained appeals revolving around intimate relationships, kissing techniques, and social attraction. Typical with brand promises, Listerine was situated as the conduit for love and successful courtship. For example, an ad in 1930 told the sad story of Smedley, a young man considered "good husband material," who, because of his breath, was unable to sustain a relationship. "He wants to get married," read the headline placed below a handsome male image, but the copy described how this stellar guy "had a fault [women] couldn't overlook." The ad's copy—typical of most Listerine ads—described how people don't know they have halitosis and friends can't be counted on to tell them: "There is no greater barrier to pleasant personal and business relations than halitosis (unpleasant breath). It is the unforgivable social fault. The insidious thing about it is that the victim never knows when he has it. And even a good friend won't tell him. The matter is too delicate to discuss."

Women didn't escape the copywriter's sad stories. Another ad in 1930 told the story of Mildred, a young attractive member of Chicago society, with a penchant for catching bouquets. "She bags the *bouquets* but never a *Beau*," was the headline. Should readers think themselves immune from halitosis, the ad painfully reminds them, "You never have it?—*what colossal conceit!*"

No doubt this ad was a forerunner to Listerine ads with the infamous line, "Often a bridesmaid...never a bride." The "Bridesmaid" theme appeared in ads in the 1930s, 1940s, and 1950s, preying on women's insecurities about failure to marry young—or worse, failure to marry at all. Consider the classic ad in figure 4.9. Although Edna caught the bouquet, she's crying because "as her birthdays crept gradually toward that tragic thirty-mark, marriage seemed farther from her life than ever." Readers were told that Edna's case was "pathetic," and like all women, her primary ambition was to get married.

Listerine appeals weren't always negative. Those ads featuring sexual content often contained an engaging image. For example, the ad in figure 4.11 contains a photograph of a couple about to kiss and the headline, "He still wants to kiss her good night." Readers were told the story of a couple, "Married eight years...but for them none of that humdrum, take-it-for-granted attitude that creeps into so many marriages." Because the wife

ISN'T SHE DUMB?

she thinks washing will remove odors

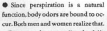

ONLY A DEODORANT CAN CHECK
BODY ODORS

● Since perspiration is a natural function, body odors are bound to occur. Both men and women realize that.

But many do not realize the folly of trying to overcome body odors with mere soap and water. It can't be done. Only a deodorant can overcome an odor. Any chemist, any physician will tell you that.

Listerine deodorizes

Use all the soap and water you want in your bath, but afterward apply Listerine to the guilty areas.

It cleanses, it freshens, and it deodorizes immediately. Tests show that Listerine overcomes odors that ordinary antiseptics cannot conquer in 12 hours. The same marvelous power that made Listerine the national remedy for halitosis (unpleasant breath) serves you again in combating this embarrassing condition.

You can't tell

Some women realize when they are troubled with body odors. For every one that does, five do not. Why take the chance of offending others when a pleasant dash of Listerine on affected areas will make you welcome?

If you haven't a bottle of Listerine in the house, get one today from your druggist. In the long run, it is the most economical antiseptic. Its action is safe. Its results are certain. Its success is a matter of record for over fifty years. Lambert Pharmacal Company, St. Louis, Mo., U. S. A.

Send for our FREE BOOKLET OF ETIQUETTE—tells what to wear, say, and do at social affairs. Address, Dept. B. O. 1, Lambert Pharmacal Co., St. Louis, Mo.

Listerine THE SWIFT DEODORANT

Ad No. 3528 R1*

Figure 4.10: Listerine was also sold as a deodorant. Run in 1931, the image is one of the earliest known nude photographs to appear in a mainstream ad. Listerine ad, "Isn't She Dumb." Domestic Advertising Collection, J. Walter Thompson Company Archives, Hartman Center for Sales, Advertising & Marketing History, Rare Book, Manuscript, & Special Collections Library, Duke University, Durham, North Carolina. Courtesy of Pfizer Pharmaceutical Group, Pfizer Inc.

used Listerine to keep her breath fresh, she was portrayed as maintaining intimacy in her marriage.

A 1932 ad described a lustful love-at-first-sight encounter. The ad in figure 4.12 shows an upscale couple in what appears to be an openmouthed kiss. Unfortunately for Gridley, the ad's male protagonist, it took only one unexpected kiss to end his chance encounter with a "beautiful and famous woman." The copy describes the carnal scene: "They had been strangers then, though across the damask of the candle-lit table their eyes met in eager challenge...he had always scoffed at the idea of love at first sight. But tonight, at their first meeting, they did not sneer. And now he was holding her in his arms ...her warm lips on his in a kiss half of yearning, half of tenderness. One kiss ...and only one. It might have carried them to the altar. Instead, it parted them forever." One kiss was enough for Gridley to discover that the noxiousness of this beautiful woman's breath was more than enough to extinguish his libido. It's likely that this message was not lost on readers who were drawn into the ad with its provocative image and pulp-fiction inspired copy.

In 1941, consumers were treated to "A Lesson in Kissing Technique." The ad features an amorous kissing couple with several quotes from distinguished writers and poets. What was the primary lesson? Those curious enough to read the copy to discover a new technique or maneuver were advised to use Listerine to eliminate offensive halitosis.

These were only a few of the Listerine ads that emphasized love and sexual intimacy. As with other brands that touted the product as a gateway to romance, Listerine was often positioned as the key to amorous wants desired by consumers. According to one source, "From its earliest days as a consumer product, Listerine had thrived by spreading anxiety about breath odor and promoting the harsh-tasting liquid's scientifically proven ability to cure this social disease."[19] It makes sense that romantic interludes should become fodder for highlighting the condition that Listerine was best able, and positioned, to control.

From 1925 to 1950, over $47 million was invested in Listerine advertising, resulting in over $187 million in sales.[20] Most emphasis was placed on Listerine's ability to eliminate halitosis, though in the late 1920s the company promoted Listerine's ability to control dandruff, body odor, and feminine hygiene conditions. After sales steadily began to climb in the mid-1940s, Listerine's parent company merged with Warner-Hudnut to

He still wants to kiss her good night

MARRIED eight years . . . but for them none of that humdrum, take-it-for-granted attitude that creeps into so many marriages. He still wants to kiss her good night. Clever woman . . . she has always known the secret of keeping dainty and fresh in all things . . . the breath particularly. After all, there's nothing like halitosis (unpleasant breath) to raise a barrier between people.

* * *

You Never Know

Your breath may be agreeable today and offensive tomorrow. The food you eat, the things you drink, the hours you keep —all bring subtle changes that may result in halitosis (bad breath). Consequently, you must ever be on guard lest you offend.

Better Safe Than Sorry

Fortunately, halitosis often yields quickly to Listerine used as a mouth rinse or gargle. Almost at once, this remarkable deodorant cleanses, sweetens, and freshens the mouth. At the same time, it halts fermentation of tiny food particles—the major cause of mouth odors. Then overcomes the odors themselves.

And remember, Listerine is safe even when used full strength—does not harm delicate tissues of the gums or mouth. *It actually stimulates them.*

When You Want To Be Sure

Fortunately for the public, many of the "bargain" imitations of Listerine are now out of business. Too strong, too harsh, too bitter to be tolerated, or lacking Listerine's speedy deodorant and antiseptic properties, such mouth washes were soon rejected by the public.

When you want a wholly delightful mouth wash, when you want to be sure of effective breath control with *safety*, use Listerine and Listerine *only*. Rinse the mouth with it morning and night and between times before business and social engagements. *Lambert Pharmacal Company, St. Louis, Mo.*

For HALITOSIS   *use* LISTERINE

If you like Listerine Antiseptic, chances are you'll like Listerine Tooth Paste. More than ¼ pound in the big, double-size tube—40¢. Regular size, 25¢.

Figure 4.11: This ad, which ran between 1932 and 1935, illustrates the positive sexual outcomes that accrue as a result of using the brand. Listerine ad, "Still Wants to Kiss Her." Domestic Advertising Collection, J. Walter Thompson Company Archives, Hartman Center for Sales, Advertising & Marketing History, Rare Book, Manuscript, & Special Collections Library, Duke University, Durham, North Carolina. Courtesy of Pfizer Pharmaceutical Group, Pfizer Inc.

ONCE WAS ENOUGH

FOUR hours ago he hadn't dreamed he could kiss this beautiful and famous woman.

They had been strangers then, though across the damask of the candle-lit table their eyes met in eager challenge. Gridley, no less than she, had always scoffed at the idea of love at first sight. But tonight, at their first meeting, they did not sneer.

And now he was holding her in his arms . . . her warm lips on his in a kiss half of yearning, half of tenderness. One kiss . . . and only one. It might have carried them to the altar. Instead, it parted them forever.

For in the instant that his lips held hers he knew that she was not the woman for him. He knew the reason, too. But she didn't . . . and probably never will. It is a matter people do not discuss.

No one is immune

Halitosis (unpleasant breath) is unpardonable—repellent in either man or woman. It breaks up many a friendship, romance, and occasionally a marriage. The insidious thing about it is that you yourself never know when you have it, and even your best friend won't tell you; the subject is too delicate. The same applies to the presence of body odors which are second only to halitosis in their power to offend others.

Why risk either? Why not make sure that your breath is sweet and agreeable? Why not take precautions against body odors?

Swift deodorant power

Halitosis yields immediately to Listerine, the quickest of deodorants. Simply gargle with it every night and morning, and between times before meeting others. Don't waste your time with ordinary antiseptics; it takes them 12 hours or more to get rid of odors that Listerine conquers instantly.

After your bath, Listerine

Body odors, including that of perspiration, are the result of a chemical action in tiny glands. No mere washing with soap and water will remove these odors. That is why we say to you: after your bath, apply Listerine to the guilty areas. It checks body odors without altering or impairing natural functions.

Keep Listerine always handy in home and office. Carry a bottle in your handbag and the side pocket of your car. It is your protection against infection in an emergency, and your constant assurance that you won't offend others.

By the way, we have a small but useful book of etiquette that tells you what to wear, do, and say at formal and informal occasions. A copy will be sent to you free if you will write Dept. 000, Lambert Pharmacal Company, St. Louis, Mo.

LISTERINE ends HALITOSIS checks BODY ODORS

Figure 4.12: Appearing in 1932, this ad told the story of a steamy first-encounter cut short by halitosis. Listerine ad, "Once Was Enough." Domestic Advertising Collection, J. Walter Thompson Company Archives, Hartman Center for Sales, Advertising & Marketing History, Rare Book, Manuscript, & Special Collections Library, Duke University, Durham, North Carolina. Courtesy of Pfizer Pharmaceutical Group, Pfizer Inc.

create Warner-Lambert in 1955.[21] Listerine continued to associated sex and controlling bad breath through the 1980s.

GENERAL CIGAR COMPANY

Faced with continual sales declines, General Cigar Company initiated in 1937 a bold and strikingly different advertising campaign for its Vintage White Owl cigars. Like many sensual appeals at the time, the campaign revolved around the implicit brand promise of sexual attraction and sexual outcomes. This time, however, the appeal was primarily targeted toward men. As such, women in tobacco ads evolved from simply decorative to enticingly available, especially in ads for White Owl cigars.

Up until then, White Owl advertising could be classified as educational. Ads concentrated on copy meant to inform the consumer. For example, an early ad was built around the claim that over a million White Owl cigars were produced in a day, resulting in lower prices. The primary visual was an image of a cigar, sometimes an owl, accompanied by copy. By the mid-1930s it was clear this advertising approach wasn't achieving the desired outcome. In the five-cent-cigar market, sales of White Owl lagged behind competitive brands. In addition, the brand lacked positioning with smokers because they considered it indistinguishable from other brands.

The new campaign—built on findings derived from the company's research department—sought to increase sales and clearly position the brand's image. Research was initiated to discover what particles were present in exhaled cigar smoke. Participants smoking cigars ("in the usual way by typical cigar smokers") blew smoke into a twin-sphere osmometer. The lab study revealed that Vintage White Owl smoke, compared to ten other leading five-cent cigars, contained fewer of the substances that cause unpleasant tobacco breath.[22] The results were formulated into a copy strategy: White Owl cigars are "easier on the breath."[23]

According to internal agency memos, the copy strategy was designed to dispel the belief that smoke from White Owl cigars was bad. "We decided to present it in a positive way through advertising."[24] The agency visualized the brand advantage as follows: "Good breath is most important when a man is kissing his wife or sweetheart. By dramatizing this romantic

Figure 4.13: A 5¢ kiss? General Cigar ad (n.d.), "Kissing." Domestic Advertising Collection, J. Walter Thompson Company Archives, Hartman Center for Sales, Advertising & Marketing History, Rare Book, Manuscript, & Special Collections Library, Duke University, Durham, North Carolina. White Owl is a registered trademark of Pinkerton Tobacco Co. LP.

moment, as in White Owl advertising, we associate women with cigar smoking in a new and powerful way. This not only helps White Owls but the cigar industry as well."[25] The strategy sought to visually take advantage of the research findings through sexual appeals.

What followed was a series of ads featuring model Shelia Carrie kissing men. Ads featured images of passionate kissing, accompanied only by a headline and the White Owl logo (see fig. 4.13). One of the headlines read, "Easier on your breath—Vintage White Owl 5¢." Other ads featured a similar image with the headline, "Every woman wants to be kissed—Vintage White Owl 5¢."

David A. Munro, an advertising industry monitor, described the campaign the following way: "She [Shelia Carrie] attempts to convey, by being flagrantly kissed on billboards & white space throughout the land, that White Owl smokers are untainted, that the subtle sex-satisfactions inherent in the cigar are peculiarly present in White Owl."[26] Munro accused the advertising agency of pandering to sex: "[JWT] played this sex angle for all it seems currently worth."

To be sure the ad claims were in compliance with regulators, JWT involved its legal counsel. The following description was provided in one memo: "To make sure the claim was sound, we had our attorney go over the findings with the head of the laboratories, and approve every advertisement before it was published."[27] Ads passing scrutiny were destined to appear on billboards and in magazines. Women were considered a secondary audience because they influenced the cigar selection process. A women might say to her husband, "If you want to kiss me, get yourself a cigar that doesn't give you bad breath." At the very least, it was hoped that the campaign would have some impact on women's negative attitudes toward men's cigar smoking.[28]

The first year of the "Kissing" campaign, White Owl sales rose above the industry average. Unfortunately for General Tobacco Company, success didn't last long. White Owl sales began to decline in 1938, only the second year of the campaign.[29] The "Kissing" campaign was discontinued shortly thereafter, but not before prompting negative mail from upset members of the public. In response to a letter by a Mr. W. J. Ryan of New York City, the tobacco company rationalized its romanticized campaign the following way: "In the selection of our illustration we have tried to keep within the bounds of good taste set by the leading publications and sound motion pictures. Good taste, of course, cannot be exactly defined. But a safe guide is established by what is acceptable to a majority of people."[30] Objections to the campaign didn't kill the campaign; lack of sales did.

Although the "Kissing" campaign was discontinued, ads for White Owls continued to employ sex-tinged images. In a series of ads emphasizing that their cigars had been improved and were "up-to-date," ads featured images of couples showing interest in each other. For example, one ad that ran in the *New York Times* in 1942 features the illustration of a sailor talking to an attractive young woman who has an accentuated figure (see fig. 4.14).

What was the White Owl promise? Possibly, it was that White Owl cigars offer more opportunity for romance and closeness. After all, ads contained only a few innocuous words—the headline: "Easier on your breath." Considering the target audience was men, however, the appeal takes on a slightly more lascivious tone. It wasn't that men desired to appear more radiant to impress others, or to attract desirable life partners, but it may have been a promise of increased sexual outcomes. Reading between the lines, the implicit argument is that smokers will be more likely to engage in sexual behavior (kissing) without worrying about cigar breath.

Figure 4.14: White Owl graduated from "The Kiss" to this 1942 ad. 1942 General Cigar ad, "Chauncey Likes Old Things." Domestic Advertising Collection, J. Walter Thompson Company Archives, Hartman Center for Sales, Advertising & Marketing History, Rare Book, Manuscript, & Special Collections Library, Duke University, Durham, North Carolina. White Owl is a registered trademark of Pinkerton Tobacco Co. LP.

CONCLUSION

Advertisements in the 1920s, 1930s, and 1940s painted a psychological portrait of America's wants and desires. Women were captivated by the glamour and celebrity of motion picture stars; advertisers used these starlets to motivate women to appear younger, more beautiful, and more radiant. Ads in popular magazines made appeals promising intimacy and romance. Not only were traditional beauty-related products pitched with sexual promises, but so were pressure cookers, flatware, and sanitary pads.

Men weren't immune to variants of the intimacy appeals, at least initially. General Cigar's White Owl brand experienced a substantial bump in sales because of a massive "kissing" campaign. Sales soon headed south, however. Perhaps men discovered that, although White Owls were "easier on the breath" by eliminating *some* offensive substances, enough substance remained to challenge the kissing campaign's veracity. A five-cent cigar is still a five-cent cigar, after all.

Whatever failure loomed over White Owl, Listerine fared much better. Naturally occurring halitosis was held at bay by the mouthwash, so appeals emphasizing the benefits and costs of this social disease worked. Perhaps some of the brand's success can also be attributed to sensual ads that offered "kissing techniques" and the secret to love after the first kiss—once you gargled and used as directed.

Aside from romance, men were also captivated for all kinds of products by photos of starlets and other cookie-cutter images that characterized women as busty, beautiful, and playful. Images of the pin-ups, associated with businesses, captured men's eyes and provided many of them with wistful and wanton images. These images, in the form of calendars, magnets, and promotional cards, adorned men's space in both the office and at home. Similarly, images of females baring almost everything could be found in pages of trade publications that were read almost entirely by men. Revealing images of women were just part of the dialogue among men in business-to-business advertising during this period, and continued into the next quarter century.

5
Intimate Intimations
1950–1975

Throughout the 1960s Virginia tourism steadily declined as more East Coast travelers visited Florida and other coastal states. In an attempt to stem the tide, in 1969 a committee of Virginia's Department of Conservation and Economic Development adopted as the state's tourism slogan: "Virginia is for Lovers." The results were immediate; in 1970 over 20 million people visited the state, and by 1971 twice as many people planned to visit Virginia as any other state. Moreover, the slogan was extremely popular with the state's residents.[1]

Adoption of the motto was surprising, however, when one considers the term "lovers" and the risqué meanings associated with it. As subtle an intimation as it was, the slogan represented an entire state—a state proud of its history and heritage—to the rest of the world. As a Virginia native and a child, I remember watching "Virginia is for Lovers" commercials featuring young romantic couples holding hands as they walked on a beach at sunset. As far as I could tell, the slogan had something to do with romance and whatever else it was young couples did when they were in love. I'm sure that I wasn't alone in my thinking, but the beauty of the slogan was its versatility. The copywriter who coined the phrase originally wrote that Virginia was for beach lovers, for history lovers, and for mountain lovers. When shortened, the motto still meant those things and more.

Perhaps the governmental committee was influenced by the times. It was the 1960s, and the slogan's debut just happened to coincide with the Summer of Love. Other advertisers were turning up the volume as American culture was heating up sexually. The general public was openly confronting, or confronted with, sexuality like never before. The introduction of the Pill in the early 1960s made possible sex without consequences. And after the Stonewall riot in 1969, many Americans were faced with homosexuality coming out of the closet. Single bars, "free love," and shifting gender roles created a sexualized cultural landscape.

To be effective, advertisers needed to express these undercurrents as a way to stay at the forefront, to stay hip, and to connect with consumers. As a result, sexual images became more visible and sexual innuendo more palpable from the end of the 1960s to the mid-1970s. During the quarter century between 1950 and 1975, the intensity and frequency of innuendo and sexual meaning increased. As early as 1947, Elliot Springs teased viewers with his sexual, yet innocent, puns and peek-a-boo shots of women's panties. Soon after, Maidenform initiated its long-running "Dream" campaign that plastered images of beautiful bra-clad women in the pages of mainstream magazines. In the 1960s, Noxzema's sexy "Swedish" spokesperson was telling men to "Take it off. Take it all off"—its brand of shaving cream, of course. At the same time, a woman with obvious control of her own sexual destiny, unusual up to that point, told viewers, "All my men wear English Leather, or they wear nothing at all."

Sex in advertising during this period was not always so flagrant, however. Flanking the more blatant ads were romantic and passionate appeals for fragrances such as Wind Song and Tabu. During this time De Beers ads cemented the association between love and diamonds with its "Diamonds are forever" slogan, which was coined in 1947. Even demure ads for Miss Clairol were mistakenly accused of using innuendo with the highly successful "Does she or doesn't she?" campaign. None of these ads, especially the most libidinous ones, were out of place in this era. It's impossible to imagine Virginia adopting its "Lovers" slogan any earlier than it did, say in 1949, for instance. But, given the cultural environment, its acceptance in 1969—in the midst of the sexual revolution—is understandable.

The second best shape in Italy

at the hottest little price in the USA. You've seen the first, in films. Now see the Fiat, in person. Fiat is the hot one. The Italians did it the way they do most things. With style. With flair. With flourish. And there's no Germanic thrift showing. This Fiat sport comes with all the extras at not a penny extra. Bucket seats, power brakes, leatherette upholstery, heater, defroster, tachometer, dual electric wipers, safety belt anchors, bumper guards, self-cancelling turn signals, help-lights and tool kit. And speaking of figures, you can't even come close to a shape like this at a price so trim and appealing. At $2639*, it's the lowest-priced sports car in its class. Every family should have at least one Fiat. **FIAT**

Figure 5.1: This Fiat ad appeared in the October 1964 issue of *Road & Track* magazine. Fiat Auto S.p.A.

AMERICA FROM 1950 TO 1975

The second half of the twentieth century began with a tremendous post-war boom. Truman, and later Eisenhower, presided over a prosperous economy that not only promised, but delivered for many, a car in every garage and a chicken in every pot. Americans needed those automobiles as they migrated from urban centers to the suburbs, due in part to Congressional action. The Federal Highway Act of 1956 built miles of new roads connecting downtowns with outlying housing developments. America's love affair with the automobile intensified and auto manufacturers soon became the nation's leading advertisers.[2]

It was also a time of political upheaval. McCarthyism and the Red Scare reflected American's sense of threat to their way of life in the early 1950s. After unparalleled success in the Second World War, American might was humbled with an uneasy truce in Korea and later failure in Vietnam. The government's credibility began to erode with a series of events including the Pentagon papers, the Warren Report, and the Watergate scandal. Demonstrations rocked the Democratic National Convention in Chicago in 1968, and race riots ravaged a number of America's cities. In addition, the assassinations of John and Bobby Kennedy, and Martin Luther King and Malcolm X, contributed to the toll taken on the nation's collective emotions and psyche.

America was also experiencing a sexual awakening. Hugh Hefner's *Playboy*, featuring its articles and pictorials of nude women, hit the stands in 1953. *Penthouse* followed suit in 1969. J. D. Salinger's *The Catcher in the Rye*, with its references to sexuality, was an instant best-seller. Elvis Presley, shaking his hips in the 1950s, opened the door for rock music in the 1960s. Sex, drugs, and rock 'n' roll were ushered in by the Beatles, Rolling Stones, Doors, Jimi Hendrix, and Janis Joplin. Female fashion also had an impact. In the late 1960s, the mini-skirt and French-inspired bikini displayed more skin. William Masters and Virginia Johnson brought attention to orgasm and helped to make sex a topic of discussion with their book *Human Sexual Response*. Congress in 1967 even got into the act with its commission that investigated the effects of obscenity and pornography.

Along with the growth of business and prosperity came an increase in consumerism. Ralph Nader, a consumer rights activist, exposed the big automakers' abhorrent safety record with his book *Unsafe at Any Speed.* In 1969 the National Association of Broadcasters began phasing out cigarette advertising on radio and television. Regulators recognized the power of television, and television advertising, to influence the general public.

MEDIA AND ADVERTISING

The biggest media development after 1950 was the widespread diffusion of television. The first television commercial, a nine-dollar spot hawking Bulova watches, was broadcast in 1941. Due to the war, however, television development was put on hold. Soon after V-J Day, televisions and television advertising proliferated at an astounding rate. For example, American homes in 1948 contained over one million television sets. By 1960, there was over 50 million sets in 45 million homes, and each family watched television an average of 35–40 hours per week.[3]

Television advertising soon evolved from single-sponsor programming (The Kraft Music Hall, The Pontiac Star Parade) to multiple-sponsored programs, similar to today's format. As a result, television ad spending took off. Money invested in commercials grew from $68 million in 1949 to over $688 million in 1953.[4] According to television historian Lawrence Samuel, "television advertising was ground central for the postwar American Dream, both with shaping and reflecting our national ethos of consumption."[5]

During the 1960s, the advertising profession experienced what was called the Creative Revolution. Emphasis was placed on art, creativity, and simplified expression of ideas. Ads exemplified a casual writing style that was much less formal than before.[6] Adoption of the new style was accelerated by the establishment of creative work teams at agencies such as Doyle, Dane, & Bernbach (DDB). One of the most admired campaigns of the 1960s, the Volkswagen Beetle ads created by DDB were extremely creative. The campaign characterized the new style of this period. Also during this era, television commercials became shorter. As a result, selling messages became more intrusive through attention getting visuals and fast-talking voice-overs.[7]

While creativity in the 1960s was highly important, advertisers also soon emphasized research, audience segmentation, and brand positioning.

Sophisticated production technology resulted in more consumer products and more consumer choices. Multitudes of brands, virtually indistinguishable from each other, soon saturated product categories. Finding a way to advertise these brands so that consumers could differentiate between them resulted in an emphasis on brand positioning. Marketing research was used to identify groups of consumers with different needs, and advertising was tailored to appeal to each group. One advertiser, Elliot Springs, relied on his own sense of judgment when it came to positioning his company's products through advertising.

SPRINGS MILLS

In the late 1940s and the 1950s, Elliot Springs, president of Springs Mills and several related firms, single-handedly changed the look of advertising with his sex-tinged advertising strategy. With ads containing taunting illustrations and deft tease, Springs is often credited with mainstreaming humorous and witty uses of sex in advertising. More important, Springs's ads were some of the most memorable—and profitable—ads of their day.

Charles Goodrum and Helen Dalrymple eloquently tell the story of Major Elliot White Springs and the development of his unique approach to sex in advertising.[8] It began when Springs, an air force ace, soon after returning from World War I, reluctantly took the helm of his father's textile businesses. After several successful years, Springs became bored with his company's standard advertising approach. Perhaps to interject some excitement, more so for him than for viewers, Springs developed a advertising strategy deliberately revolving around sex. Beginning in 1947, ads containing sexual images and double entendres were used to sell Spring Mills fabrics and related products such as sheets and pillowcases, and innerwear.

Springs conceptualized the ads himself, often writing the copy and having illustrators in New York develop just the right image of a pretty girl and her partially exposed underwear. Showing too much skin in too lecherous a manner was considered tasteless by Springs. As far as he was concerned, complete nudity defeated the purpose. Although Springs believed that sexy images of attractive people grabbed readers' attention, it was the glimpse of the forbidden—a woman's panties or garter belt—that drew

A buck well spent on a Springmaid Sheet

This buck may look more like 47¢—which is what *most* bucks are worth these days. But not *this* "dearslayer." Any buck spent on a SPRINGMAID sheet gets you value of *100 cents* on the dollar— as any two smart squaws know.

Because they stand up so well to wear and washings and yet are soft and beautiful, any number of bucks couldn't get you a better sheet value. We sent them to an independent testing laboratory and, honest Injun, what happened to them would make Custer's Last Stand look like a Vassar Daisy Chain. First, they were washed 400 times—abraded 100 times warpwise and 100 times fillingwise.

That was equal to a whole generation of constant use! And those sheets came out looking like—you guessed it—a million bucks, with a lot more wear left in them, too! But don't take our word for it! See for yourself their luster and even yarns. And compare the "washability" of SPRINGMAID sheets and pillowcases with any other sheet on the market. We're betting plenty of wampum every time that you'll put your buck on a SPRINGMAID sheet—*and it'll be a buck well spent!*

SPRINGS MILLS, Inc.

Figure 5.2: "A buck well spent . . ." Elliot Springs believed the images in his ads attracted attention, and his wily puns piqued readers' interest.

people in. "He believed the best way of stopping readers who were scanning two hundred ads in a *Saturday Evening Post* was to show them something they didn't ordinarily see, but show so little of it it forced the readers to use their imaginations."[9] The images and ambiguous headlines enticed readers, arousing their curiosity enough so that they would read the copy.

Consider, for example, a 1948 magazine ad showing three female performance skaters waiting backstage for their cue. All three are lifting the backs of their short skirts to warm their derrières at a portable coal-fired heater. The headline reads, "Protect yourself." People curious enough to want to determine what *protection* had to do with women's rears were required to read the copy. They discovered that Springs Mills developed a flame resistant fabric during the war. "Protect yourself" wove together the ambiguous headline and the image to demonstrate a feature and benefit of Springs Mills' fabric. Good advertising, believed Springs, made a connection between the titillating image and the promoted brand. If not, consumers would feel manipulated and shun future ads, much less buy the product.

Much like David Ogilvy's principles of successful advertising espoused in his semi-autobiographical books, Elliott Springs developed his treatise on sex in advertising. The following is Goodrum and Dalrymple's characterization of Springs's beliefs: "Sex was phenomenally effective in getting the attention of a jaded reader. It worked, however, only if used with certain correlative devices: 1) You had to treat the reader as an intelligent peer; 2) Once you had the reader's attention, you had to offer some product benefit to justify stopping him, otherwise he would resent your impudence; 3) The actual sex image should be used not only with humor—a light touch—but with respect. The 'object' must not be being taken advantage of. And 4) the most effective use of the sex should be what we now call The Tease."[10] According to Springs, a peek-a-boo shot—a fallen sleeve revealing a bra strap, gusts of wind raising skirts enough to expose underwear—grabbed attention better than images of nude models. His diligent adherence to his principles was reflected in his advertising.

It's important to note that Springs's campaigns were not, at least initially, handled by national advertising agencies such as J. Walter Thompson and N. W. Ayer. None of them wanted his business, perhaps because of the sexual images and double entendres that Springs insisted on inserting into his ads.

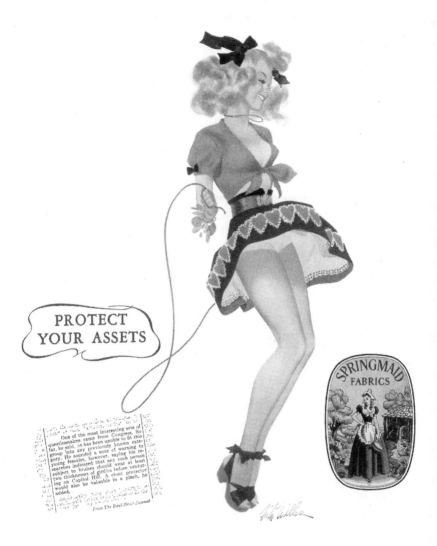

PROTECT YOUR ASSETS

SPRINGMAID FABRICS

One of the most interesting sets of questionnaires came from Congress. So far, he said, he has been unable to fit this group into any previously known category. He sounded a note of warning to young females, however, saying his researches indicated that any such person subject to bruises should wear at least two thicknesses of girdles before venturing on Capitol Hill. A chest protector would also be valuable in a pinch, he added.

From The Wall Street Journal

SPRINGS MILLS, Inc.

(This advertisement is from a series of ads conceived by Elliott White Springs, president of Springs Mills from 1931 until his death in 1959. The ads appeared in general circulation magazines in the 1940's and 1950's and helped establish the Springmaid® brand name as a consumer favorite.)

Figure 5.3: Springs directed his illustrators not to "show too much." Provided by Springs Industries, Inc. Provided by Springs Industries, Inc.

It might have been because Springs was stubborn when it came to projecting the perfect image—revealing, but not too scandalous. Thus, in contrast with most large advertisers of this era, the Springs Mills' campaigns were conceptualized by the president of the company and handled in-house.

Elliot Springs's advertising approach was different than others' at the time because he used sexually captivating images in a humorous and lighthearted manner. Explaining his initial strategy in 1946, Springs wrote: "We'll take a typical sexy ad and revise it into a cartoon. Or take a cartoon and revise it into a sexy ad. This should please everyone."[11] Overall, Springs's strategy worked: Springs Mills' campaigns had very high brand-name recall among consumers. For example, Springs's advertising from 1947 to 1951 was remembered better than any concurrent advertising campaign, even those produced by top-rate agencies. His strategy also proved successful in regard to monetary return. Sales of Springmaid sheets increased until Springs's death in 1959.

MAIDENFORM'S "DREAM-Y" ADS

"I dreamed I held the world on a string in my Maidenform bra," declared the headline in a circa-1950s Maidenform advertisement. The model in the ad, clad only in her bra from the waist up, did indeed hold the world's attention. So did the other models, photographers, and writers associated with Maidenform's infamous bra campaign, a promotional effort that *Fortune* magazine judged as one of the five classic advertising campaigns of all time.[12]

The enduring "Dream" campaign, lasting twenty years (from 1949 to 1969), contained images of women in their Maidenform bras dreaming about life in exotic locations, fun situations, and creative contexts. The headlines contained the line, "I dreamed I . . . in my Maidenform bra." The blank was filled in with over two hundred different themes throughout the life of the campaign. The "Dream" theme provided tremendous continuity, a plus in advertising, because the number of clever and creative ways to display the product was limited only by the imagination.

Maidenform's "Dream" campaign wasn't the first to feature photos of bra-clad women in advertising. It was, however, one of the first instances of women's breasts being flaunted so blatantly in mainstream magazine ads.

I dreamed
I barged down the Nile in my *maidenform* bra

Sweet Music!..Maidenform dream bra...features spoke-stitched cups for Cleopatra curves! All-elastic band for freedom of fit;

Figure 5.4: "I dreamed I sailed down the Nile in my Maidenform bra." Maidenform, Inc. All Rights Reserved.

The idea of nearly topless women in realistic or imaginary settings was daring and titillating, and the models were beautiful and glamorous. One of the advertising agency principles associated with the campaign, Norman B. Norman, described the Maidenform models as "striking, blatant, voluptuous."[13] Kitty D'Alessio, a designer who worked for Norman, said, "We always did a three-quarter pose to make them look as attractive as possible. The models had gorgeous, incredible figures to begin with. They all had those flat midriffs and kept themselves in shape."[14] The combination of the women and the writing was responsible for a bra campaign that busted the norms of women's innerwear advertising, and had fun doing it. More important, it put Maidenform on the map, making it one of the top women's bra brands in the country.

Maidenform's roots were as a dress boutique, not as a manufacturer of women's intimates. In 1922 Ida Rosenthal and Enid Bissett became partners in a custom dress boutique named Enid Frocks, located on Fifty-seventh Street in New York City. At that time, boyish-look fashion was in. Women wore clothing that neutralized their figures. Bandeaux deemphasized their breasts and loose-fitting dresses veiled women's curves. Bissett went the opposite route by modifying the restricting bandeaux to create a brassiere that emphasized the natural shape of the breasts. According to Ida Rosenthal, "Nature made woman with a bosom, so nature thought it was important. Who am I to argue with nature?"[15]

The original Maidenform bras, described as "little more than strips of cloth with strategic tucks," were originally given away as premiums with the dresses.[16] As the bras became popular, the ladies started selling them for a dollar apiece. In 1925 Bissett, with Ida and William Rosenthal, founded the Enid Manufacturing Company. By 1928, they stopped making dresses and focused exclusively on designing and manufacturing bras. William Rosenthal, Ida's husband, was involved in the design process. His sister, also working at the company, borrowed assembly-line production methods to keep up with demand. Whereas one woman could produce only three or four bras in a day, as a member of an assembly line she could help produce hundreds of bras in the same amount of time.[17]

By 1930, the company's name was changed again, this time to Maiden Form Brassiere Company. The name was chosen because the company's product, including its line of signature bras, emphasized the woman's physique—a *maiden's* form, not the physique of a boy. Moderately priced and made of good material, Maidenform bras were known as a good value. In 1949, the same year the "Dream" campaign was introduced, Maidenform introduced bras with different cup sizes. It was one of the first companies to do so.

The "Dream" campaign wasn't Maidenform's first foray into advertising. The company ran small ads in New York City newspapers as early as 1925. Beginning in 1930, larger ads were placed in newspapers and national magazines such as *Life*. In 1938, Maidenform hit the airwaves when it sponsored the music program, "Console and Keyboard." Surprisingly, the bra company was an "official" sponsor for the 1939 New York World's Fair. Its name was plastered all over the city in Fair promotional materials.

In 1949, writers at William Weintraub, Maidenform's advertising agency (which later became Norman, Craig & Kummel, Inc.), were developing new ideas for an upcoming campaign. It was then that Mary Fillius, a Weintraub copywriter, introduced the "Dream" idea that proved so popular. Dr. Joseph Coleman, Maidenform's advertising director as well as the Rosenthal's son-in-law, liked the idea immediately.

Although Fillius is credited with initiating the "Dream" concept, the attribution is somewhat controversial. According to advertising professional Joe Saccro, the idea behind "Dream" was originally developed by his art-director buddy, Herman Davis.[18] Fillius helped to develop Davis's idea when they both worked at the Lester Harrison agency. The original line was: "I dreamed I went shopping in my Seamprufe slip." Unfortunately for Seamprufe, someone at the underwear company decided they didn't like the concept. Fillius, who later migrated to Weintraub, was out of ideas for Maidenform when Sacco suggested she use the "Dream" theme. The rest is history. Coleman okayed the idea, and after some development, "Dream" ads began appearing in women's magazines.

The campaign was described as "a glamorous young woman depicted in a print ad doing just about anything imaginable in her Maidenform bra."[19] Maidenform described the psychology behind the campaign as an example of wish-fulfillment. Women, forced back into traditional roles after men returned from the war, could dream about exotic places and off-limits situations. The campaign was popular among women because it appealed to their aspirations to realize both their personal and professional "dreams." According to Maidenform, the campaign contributed to women's needs for independence and romance.[20]

Many of the themes, however, had little to do with what feminists would truly consider *autonomous* situations. For example, many ads contained "dreams" revolving around stereotypically female activities or situations that were simply playful. Consider a few of the headlines: "I dreamed I... went to a masquerade; was an outdoor girl; had tea for two; was an autograph hound; played Cleopatra; was an Egyptian dreamboat; was made over; danced the Charleston; was queen of the Westerns; went to the theater; went cruising; stopped traffic; went on a tiger hunt... in my Maidenform bra."

Consider the first full-page "Dream" ad of 1949: "I dreamed I went shopping in my Maidenform bra" (see fig. 5.5). The woman in the ad, sitting on a display table in John Frederic's hat salon, was admiring herself wearing a fashionable hat. The copy in the ad read: "Wake me quick... this dream's too lovely! Designer hats... millions of them... peacock-bright, moon-dark, sun-spangled. What could be lovelier? Only my figure... so pretty in my Maidenform bra? I never dreamed that I could be so curve-sure, so secure, 'til I discovered Maidenform!" At the time, this ad might have articulated legitimate dreams for fashion-conscious, middle- and upper-class women, but few can agree that it espoused "girl power." It did sell bras, however. The ad promoted Maidenform's Chansonette bra. Consisting of white cotton broadcloth with circular-stitched cups, the Chansonette soon became a top-selling bra and remained one for over thirty years.[21]

Feminists might have preferred headlines such as "I dreamed I... got the big deal; I got him to sign the dotted line... in my Maidenform bra." One can only imagine the visuals that would have accompanied those headlines. As a post-"Dream" campaign might reveal, I think it would be difficult to show bra-clad women in a powerful, pro-feminist ideal, regardless of the scenario.

Almost without exception, models were clad in a skirt and a Maidenform bra—without outerwear above the waist. According to D'Alessio, the model had to be just right. Photographers approved each model, making sure she had the precise look for the designated theme. Shoots often took an entire day.

Maidenform invested $180,649 in advertising the first year of the campaign. The company claimed the ads were successful because they "satisfied the secret longings of the sentimental women of the fifties."[22] The

I dreamed I went shopping in my *maidenform bra*

Wake me quick...this dream's too lovely! Designer hats...millions of them...peacock-bright, moon-dark, sun-spangled. What could be lovelier? Only my figure...so pretty in my Maidenform bra! I never dreamed that I could be so curve-sure, so secure, 'til I discovered Maidenform! Maybe you've dreamed of a bra with letter-perfect fit like this! Shown: Maidenform's Allo-ette® in white rayon satin. Just one of a vast and varied collection of styles, fabrics and colors. There is a *Maiden Form*® for every type of figure

PHOTO BY PAULICAS. DREAM SETTING AND SCENE HATS BY JOHN-FEDERICO. ©1949, MAIDEN FORM BRASSIERE CO., INC. ®REG. U. S. PAT. OFF.

Figure 5.5: "I dreamed I went shopping . . ." was one of the earliest Maidenform "Dream" ads. Maidenform, Inc. All Rights Reserved.

target market was women of all ages. When Maidenform ads started running in *Seventeen* magazine, themes took a more youth-oriented tone: "I dreamed I was an autograph hound for *Seventeen* Magazine...."; and "...had a mod mod world on a string in my Maidenform bra."

Women were expected to identify with the models and to project themselves into the ad. In addition, Maidenform's ad director, Joseph Coleman, told *Madison Avenue* that the selection of "Dream" themes was "rigidly controlled by three factors. It must be at least quasitopical, pitched to the current fashions, and adapted to the particular line that Maiden Form is then producing. From the beginning we were determined that we would work for artistic ads in impeccable taste."[23]

It's estimated that over two hundred different "Dream" themes were advertised over the life of the campaign. Initially, six different themes were produced each year.[24] To save money, fewer original concepts were produced toward the end of the campaign. Considering rising advertising costs, the expense of top talent, and elaborate scenes constrained only by dreams, it is not surprising that Maidenform produced fewer ads. The company did continue to saturate the market with advertising, however. The ads appeared in the pages of *Vogue, Harper's Bazaar, Glamour, Mademoiselle*, and many other women's magazines.

In a 1990 interview, D'Alessio, who eventually left Norman, Craig and Kummel to become president of Chanel, Inc., disclosed some interesting details about the "Dream" campaign. A group of people at the agency would get together and brainstorm themes, she said. Ideas were written on three-by-five-inch note cards. The batch of ideas were then narrowed down to four or five good ideas that were eventually produced. "We tried to inject fashion as well as some humor, so the ad would be fun. People looked for them because they were campy," commented D'Alessio.[25]

D'Alessio also shed light on the status of advertising intimates at the time. "It's odd, here in the '90s lingerie photography is commonplace," said D'Alessio. "...in those days lingerie was a difficult thing. The models were paid double hourly rate, as it was undesirable to be photographed in a bra; today, it's nothing."[26] Bras worn by the models were custom made. Executives at Maidenform made decisions about what product-line to feature, a new or existing line, and designers would tailor the specific product to the model's form.

Several well-known photographers produced images for the "Dream" campaign. One of them was Richard Avedon, renowned for his work for Calvin Klein and his own artistic achievements. Avedon was the photographer for the "I dreamed I was a knockout" ad featuring model Sandy Christopher. Clad in boxing shorts and a bra, Christopher leaned provocatively on the boxing ring ropes. With a big, sensual smile, she was supposed to be a cross between wrestler Gorgeous George and Marilyn Monroe.[27]

Avedon shot another provocative ad for Maidenform, the western-style "Wanted" poster: "I dreamed I was Wanted in my Maidenform bra" (see fig. 1.7). Meant to resemble a *Wanted* poster, the model—Sara Dolley—was partially turned toward the camera (in the signature ¾ pose) much like a gunslinger turning to face an assailant. There is little doubt Dolley was "wanted," but probably by male viewers. Looking good, she oozed with sex appeal as she gave viewers a come-hither look, her mouth turned up slightly at one corner. In addition to her bra, she wore a hat created by either John Frederic or Mr. John, both trendy New York hat designers.[28] The next year, French designer Yves St. Laurent introduced a line of cowboy-style hats.

Many of Maidenform's "Dream" ads took place in public settings. It's one thing to see a bra-clad woman in a setting without any context, but Maidenform ads positioned their models outdoors and on the street. Consider an ad with the headline, "I dreamed I was an Outdoor Girl in my Maidenform bra." In this 1957 ad, appearing in *This Week, Vogue,* and *True Story,* a woman is looking at an image of herself on a billboard. In the image, she's smiling as she sits at the steering wheel of a car, clad only in her bra, driving gloves, and scarf that blows in the breeze. "I'm the nicest sign of the times…openly admired by thousands," read the copy. This ad may have been what critics were referring to when they said that Maidenform's ads had more to do with exhibitionism than women's dreams of independence.

In a sense, the ads appealed to the male fantasy of imagining what women look like with their clothes off. Just consider the not-so-implicit selling point of X-Ray glasses sold to boys in the backs of comic books. The ads promised young voyeurs they could see through anything, especially clothing. A man with a lecherous grin watched a particularly buxom young woman as she walked by him. Although boys don't buy bras, Maidenform ads inadvertently put boys one step closer to their fantasies with its sexy, bra-clad models in mass-circulation magazines.

Maidenform's advertising campaigns were seasonal—running heaviest during the fall and spring fashion seasons. During these campaigns, Maidenform would spend millions to reach women consumers, saturating magazines and television with its advertising. Consider, for example, the company's advertising strategy in the spring of 1966.[29] Six different products (bras and girdles) were advertised in magazines. The largest promotion was the "Dream" campaign for the Dreamliner Bra. The ad ran in eleven magazines, reaching over eighty million women readers. The campaign also included a maternity and nursing bra, and girdle promotion. Overall, the company ran thirty-seven full-page ads with a readership of over 200 million women.

Maidenform's 1966 Spring campaign also contained a television "spotacular" consisting of sixty-second commercials. The television ads emphasized Maidenform's Tric-o-lastic lace bra and Concertina girdles. The television plan reached eight of every ten women. Those eight women saw the commercial, on average, five times that spring.

The "Dream" theme added extra continuity to other Maidenform lines and promotional efforts. For example, a line of swimsuits was advertised with the headline, "Who's the dream in the...?" Maidenform also sponsored a very popular promotional contest where people mailed in their own versions of the "I dream" theme. The winner earned $20,000 by telling Maidenform, in twenty-five words or less, why they liked their bra.

Eleven years after the "Dream" campaign ended in 1969, Maidenform's ads returned to a similar "dream"-style campaign. In 1980, the company initiated the "Maidenform Woman" campaign created by Daniel & Charles agency. Each ad contained the headline: "The Maidenform woman. You never know where she'll turn up." Women, shown in their bras *and panties* this time, were featured in an array of settings. Although some of the ads positioned women in contexts of strength and authority (as doctors and lawyers), the campaign was criticized by feminists who claimed the ads contributed only to the degradation of women.

The copy style in the newer ads was similar to that in the original "Dream" campaign. For example, the copy for an ad with a horse race theme reads, "She's picked an unbeatable combination in sleek, satiny Sweet Nothings...In colors that are sure to be your odds-on favorites." In an ad with a basketball theme, the copy reads, "She's bound to score points when she's wearing sassy Cotton Continentals…in a basket full of fast-breaking colors."

Maidenform's reincarnations and extensions of the "Dream" theme were effective, but they could never regain the magic and brilliance of the original campaign. According to advertising creative Joe Sacco, the "Dream" campaign was "one of the hardest-hitting, highest-longevity advertising campaigns ever created."[30] Maidenform invested over $20 million in advertising during the twenty-year "Dream" campaign. It paid off in sales—revenue tripled from 1949 to 1969—and the popularity of the campaign. According to Anita Coryell, "The ads were parodied in editorial cartoons and on greeting cards. No costume party or parade was complete without someone dressed up in an 'I Dream' spoof."[31] In 1961, a Gallup and Robinson poll revealed that thirty-seven out of one hundred women could recall a specific Maidenform ad—twice as many as for Maidenform's leading competitor.[32] By 1997, however, Maidenform had filed Chapter 11 and was in financial reorganization. Women are still buying Maidenform bras, however—the company reemerged from bankruptcy in 1999—but the brand's prestige and the image it once enjoyed have eroded.

DE BEERS DIAMONDS

Whereas Maidenform ads were clever and attention getting, De Beers ads were about imbuing minerals with romance. Since the 1920s, De Beers Consolidated Mines and its U.S.-based advertising agencies have successfully linked its cartel-controlled diamonds with romance and love through deliberate advertising strategies. At no time was this more apparent than with its "Diamonds are forever" slogan, coined in 1947, and its romantic appeals in the 1950s, 1960s, and beyond.

N. W. Ayer copywriter Frances Gerety created the infamous "Diamonds are forever" tagline in 1947.[33] It was—and continues to be—a great line because, as with all good advertising slogans, it has multiple but related meanings. Diamonds, one of the hardest of naturally occurring substances, last a lifetime (beyond a lifetime actually). Similarly, marriages and the love they symbolize are supposed to last forever. De Beers ran many cam-

The Best Offer a Girl Ever Had!

You get Cannon Bath Towels for Rinso Blue boxtops at your Singer Sewing Center

HERE'S HOW EASY IT IS TO START COLLECTING LUXURIOUS CANNON TOWELS: Just see details of the offer on the back of your Rinso Blue package. Then take your Rinso Blue boxtops to the nearest Singer Sewing Center and get a big, beautiful, full-size Cannon bath towel in exchange. Take your choice of lovely pink, yellow or aqua stripes on snowy white.

If you love fresh air and sunshine, you'll love the sunshine whiteners in Rinso Blue. Even indoors, right in your wash, the sunshine whiteners in Rinso Blue get clothes so fresh and white they sparkle with whiteness! Colors come out brighter, too!

Figure 5.6: 1958 Rinso Blue ad, "Best Offer a Girl Ever Had." Domestic Advertising Collection, J. Walter Thompson Company Archives, Hartman Center for Sales, Advertising & Marketing History, Rare Book, Manuscript, & Special Collections Library, Duke University, Durham, North Carolina. Rinso ad reproduced courtesy of Unilever PLC and Unilever N.V. or their subsidiaries, copyright holders.

paigns positioning diamonds as symbols of *new* love with engagement rings, and tokens of *enduring* love as gifts for women on special occasions. *Advertising Age* liked the tagline so much, they selected it as the best slogan of the twentieth century.[34]

In the 1920s, De Beers campaigns associated diamonds with artwork. In the late 1930s, De Beers initiated an approach designed to increase consumption of diamonds. The company engineered and fostered the belief that diamond engagement rings were the best way for young couples to represent their love.[35] This proved to be an excellent strategy for De Beers, because the company, founded in South Africa in 1880 by Cecil John Rhodes, controlled 80 percent of the worldwide diamond market.[36] Thus, increasing large-scale consumption would increase prices and fatten De Beers's margins.

Sales and favorable attitudes towards diamond gift-giving soared when the emphasis on engagement rings was combined with Gerety's slogan. The ads contained images of young couples picnicking or embracing in idyllic settings. A full-page ad running in *Life*, *Look*, and the *Saturday Evening Post* in 1957, contained a soft photograph of a romantic couple on a blanket sharing a bottle of wine. Tall trees surround the couple but soft radiant sunlight creates warmth in the image. "In the magic time when love is new, the hours are filled with sweet delights, the world's a place for dreaming. You'll cherish these moments, and recall them always, in the clear, bright lights of your engagement ring."

The ad, and many others like it, exemplified De Beers' strategy of linking marriage with diamond rings. According to business professors Donna Bergenstock and James Maskulka, "Men were encouraged to view the gems as palpable symbols of love and devotion, while women were persuaded that a diamond ring was an engagement necessity."[37] The mere act of giving a woman diamonds was presented through advertising as an expression of love and a lifetime commitment.

A second strategy for increasing diamond consumption was encouraging "trading up." In mature markets where diamond-giving is the norm, trading up means that consumers purchase more expensive diamonds and give them as gifts on special occasions, such as anniversaries and birthdays. Second or third diamond purchases are usually more expensive than the initial engagement ring. A strategy for fostering diamond gift-giving involved creating appreciation for the value of diamonds through education. Advertising developed by N. W. Ayer educated men and women on diamond quality. As a result, many ads contained information about the "four C's" (cut, color, carat, and clarity).

An ad exemplifying "trading up" featured a distinguished older gentleman examining a diamond ring while sitting at a jeweler's counter. The headline read, "Most valued symbol of your devotion." In the ad, men were told, "Beyond all other gifts, a diamond best reflects the depth of your devotion." In a similar ad run in 1964, an attractive older couple nuzzles together on one side of the ad. On the left-hand side, different types of diamond jewelry are shown. "Diamonds bespeak an ever-growing love." These ads, designed to educate consumers while also creating demand, prompted Bergenstock and Maskulka to argue that size did matter. "The size and quality of the diamond were even supposed to signify the degree of love a couple shared."[38]

De Beers' advertising promotions worked as intended. In the 1960s, over 80 percent of couples symbolized their commitment with engagement rings.[39] For the first time, engagement rings became a necessity, and young men were advised by De Beers to invest two month's salary for the proper-sized ring. According to one source, "in its print advertisements, De Beers convinced engaged couples that a diamond represented the love they felt for each other."[40] Market research also revealed that more men and women associated diamond buying with love than ever before.

De Beers has continued to instill its "diamonds = love" formula in consumers' hearts and minds. The enduring slogan, "A diamond is forever," has been used in a multitude of campaigns since its inception. J. Walter Thompson, De Beers' international agency at the time, developed a stunning and very effective campaign in 1993 referred to as "Shadows." A series of television commercials emphasized the highlights of a couple's life. No people were shown, only their silhouettes. The diamonds, shown in brilliant color, marked life events appropriate for diamond giving, such as engagement, birth, and the twenty-fifth anniversary.[41]

The "Shadow" campaign was popular with viewers. Emphasizing anonymous shadows, it allowed viewers to project themselves into the situations. Ad measures such as recall and recognition were in the 80 percent range (much higher than the norm), and consumers' perceptions of diamonds as expressions of love jumped significantly. In addition to building confidence and favorable attitudes toward diamonds, sales increased above expectations.[42] In four years, De Beers sold more than $50 billion worth of diamonds. Not too shabby considering it only invested $55 million to promote the "Shadow" campaign. The campaign left little doubt that diamonds were a girl's best friend.

Thus, De Beers's campaigns have successfully created demand by equating the product (diamonds) with love and the expression of love. Through its advertising, the company sold its gems with purposeful strategies revolving around engagement and life events. "Through the last five decades, De Beers' and N. W. Ayer's vision has gradually been realized. Diamonds have become an integral part of romance, courtship, and marriage rituals worldwide."[43]

Images of attractive couples in romantic settings helped to sell the dream. Combined with the slogan "A diamond is forever," De Beers's advertising convinced people that diamonds would ensure their continued love. According to one source, N. W. Ayer's tagline "became a part of the American psyche, convincing people that buying a diamond was a gesture of love."[44] A 1966 De Beers ad describes the company's approach succinctly: "…only a tangible expression will voice the love you bear your wife. On this day the diamond jewel—love's symbol transcending all earthly values—will bring you both a special day."

NOXZEMA

Unlike De Beers, other advertisers use more salacious and overt sex appeals. In one the sexiest ads on television at the time, Noxzema promised to "Take it all off." The infamous line, "Take it off. Take it all off," was uttered by a Scandinavian beauty in a 1966 Noxzema shaving cream commercial. The ad and its classic use of double entendre became a symbol of the times during America's sexual revolution.

Noxzema, a medicated skin-care products brand, initiated the provocative television campaign to reintroduce its aerosol shaving cream. The company was best known for its blue glass jars of cold cream, but it also developed a line of related products. Noxzema's parent company,

gives
you
the glow
of a girl
in
love...

EYES BY AZITA

Angel Touch
by POND'S

new liquid makeup...
glows on in seconds...lasts for hours!

Just touch on ANGEL TOUCH—and a light from *within* seems to glow through your skin! It can happen to *you!* ANGEL TOUCH is the liquid makeup that gives your complexion the come-touch-me *texture*, the tender color, the luminous *glow* of a girl in love!

try it tonight...people will think you're in love!

In 9 soft-and-subtle shades
$1. Also available in purse-
size plastic bottle, 59c.

For the finishing touch,
Angel Touch Face Powder
in complementary shades:
$1, 50c, 25c.

All prices plus tax.

©1960, CHESEBROUGH-POND'S INC

Figure 5.7: 1960 Angel Touch ad, "Glow of Love." Domestic Advertising Collection, J. Walter Thompson Company Archives, Hartman Center for Sales, Advertising & Marketing History, Rare Book, Manuscript, & Special Collections Library, Duke University, Durham, North Carolina. Angel Touch ad reproduced courtesy of Unilever PLC and Unilever N.V. or their subsidiaries, copyright holders.

Noxell Corporation, also owned Cover Girl cosmetics. The "Take it off" campaign consisted of a series of commercials running from 1966 to 1973. During the campaign, the Noxzema ads were considered "the most overtly sexual to run up until that time."[45]

The signature commercial featured former Miss Sweden bombshell, Gunilla Knutson. In her heavy Scandinavian accent, Knutson gave men advice about shaving. "Men, nothing takes it off like Noxzema medicated shave." Then she purred, "Take it off. Take it a-l-l off."

Everything about Knutson was sexy. The way she looked. The way her long hair cascaded over one eye. The way she stared at the viewer. The way she spoke. Even the string of pearls she held in her hand was sexy. When Knutson wasn't telling men what to do, horns blared the burlesque "The Stripper" tune, while shots were shown of a man quickly pulling a razor across his face. He was taking it off all right.

The sexual tone of the double entendre goes without saying. As far as the network censors were concerned, however, Knutson was referring to whisker removal. "Take the *stubble* off. Take all *the stubble* off," was the literal translation. It was a shaving cream ad, after all.

Considering that the ad was drenched in sex, however, the tongue-in-cheek interpretation was clear. The soundtrack was a *striptease*, and beautiful Knutson teased viewers with her bedroom eyes and sultry inflection. The only nonsexual exception might have been the female voice-over at the end of the commercial who sings, "The closer you shave, the more you need Noxzema. Noxzema medicated comfort shave."

The campaign was designed to promote Noxzema's aerosol shaving cream. Although a lot of men were shaving with electric razors, a sizable segment was still shaving with a blade. These men wanted a foamy, smooth shave that wouldn't burn. The campaign appealed to male consumers by grabbing their attention and showing them how easy it was to shave with Noxzema.

Obvious advertising objectives included creating excitement for the brand while expanding the company's shaving cream market share. Noxzema's ads also served to associate its shaving cream brand with attractive women like Knutson. In a sense, Noxzema became a sexier brand in consumers' minds because of the association. It didn't stop there, however. Noxzema's use of innuendo and drippy sexuality influenced ads for other

LISTERINE IS FOR BREATH-
TOOTH PASTE IS FOR TEETH

*Listerine stops bad breath
4 times better than tooth paste!*

LISTERINE KILLS BAD BREATH GERMS
TOOTH PASTE DOESN'T EVEN REACH!

Germs all over your mouth and throat cause most bad breath. Tooth paste can't even reach most of these germs, let alone kill them. You need a free-flowing liquid antiseptic—Listerine Antiseptic—to do that!

Tooth paste reaches only this small area around your teeth and gums. Besides, no tooth paste is antiseptic. Listerine Antiseptic kills germs as no tooth paste can—on contact, by millions.

Listerine is amazingly "wet"— far more fluid than any tooth paste. The Listerine way" kills germs on four times more germ-laden surface— stops bad breath for hours on end.

*See directions on label.

Every time you brush your teeth, REACH FOR LISTERINE

TUNE IN "THE LORETTA YOUNG SHOW" AND "OVERLAND TRAIL" NBC-TV NETWORK

Figure 5.8: Listerine (1960). Domestic Advertising Collection, J. Walter Thompson Company Archives, Hartman Center for Sales, Advertising & Marketing History, Rare Book, Manuscript, & Special Collections Library, Duke University, Durham, North Carolina. Courtesy of Pfizer Pharmaceutical Group, Pfizer Inc.

brands. According to one source, Noxzema's "Take it off" campaign "was in the vanguard in terms of its overt erotic overtones and helped to kick off the wave of ad campaigns relying heavily on sexual innuendo that endured well into the 1970s."[46]

MISS CLAIROL

In the 1950s, advertisers could flaunt bra-clad women and sell bed linen with blatant innuendo. Yet an innocuous headline for a women's hair coloring product was off limits. At the time, for example, Hearst publications had a policy forbidding articles about, as well as advertising for, women's hair coloring products—respectable women didn't color their hair.[47] When Clairol, a leading marketer of hair colorants, submitted its first national ads to *Life* magazine in 1956, they were rejected because it was a hair colorant and the editors considered the ad's headline, "Does she or doesn't she?" too suggestive. Only when female employees were polled—not one of them interpreted the headline as sexual—did *Life* decision makers acquiesce.

The full headline read: "Does she or doesn't she? Hair color so natural only her hairdresser knows for sure!" It was conceived by Foote, Cone, & Beldings' junior copywriter Shirley Polykoff, herself a bleached blonde. She had the empathy and insight necessary to create an effective concept for Clairol's 1956 launch. Since her teens, Polykoff had altered her hair color. She knew firsthand the stigma associated with hair coloring. At the time, hair coloring was looked down upon. Only actresses, prostitutes, and misguided women were known to dye their hair—respectable housewives maintained their natural color. All that changed with Clairol's groundbreaking advertising campaign. According to one source, "Clairol invested heavily behind the new Miss Clairol advertising campaign in an effort to reassure women that, in coloring their hair, they would lose neither their naturalness nor their respectability."[48]

The ads were successful because Polykoff's headline hit the nail on the head. It played at the heart of Clairol's color advantage—that no one will know that you're coloring your hair. Unlike other formulations that coated the hair, Miss Clairol's dye penetrated the hair strand so that it looked natural. In addition, Clairol's one-step hair coloring process could easily be performed at home. Until that time, hair coloring was an involved process usually done at the salon.

To combat the sexual stereotype that only fast women used hair coloring, images of attractive, but natural, beauties were shown in the ads. The women were described as "wholesome looking models [who] portrayed the girl-next-door image."[49] In a memo to Clairol executives, Polykoff described the type of models she thought belonged in the ads: "Cashmere-sweater-over-the-shoulder types. Like larger-than-life portraits of the proverbial girl on the block who's a little prettier than your wife and lives in a house slightly nicer than yours."[50] Children were also included in the ads to dispel the "fast" connotation associated with hair coloring.

Besides the legendary Miss Clairol headline, Polykoff is also credited with conceiving other catchy headlines for Clairol products. For example, she created in 1965 Nice 'n Easy's line, "The closer he gets, the better you look." Polykoff also penned a series of blonde headlines including: "If I've only one life to live, let me live it as a blonde!"; "It is true...Blondes have more fun."

The "Does she or doesn't she" campaign consisted of both print ads and television commercials. Although the campaign's headline wasn't in the same ballpark as Noxzema's "Take it off," some of Clairol's commercials were energized with a slight sexual charge. Consider the following description of an early Miss Clairol commercial: "[It] featured a housewife, in the kitchen preparing hors d'oeuvres for a party. She is slender and pretty and wearing a black cocktail dress and an apron. Her husband comes in, kisses her on the lips, approvingly pats her very blond hair, then holds the kitchen door for her as she takes the tray of hors d'oeuvres out for her guests."[51]

The campaign was an immediate success. Sales of Clairol products increased tremendously, and hair coloring became the norm. After six years, Clairol's sales were up over 400 percent and 70 percent of adult women were coloring their hair.[52] According to one source, Clairol "practically invented the American hair color market with its breakthrough advertising in the 1950s, and the company ran away with a huge market share."[53]

FRAGRANCE ADVERTISING IN THE 1960s

As the first crop of baby boomers reached adolescence, fragrance advertising began to reflect the sexually progressive social changes taking place in America. Ads for Tabu, English Leather, Chanel, and Faberge provided consumers with a wealth of romance, innuendo, and carnality in the pages of magazines and on television screens.

Tabu was, and still is, a perfume with a great deal of staying power. Introduced in 1931 by Dana Perfume, the Tabu brand has been bought and sold by conglomerates. It's still available at merchandisers and drugstores, but to many people Tabu is best remembered for its passionate image advertising (see fig. 5.9). Running for many decades, its captivating signature ad depicted a male violinist lustfully embracing his female piano accompanist. One could safely assume the musician was swept away by the woman's fragrance.

The amorous ad broke in 1941 issues of *Vogue* and *Harper's Bazaar*, but appeared in magazines throughout the 1950s, 1960s, and 1970s. The ad's tagline read, "Tabu, the forbidden fragrance by Dana." Of course the name "Tabu" conjured up pictures of sensual scenes: "taboo." Today the Tabu brand is owned by New Dana Perfumes. A new extension, Dreams by Tabu, was introduced in the late 1990s. In addition, the image of the musicians was updated to reflect the times, as well as a different style of art.[54] In the 1990s version, reworked by McCabe & Company, a nude male model is shown kissing a female artist who was painting *his* picture. "Blame it on Tabu," reads the re-model-ed tagline.

The original Tabu ad was powerful. Today's grandmothers still remember the ad because it was so captivating. It symbolized the moment when people are swept up in the throes of passion. Even William Safire, political columnist and former Nixon speechwriter, admits to being under Tabu's spell. "... to this day, whenever I write of a word that cannot be used in a family newspaper because it is taboo, I see myself with a violin in one fist and my face buried in the neck of some poor woman who only wanted to play the piano."[55]

Tabu wasn't alone, of course. Other fragrances have been promoted with libidinous themes. Consider, for example, a 1960s ad for English Leather cologne. As noted earlier, the commercial contained a particularly

Figure 5.9: Tabu (1965). "Forbidden Fragrance." Domestic Advertising Collection, J. Walter Thompson Company Archives, Hartman Center for Sales, Advertising & Marketing History, Rare Book, Manuscript, & Special Collections Library, Duke University, Durham, North Carolina; New Dana Perfumes; Parfums de Coeur.

risqué line uttered by a sexy woman: "All my men wear English Leather, or they wear nothing at all." As with most double entendres, her innuendo could easily be dismissed—she's simply talking about her men (changed to "man" in a '90s version of the ad) wearing cologne. When coupled with other elements in the ad, however, her meaning is easily interpreted as sexual. Her tone of voice, for instance, suggests that she may be referring to clothing. In addition, the woman's sense of awareness contributed to the ad's arousing nature. It was obvious that she told her men what to do instead of the other way around. In addition, she could be insinuating that she's a player and can brag about it. The power theme played on notions of changing gender roles as reflective of the times.

On the romantic side, women in Prince Matchabelli's Wind Song commercials got what they wanted without saying anything at all. It was the scent of Wind Song's perfume that mesmerized men (see fig. 5.10). The commercials were stamped with a lovely and memorable jingle: "I can't seem to forget you, your Wind Song stays on my mind." The tune was written and performed by prolific jingle-man Fred Stark. Print ads took advantage of the tune's imprint on viewers' memories with the following headline: "He can't get you out of his mind when Wind Song whispers your message." Full-page, black-and-white Wind Song ads featured close-up images of handsome men staring off the page, lost in thoughts about their women. The men in the ads displayed the effect of a woman's power of attraction via fragrance.

The print campaign for Wind Song debuted in 1952, and television commercials first appeared in the 1960s.[56] The ads didn't have a lascivious nature. The Wind Song man was thinking only about the woman who captured his imagination and his heart. The ads played on the connection between remembrances of lovers and the perfume or cologne they wore. In essence, Wind Song advertising directly appealed to the Pavlovian link between sex and scent. Most of us have experienced being transported back in time by a whiff of an ex-lover's cologne. In an interesting twist, Wind Song sought to position itself as the link to romantic associations between partners.

Sexual promises were offered in fragrance advertising for a multitude of brands. A series of 1965 ads for Emeraude by Coty featured close-up images of beautifully seductive women. The headlines told women how to get their men to behave like, well, more like the men they should be. "Want

He can't get
you out
of his mind
when
Wind Song
whispers your
message

Wind Song
flowers into fragrance
that is yours alone...
for Wind Song
was created
to express itself differently
on *you*
than on any other woman
in the world.
Let Wind Song
do the talking for you!

2.50—5.00

WIND SONG
COLOGNE PARFUMÉE
PRINCE MATCHABELLI

Figure 5.10: "I can't seem to forget you . . ." (1965). Prince Matchabelli's Wind Song. Domestic Advertising Collection, J. Walter Thompson Company Archives, Hartman Center for Sales, Advertising & Marketing History, Rare Book, Manuscript, & Special Collections Library, Duke University, Durham, North Carolina; Parfums de Coeur.

him to be more of a man? Try being more of a woman." A similar headline read, "What him to be more of a Romeo? Try being more of a Juliet." What was the secret? A quick spray of Coty perfume. If women needed help to be more outgoing, Revlon offered them aid. Ads for Revlon's Intimate perfume read: "What makes a shy girl get Intimate?" The copy described what Revlon was really promising. "It's the fragrance that does all the flirting for her. The uninhibited perfume that makes things happen. What kind of things? That's her affair."

Like the other perfume marketers, Chanel No. 5 ads contained similar promises. Chanel's 1965 campaign consisted of two-page magazine spreads with images of attractive men and women nuzzling. The headline said it all: "Caught...By the spell of Chanel." Fragrance advertisers were obviously under the spell of seduction. They used romantic themes, innuendo, and sexual promises to build provocative images for their perfumes and colognes—and consumers responded with their dollars.

CONCLUSION

As America experienced the sexual revolution, so too did advertising. Considering what most American consumers had seen up until 1950, they hadn't seen anything yet. The nude pictures in the 1930s were seductive, but they were not disseminated in mass-marketed magazines. In the 1950s, viewers witnessed bra-clad bombshells and musk-related sexual promises that reflected America's increasing sexual liberalism. Even state slogans with possible sexual meanings, like that of Virginia, were a sign of the times.

The period between 1950 and 1975 began with Elliot Springs and his desire to spice up his company's advertising through sexy ads. Springs codified the use of humorous double entendre and sexual imagery in mainstream advertising. His use of the "Tease" was remarkable because it was often more successful at attracting consumers' attention and increasing sales than standard approaches for other national brands. He strongly believed that consumers would respond favorably to an advertiser that titillated them and gave them an opportunity to figure out the relevance of a double entendre. He was right. But who at the time would have guessed a fabric manufacturer could successfully employ a sexual ad strategy?

Americans also got an eyeful of bra-clad women in the pages of mass-circulation magazines. Maidenform models, in their three-quarter poses, provided provocative images of women in their bras as early as 1949. But Maidenform wasn't alone. Soon bra-encased breasts abounded in print ads. Following Maidenform's lead, Playtex, Bali, and Peter Pan were a few of the bra brands that advertised heavily during this period. Maidenform's ads were also remarkable because they placed women in dream sequences and public settings. Unlike other bra brands, Maidenform models weren't portrayed in simple poses with portrait-type backgrounds. Maidenform's models were driving cars, floating down rivers, and standing next to stagecoaches. Overall, Maidenform's "Dream" campaign was remarkable considering that women clad only in bras from the waist up wouldn't appear on network television until almost forty years after Maidenform's first "Dream" ad.

The ads here could not possibly include every instance of sexual promotion during this period. Several automotive ads were adorned with decorative images of sexually attractive women standing next to (or lying on top of) cars. A campaign for Fiat in the 1960s, for example, compared the shape of its cars to the shape of attractive, young women—"The second best shape in Italy" (see fig. 5.1). The ad, appearing in *Road & Track* magazine, was an obvious attempt to woo male auto enthusiasts with a woman's profile. In addition, the automaker attempted to associate the curves of its Spider with the curves of its bikini-clad model. In airline promotion, attractive stewardesses (flight attendants) in short skirts were shown in ads to attract male business travelers. It seemed as if a sexual charge was pervading everything in America. It wasn't, of course, but compared to earlier decades, sexual content was more visible. And there was no going back.

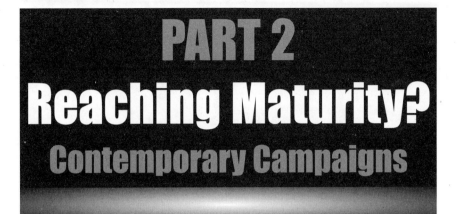

PART 2
Reaching Maturity?
Contemporary Campaigns

6
Packaged Goods
Intimates and Underwear

Picking up where the infamous "I Dreamed" campaign left off, a woman in a 1976 television commercial "dreamed" she was a "knockout" in her No-Show Natural Maidenform bra. The commercial contained a chorus line of dancing women in their top hats, cuffs, and partially revealing vests. They wore Maidenform bras under their vests, and leotards under their bras.[1]

Less than twenty-five years later, Victoria's Secret supermodels strutted their stuff in top hats, bras, and panties—sans the leotards.

If coy old Rip Van Winkle had dozed off in 1976, he would have had a heart attack when he flipped on the tube in the 1990s: Marky Mark grabbing his crotch, bare-chested Kate Moss letting us peek at her Calvin Klein waistband, and "Hello, boys"—Wonderbra's Eva Herzigova—chatting with her uplifted breasts. Business writer Robin Kamen made the observation in 1994 that "underwear is busting out all over. . . . Corsets for women and skin-tight skivvies for men nearly pushed the clothing off the runways at the latest fashion show in New York. Advertisements for men's boxer shorts pop out from hundreds of billboards; guys are dropping their trousers on the sides of city bus shelters."[2]

Kamen's observation was accurate. Intimate apparel and underwear advertising came into its own in the last quarter of the twentieth century.

Figure 6.1: Buffalo by David Bitton (2002).

Figure 6.2: "Draw Your Weapons," Lily of France, 2000 © All rights reserved.

Before 1975, underwear was, well, underwear—more so for men than women. It was a commodity product, with little difference between brands. The category was dominated by no-nonsense basics—the frill-less white and beige variety. Fit, comfort, and durability were the defining product features. Most of that changed with shifts in consumer preferences and groundbreaking advertising by Jockey, Berlei, Playtex, and Fruit of the Loom. These brands punctured the nudity boundaries in network and cable television, and magazines. Calvin Klein, Wonderbra, and Victoria's Secret followed suit with carnally charged campaigns that branded intimates and underwear as sensual fashion.

Intimates and underwear advertising doesn't have to be sexy. Today, several innerwear marketers earn revenue without resorting to sexiness. They do so by emphasizing comfort, style, and color. Their ads may even include attractive models, but don't everybody's? Other innerwear marketers—like Vassarette and Jockey—put a sexy spin on their "comfort" advantage. These brands argue that you can be sexy and comfortable at the same time.

Then there are those brands who go for broke, who use sex as the product attribute. Heralding "Unite and Conquer" and "Draw Your Weapons," Lily of France's X-Bra promises to turn breasts into guy magnets (see fig. 6.2). Lovable-brand ads claim their bras make men beg: "It's true that the alluring fashion of a Lovable bra has driven more than one man to his knees. But who's complaining?" Other brands, like Buffalo, DKNY, Tommy Hilfiger, and Guess, don't say anything at all. The models' poses in these ads, photographed to rouse sexual interest, say it for them. These marketers realize that people want to feel sexy. Millions of consumers, if not all of us at some level, want to be attractive to others. We know, intellectually, that underwear doesn't make the difference. Or does it? At an emotional and visceral level all bets are off.

MEN'S UNDERWEAR: RAISING THE BAR

Jockey

Jockey International, an innovative underwear manufacturer since 1876 (formerly Cooper's Underwear Company), created a remarkable campaign

Call 1-800-TWO-XIST (896-9478) Ext. 22 For An Underwear Catalogue

Figure 6.3: A napping underwear model.
Courtesy 2(x)ist, © David Morgan, www.dmny.com.

for its signature men's Jockey briefs in 1976. The ad was noteworthy because it featured Baltimore Orioles pitcher Jim Palmer and eight other athletes clad in their briefs. The campaign's tagline was "Take away their uniforms, and who are they?" Up to that point, beefcake images of men in their skivvies were rare, at least in mainstream advertising. Underwear advertising hasn't been the same since.

Soon just a briefs-clad Palmer appeared in Jockey ads. The advertising was so successful that Palmer became Jockey's official spokesperson-model in 1980. Jockey's CEO gave *Forbes* one of the main reasons Palmer was chosen as their underwear poster boy: "Women buy 70% of men's underwear. They think Jim Palmer is sexy—incredibly sexy."[3] Palmer was handsome, tall, tan, and athletic. Instead of a nameless model, Palmer was a real person who had accomplished some significant feats. He was a multiple Cy Young award-winner and destined for baseball's Hall of Fame. So Palmer was not only "sexy" but a well-known professional athlete. Jockey maximized Palmer's appeal by featuring him in an array of ads and promotional material for the company.

In 1980, Palmer solidified his status as men's underwear's first sex symbol. Palmer was pictured in a pair of Jockey's stylishly cut Elance fashion briefs. Sitting in a classical-style pose with one leg raised, Palmer rests one arm on his thigh, and the hand of his other arm on his hip. In such a stance, Palmer gives viewers a full shot of his bikini briefs. According to brand researcher Jay Pederson, the ad was so popular that Jockey reproduced it as a poster and sold it to consumers.[4] Jockey didn't directly profit from the posters—proceeds went to Palmer's preferred charity, the Cystic Fibrosis Foundation—but the attention caused by the posters created much profitable awareness for the brand. By 1982, Jockey had 65 percent of the men's fashion underwear market.

Jockey's success in the early 1980s opened the door for other innerwear brands wanting to use a sensual approach. According to Pederson, "Palmer's ad campaign brought the element of sex-appeal directly before the underwear consumer, and other companies were quick to follow."[5] In 1983 two underwear marketers outdid Jockey's sex appeal with their own brands of scintillating advertising: Calvin Klein and Berlei.

Calvin Klein

Calvin Klein's underwear advertising, initiated in 1983, contained images of men and women that transcended gender. The designer Calvin Klein may have followed Jockey's lead, but he quickly took the reins and commanded the spotlight with his own brand of underwear advertising. As a result, Klein's advertising was, and is, some of the most sensual, stylish, and controversial to date.

Enjoying the success of his designer jeans line, Klein introduced the world to his men's, and a year later, his women's underwear lines. "For Calvin, underwear was pure sex," said writers Steven Gaines and Sharon Churcher. "Calvin believed that most men were often much sexier with their underwear on."[6] That's how his models were shot, in little else than their white-cotton Calvin Klein briefs. Klein's Y-front briefs were similar to those produced by Jockey; in fact, they were made by the same manufacturer.[7] Klein's underwear even had the wide elastic waistband with the brand name stitched across it. A primary difference, however, was price and advertising. A pack of three Calvin Klein briefs was priced at $14.50. In 2002, a three-pack of Jockey briefs is still less than half of what Klein was getting for his underwear in 1983. However, today the styles are very different.

The advertising justified the price and made the distinction between the two brands. Klein's campaign began with a rousing image. Shot by photographer Bruce Weber, the first model was Olympic pole-vaulter Tom Hintinaus. Tan, muscular, and clad only in white Calvin Klein briefs, Hintinaus was an impressive figure at six feet, three inches and 185 pounds. Weber photographed the athlete on a rooftop in Santorini, the southernmost Greek island. Consider a description (not the copy) of the print ad's image: "The pole vaulter was captured from below the apex of the bulging briefs, the corona of his penis clearly discernible through the soft cotton material. The crisp, clean white of the briefs, matching the pure white of the stucco behind him, stood out in brilliant relief against his tanned skin."[8]

The shot appeared on a colossal billboard seven stories above Times Square in September 1983. The spectacle triggered media attention in New York and around the country. Klein contributed to the controversy by renting twenty-five bus shelters throughout Manhattan to display the poster. Overnight, all the posters were stolen.[9]

According to Barbara Lippert, Hintinaus was "an Adonis for the Reagan age: trim, tan and muscular. The man was clearly an object, but the bold graphic design and the look of the photography elevated sex in advertising to a new art form."[10] The image soon appeared in print, gracing the pages of men's and women's magazines in what amounted to a $500,000 campaign.

Fruit of the Loom

In 1990 the first set of underwear-clad males appeared on network television. Produced by Grey advertising, the television spots showed male celebrities wearing Fruit of the Loom underwear and little else. The tagline for the campaign was "Who's underwear is under there?" Hunky male celebrities Patrick Duffy, Ed Marinaro, and James DePaiva appeared in the spots.[11]

Previously, the company had run a print campaign featuring men in briefs, with the tagline "We fit America." In a 1989 print ad from the campaign, a man appeared in a pair of fashion briefs and matching tank top. Unlike the Jockey ads from 1980, the man posed like a Chippendale dancer, pulling up his tee shirt while looking at the camera with a sensual gaze. Raising his shirt, the model not only reveals his abdomen but also draws attention to his briefs. An outline of the model's penis is clearly visible. In a sense, the Fruit of the Loom model was more prurient than Jockey ads featuring Jim Palmer. The Jockey campaign featured Palmer in a classical pose, looking away from the camera. Palmer may have been "sexy," but he exemplified the look of an aloof *male* pinup as opposed to a salacious *female* pinup.

Marky Mark

In 1992 Klein once again captured attention when he signed rap singer Marky Mark—more commonly known today as Mark Wahlberg—to a $100,000 advertising contract. Wahlberg became a new celebrity model for Calvin Klein jeans and underwear. The union appeared to be a perfect match. Wahlberg was a successful rap songster, very popular with younger audiences. He was muscular and good-looking—necessities for Klein's male models. More important, Wahlberg was a walking Calvin Klein poster. He was notorious for wearing his jeans so low that his underwear waistband was visible, much like the Tommy Hilfiger waistband that was a fixture on male rappers in the 1990s. "Marky Mark," remarked Bloomingdale's vice president Kal Ruttenstein, "is the male equivalent of Brooke Shields."[12] (Ruttenstein was referring to Klein's successful jeans advertising that had starred Shields twelve years before.)

The campaign, photographed by Herb Ritts, was attention-getting and provocative. According to one source, Wahlberg "stretche[d] his already tight underpants across his crotch so snugly that the shot had to be airbrushed before it began appearing in magazines and bus shelters in October 1992."[13] Like other Klein ads, Wahlberg was shot posing in his underwear, sometimes wearing jeans that were unbuttoned or pulled down. In one of the ads, Wahlberg is shot from just above the knee to the top of his head. Smiling, and his arms at his sides, Wahlberg is cupping the bottoms of this boxer briefs, pulling them up a few inches on either leg. The ad is shot in black-and-white, emphasizing the then rap star and his Calvins.

In another famous image, Wahlberg, with a serious look on his face, is sitting shirtless with a bare-chested Kate Moss straddling him—her breasts pressed against his neck. Both are wearing low-riding jeans so that their waistbands are visible. Klein aired two thirty-second commercials based on these shoots. In one, Wahlberg grabs his crotch. Ritts described the ads as "almost kind of funny, yet sexy . . . because Marky Mark and Kate Moss had their own personality, especially Marky."[14] By all accounts, the campaign did sell underwear—lots of it. Three months after it began, sales increased 34 percent year-to-date, and within a year the Calvin Klein's men's underwear group grossed $85 million. Wahlberg's contract wasn't renewed, however. Several reasons were offered. One reason concerned Wahlberg's uneasiness about being a gay pinup, and he said so, publicly. Obviously, Wahlberg's remarks didn't bode well with the gay community—a meaningful proportion of Calvin Klein customers.

In more recent ads, Kate Moss rode male model Michael Bergin's back in a memorable ad that singed reader's fingers. And in the mid-to-late 1990s, Antonio Sabato Jr. had his hands down his boxer briefs as he gazed intently at the camera. These ads, while attention getting, hardly seem as provocative and cutting-edge as Klein's early men's underwear ads.

INTIMATES: BUSTING BOUNDARIES

Berlei

In 1983 Berlei U.S.A., a lingerie maker and subsidiary of an Australian conglomerate, was the first marketer to air a television commercial featuring a nude woman. The spot introduced Berlei's line of "Silkiss" silk lingerie for women. The commercial, risqué even by today's standards, featured a sexy blonde extolling the virtues of silk intimates.

The commercial begins with actress-model Debra Diehl sitting stark naked—legs slightly spread—with her back to the camera. Sitting in front of her vanity, Diehl slowly slips on a pair of silk bikini panties. To emphasize the feel of the fabric once they are on, she caresses her derrière with her right hand. She then slips on her bra. Now that she's *clothed*, Diehl swings her head around and runs her hand through her golden locks. As she looks lustfully into the camera, the stirring voice-over begins: "I love silk. It makes me feel so, so, mmmm. Ahhh. With soft Italian silk from Berlei. Berlei knows how to bring out the best in me. Ohhh."[15]

Regarding the copy, *New York* writer Bernice Kanner said it was, "Not exactly a script that would win an Oscar. Then again, this script doesn't need great writing: It's got a great body."[16]

If the ad doesn't sound familiar, it's for a good reason. The commercial ran on only a few local New York cable stations because the networks refused to run it. They rejected the ad for a couple of reasons. One, the model was nude. Two, she wore lingerie. Either way, the spot violated the broadcasting code for acceptable underwear advertising. Networks were still adhering to the National Association of Broadcasters' voluntary Code of Conduct. Established in the 1960s, the Code restricted advertising for birth control, astrology, and hard liquor. It also stipulated that live models could be shown in lingerie, but only if the lingerie was worn *over* clothing. Explaining why the Berlei spot was rejected, an ABC spokesperson told *New York* magazine: "We don't allow nudity on our air or live models wearing only undergarments, except if they're pictured on packages, as a small part of the overall ad."[17] Cable operators, on the other hand, could do as they pleased.

Despite the ban, the ad did attract national attention. Phil Donahue

THE MAIDENFORM WOMAN.
YOU NEVER KNOW WHERE SHE'LL TURN UP.

The evidence is in and Pretty Me™ is the winner. Simply feminine,
this front-close bra and matching bikini are lustrous super-satin with fan-shaped
lace appliqués. Unquestionably natural in softcup (shown), underwire, or
light fiberfill. In sensational colors....and that's the whole truth.

Pretty Me by Maidenform.

Figure 6.4: The "Maidenform Woman" ads appearing in the
1970s and '80s could trace their roots to the original "Dream" campaign.
Maidenform, Inc. All Rights Reserved.

devoted a program to the Berlei spot. According to advertising professional and columnist Art Ross, the spot caused quite a debate. Recounting the argument, Ross said a Berlei spokesperson, Diehl, and most of the women in the audience considered the ad "quite acceptable, ineffective, cute, sensuous, and a 'turn on' for them and their husbands/boyfriends."[18] Not everyone fit Ross's assessment, however. Dorchen Leidholdt, a cofounder of Women Against Pornography and a guest on the show, didn't like the way the ad sexualized Diehl. She later published her comments on the commercial: "We see the model exactly as a 'Peeping Tom' squinting through a keyhole would see her: as a delectable pair of thighs, as a perfectly rounded behind, as a piece of meat."[19]

Leidholdt had a point, but her perspective was contrarian. Her view could hardly stem the tide of what was to come in women's underwear advertising. As pioneering as the Berlei ad was, it would be four years until a bra-clad model was shown in a network television commercial—and then only for three short seconds.

Three Seconds of Fame: Playtex's Cross Your Heart Commercial

When it came to advertising, Playtex was an innovator. The company was the first to advertise bras and girdles on network television, beginning in 1955. Playtex also claims to be the first marketer to sell its intimate apparel as a "packaged good," although Maidenform makes the same claim. More important, it was the first advertiser to air a bra-clad live model on network television.[20] The spot ran in May 1987.

Playtex Apparel, Inc. (formerly International Latex Company; now owned by Sara Lee) advertised prodigiously in the latter half of the twentieth century. Unlike Maidenform and other intimate apparel advertisers, it concentrated most of its ad dollars on network television. Some of its better selling bras included the Playtex Living Bra, Cross Your Heart, and Eighteen Hour bras, as well as the intriguingly named girdle, I Can't Believe It's a Girdle.

The Cross Your Heart bra, known for its criss-crossed elastic support, was marketed to average- to full-busted women, ages eighteen to fifty-four. The bra's primary selling point, that it "lifts and separates," was more familiar to Americans than the Pledge of Allegiance. In Playtex commercials, because of the NAB Code of Conduct, Playtex displayed its bras on mannequins. If a live model was used, she was only allowed to wear the bra if it was worn over leotards, much like the dancers in the 1976 Maidenform ad.

Early in 1987 the networks decided to relax the NAB-era restriction. Playtex and its agency, Grey Advertising (the same agency that produced the Fruit of the Loom commercials), were the first to test the new restrictions. According to Playtex executives, the new rule allowed them to display the Cross Your Heart bra in a manner that was more realistic and chic than before. In May 1987 the company aired two fifteen-second spots showing live models. According to writer Deborah Mack, the commercial "showed very brief shots of women, seen from the waist up, clad only in a bra."[21] The shots were very brief indeed, each lasting only three seconds.

Critics also noticed the spots. The brief shots of partial nudity put Playtex in the crosshairs of moralists. *Advertising Age* writers Pat Sloan and Carol Krol said the Playtex spots "incurred the wrath of self-appointed guardians of family values such as the American Family Association's Rev. Donald Wildmon to the Eagle Forum's Phyllis Schafley."[22] This wrath may have been what kept advertisers from immediately following suit with their own bra-clad models. Grey's chairman, Edward Meyer, defended the ads by explaining: "All we're trying to do is get advertising brought up to the same standards as the media that surrounds it."[23]

In regard to sex in advertising, things haven't been the same since the Playtex ads. Many of my undergraduate students, born in the 1980s, can't recall a time when bra-clad models *weren't* advertised on television. The Playtex ads were a first, but the ads weren't particularly sexy. According to Betty Friedman, who oversaw the creative work for the Playtex account, the "bras are not particularly revealing.... We are not doing cheesecake. We are showing a product."[24] In addition to rejuvenating the brand in consumers' minds by stimulating awareness and interest, the commercials opened up the corral gate for the advertising cavalcade that was to come.

Calvin Klein Intimates

Advertising for Klein's women's line was no less provocative than for his men's. Early campaigns were shot in black-and-white by photographer Denis Piel. As with men's images, the ads were artful and erotic. They ran

Figure 6.5: La Perla Campaign. Photo Dominique Issermann.

in *Glamour, Mademoiselle, Seventeen,* and *Vogue. Interview* magazine accepted a bare-breasted version of the ad. The tan model, eyes closed, reclined on what appeared to be a white surfboard. One of her arms is behind her, the other is bent so her hand rests on her forehead. The model's back is arched, drawing attention to her body and white Calvin Klein briefs. Similar to the men's line, the women's panties had an elastic waistband with "Calvin Klein" stitched around it. Her white undershirt, a tank top, is pulled up to reveal her breast. In the PG-version, the model's tank is pulled up to the crease just below her breast.

The ads were effective. In 1984 Calvin Klein sold four hundred thousand pairs of women's underwear. With prices above the competition, at a sizable profit margin per pair, the company made a substantial profit. "The woman buying $7.50 panties doesn't get much that she can't find at $3. The difference is that insecure people feel better wearing designer labels—and there are plenty of insecure people out there," said *Forbes'* Jeffery Tracht-enberg.[25] More than just insecure people were buying his underwear. Klein tapped into an unrealized market—people who wanted fashionable and sexy underwear.

Klein struck again, this time with a scintillating underwear ad in 1985. Reeking of a ménage à trois, the Weber photograph oozed carnality. Two men, a naked woman sandwiched between them, were shown lounging on a towel-covered mattress. The men were wearing underwear, but nothing else. It is images like this one that contributed to the erotic identity of Calvin Klein's advertising in the 1980s.

Calvin Klein's underwear advertising continued to exude a similar pattern of gorgeous models clad only in their intimates. With few exceptions, the images are shot in black-and-white. The models are solitary figures alluringly stretched across a two-page spread. For example, in the mid-1990s, Klein house model Christy Turlington (re)introduced women's intimates in beautiful multi-page layouts. Most recently, Turlington is back—this time crawling across the floor in a tee shirt and black Calvin Klein briefs.

Klein took the everyday look out of intimates and underwear advertising, and replaced it with a sexualized fashion style. He also set the rules for anyone who wants to brand their underwear with a sexy image. Those that have taken a page from Klein's rulebook include Tommy Hilfiger, Ralph Lauren, Donna Karan, Guess, and other brands such as La Perla,

Adrianne, and Victoria's Secret. One brand, Wonderbra, took Calvin Klein's sex appeal and had some fun with it.

The One and Only Wonderbra

What does a $20 billion global foods conglomerate have in common with a cleavage-enhancing push-up bra? If you guessed "packaged goods" and "cheesecake," you're on the right track. If you guessed "Wonderbra," you hit the jackpot. And a pot of gold is what Sara Lee earned when it introduced the Wonderbra to American women in 1994. Sara Lee Corporation, the same company that manufactures and markets packaged meats, frozen baked goods (including Sara Lee cheesecake), and shoe care products, is also a leading marketer of hosiery, underwear, and women's intimates. Its intimates brands include Playtex, Bali, Lovable, and Wonderbra, as well as the license for Polo/Ralph Lauren intimates.

Sara Lee introduced the Wonderbra, a figure-enhancing push-up bra, with a memorable and provocative promotional campaign in 1994. Ads featured a Wonderbra-clad Eva Herzigova, a stunning former Guess jeans model born in Czechoslovakia, coupled with catchy headlines proclaiming "Your dad's worst nightmare," "Newton was wrong," and "Hello, boys."

The Wonderbra hit America with a bang. An inventive publicity campaign created media buzz and massive consumer interest. Promotional efforts included events like the "Cleavage Caravan," armored cars loaded with Wonderbras, making deliveries to department stores. Press releases hawked impending "Bra Wars" once Wonderbra was available in the U.S. News stories picked up on the release and covered the events.[26] For example, *Marketing News* writer Cyndee Miller commented, "Cleavage fever is busting out across the U.S., setting off a battle of the bosom-boosting bras."[27] The result was a great deal of excitement and anticipation, so much so that maintaining adequate Wonderbra supplies was a challenge for some retailers.

Originally a North American invention, the Wonderbra was available only in the United Kingdom until 1993. The Wonderbra was created by Canadelle, a Canadian company, who granted the Gossard Group a thirty-year license back in the 1960s. The bra contained unique design elements to create deep, dramatic cleavage with a push and plunge effect.[28] Unfortunately for Gossard, the license expired as demand for push-up bras began to soar. At the time, Gossard's annual Wonderbra sales went from 250,000 in 1991 to 1.5 million in 1993. To make matters worse for Gossard, Canadelle had since been purchased by Sara Lee and it wanted to keep the license in the family. As a result, Playtex was awarded both the U.K. and U.S. licenses. Gossard responded by introducing a top-selling push-up bra of its own. As an interesting twist-of-fate, Gossard is now part of the Sara Lee family.

Several reasons are given for the increased demand for push-up bras in the early 1990s. For one, women were ready for figure-flattering curves after the waif-look of the 1980s. Calvin Klein model Kate Moss—considered a waif by many—added to the Wonderbra excitement when she reportedly said, "They are so brilliant, I swear, even I get cleavage with them."[29] According to *Marketing News* writer Cyndee Miller, female baby boomers were also looking for something to rejuvenate their sagging bustlines, something other than breast augmentation.[30] The Wonderbra provided a way to enhance one's curves for a mere twenty-six dollars.

One of the goals of the campaign was to set Wonderbra apart from its competition. Before it was introduced, over 25 percent of bra sales in the United States were push-up bras. Maidenform controlled 70 percent of the push-up market with over ten different lines. In addition, Victoria's Secret introduced its Miracle Bra just months before the Wonderbra release, partly in response to anticipated demand for the Wonderbra.

In addition to public relations, Sara Lee invested an estimated $5 million to launch Wonderbra with print and outdoor advertising. As soon as the bra was available nationally, ads began appearing in *Cosmopolitan*, *Mademoiselle*, *People*, *Vogue*, *Glamour*, and *Allure*. A huge billboard was unveiled in Times Square and outdoor ads were posted in major cities.[31] The result was over $120 million in Wonderbra sales the first year. The promotional campaign was so successful that sales of push-up bras increased for all brands.

The ads, created by TBWA Chiat/Day, New York, were simple and likable, yet powerful. Exemplifying classic branding strategy, all ads—including print and outdoor—were similar in look and approach. Two-thirds to three-quarters of each ad consisted of an image of Herzigova clad only in a Wonderbra. Slender, blonde, and beautiful, she was photographed looking at the viewer, typically with a devilish grin.

With sensual eyes emphasized by dark eye shadow, Herzigova was visible in close-ups from head to mid-torso, or to just below her bra. Despite the model's breathtaking beauty, the bra and its contents were stage-center. The ads were targeted toward women and appeared only in magazines with high female readership. For women the ads were aspirational—or instructive—rather than seductive. The ads touted the Wonderbra as the key to enhancing one's physical assets. Men simply found the ads tantalizing. Collectively they could be heard to say, "Okay, you've discovered my weakness—keep teasing me."

The ads also made effective use of white space. Everything was printed in black-and-white except for a little yellow tag centered at the bottom of the page. The tag read, "The One and Only Wonderbra." Because it was in color, the tag stood out and helped to differentiate the Wonderbra from other push-up imitators.

The interplay between the images and headlines was simple and playful. Directly under the photograph was a catchy headline; some of the more ingenious headlines read, "Mind altering and legal, too," "Manage your assets," and "Who cares if it's a bad hair day." One of the original ads featured only numbers: "36-24-36." The first number originally read "26" but it was crossed out and a big "36" was written under it. No copy points or explicit selling points were needed. The clever interplay between the headlines and the images made for an award-winning campaign. In 1995, the campaign won a Clio for "best of print."

The ad campaign was created in such a way as to counter feminist criticism. Sara Lee argued that, first of all, the campaign was created by women, so how could it be anti-woman? Second, feminism was about making choices. With the Wonderbra, women had more fashion and style options to choose from. Susan Malinowski, vice president of marketing at Maidenform, told *Marketing News*, "Women are tired of being so serious and being so politically correct, and they're tired of being forced to act in ways contrary to their feminine nature."[32]

The campaign was designed to appeal to women's desire to feel younger and more appealing. As a result, the ads emphasized empowerment—that women can wear whatever they want, and that women can be comfortable, confident, and sexy all at the same time. That message was credibly presented in the ads. There is a difference, however, among levels of choices that women can make. Whereas feminism is about freedom to make decisions, it's also about freedom from stereotypes such as sexual objectification. "Replacing dressing-for-success with dressing-for-sex is no leap forward," asserted *Time* writer Margaret Carlson.[33] Still, does such a message have resonance with women? Absolutely. The campaign spoke directly to what executives doubtlessly uncovered in countless focus groups. The message may not be entirely pro-feminist (pandering to the desire for attention), but for those who want to appear busty in a breast-crazed culture, they have the option to do so.

The message isn't lost on women who wear push-up bras. Consider the following e-mail "confessionals" that appeared on the Wonderbra Web site: "I just got the AIR WONDER. It is the most amazing bra ever made. I feel so confident in it. The bra makes me look like I had a breast enlargement by the finest surgeons but without the money and pain! good job wonder bra!" Another women was so pleased with the Wonderbra's effect on men that she was compelled to share her nightclub experience: "One night in a club I was wearing my wonderbra and was getting quite a lot of attention even to the point of two men [coming] over to tell me what a wonderful chest I had!! But the funniest thing happened, a chap was walking across the room but staring so hard at my chest that he suddenly fell down the stairs much to the amusement of myself and all my friends, but my Wonderbra certainly attracted a lot of attention that evening!!!"[34]

As these testimonials demonstrate, Wonderbra *is* about empowering women. How women choose to use that power or how they construe that power, is for them to decide. One thing is clear, the Wonderbra causes men to behave like idiots.

Needless to say, the initial Wonderbra campaign was a major success. For instance, overall bra sales increased after Wonderbra was introduced and push-up bra sales increased from 25 percent of the bra segment to 32 percent within two years.[35] In 1995 Wonderbra became the top brand in department store bra sales. When sales of all Sara Lee bra brands were combined in 1997—Wonderbra, Playtex, Bali, and Hanes Her Way—its sales surpassed those of all other bra marketers.

More important, the Wonderbra was a must-have for women when it was introduced. *Forbes* listed the Wonderbra as a product of the year in 1994. As styles changed and interest has waned, Wonderbra is still introducing new product enhancements to augment flattening sales. Recently Wonderbra introduced its "Three degrees of wonder" bra. Adjustable push-up cups offer women the "choice" to be as sexy as they want to be. And this appeal must be working. In 2001 sales of Wonderbra were up 14 percent with sales driven by the adjustable-cleavage bra.

Victoria's Secret

"What is sexy?" asked a recent Victoria's Secret ad. The question was merely rhetorical. Victoria's Secret is sexy. Without a doubt, Victoria's Secret is the sexiest brand of women's lingerie and underwear in America—probably the world. The company, a subsidiary of Intimate Brands, Inc., achieved its top-shelf status with a consistent image of sexy supermodels clothed in little more than Miracle Bras and skimpy panties. It's an image that leaves men wide-eyed and drooling. The company's well-cultivated image strikes the ideal balance between alluring decadence and upscale sophistication. More important, Victoria's Secret has creatively—and very lucratively—plastered its image across America with promotional efforts that include advertising, catalogs, Web-based fashion shows, and, most recently, what amounted to an hour-long "infomercial" on prime-time network television.

Victoria's Secret wasn't always so successful. A trouncing by Wonderbra in 1994 gave the lingerie-marketer a lesson in successful promotion. As noted, the Miracle Bra, Victoria's Secret's version of the padded push-up, hit shelves three months before Sara Lee launched the Wonderbra. Victoria's Secret promoted its push-up with a few pages in its catalog and in-store displays, but the bra didn't have a chance. Sara Lee's promotional effort buried the Miracle Bra. "We got creamed in terms of awareness," Grace Nichols, president of Victoria's Secret Stores, told *Forbes*. "It was a really big kick in the pants for us."[36]

Like a prize-fighter who recovers after being hit with a lucky jab, Victoria's Secret learned from its mistake. The company boosted its annual marketing budget from $5 million in 1993 to over $110 million in 2000. In addition to more spending, management placed a heavy emphasis on branding. In 1996 the chairman of Intimate Brands, Leslie Wexner, decided that Victoria's Secret was going to be the best at marketing its bras.[37] The

Figure 6.6: Victoria's Secret catalog cover. Courtesy of Victoria's Secret.

decision resulted in profit margins for its bras three to five percentage points higher than for its other products. Cindy Fields, Victoria's Secret catalog president and CEO, said in 1999 that bras "are absolutely what Victoria's Secret is best known for."[38] According to PaineWebber financial analyst Richard Jaffe, "The company realized the importance of bringing out exciting new products and promoting them."[39] The strategy paid off. Revenue topped $3.3 billion in 2000, with exceptional year-over-year growth. Thanks to its sexy television commercials and print ads, Web presence, and store displays, Victoria's Secret soon ranked ninth among "most recognized brands."[40] It had ranked twenty-sixth only two years before.

Although the company has cultivated a faux English origin, Victoria's Secret has New World roots. Roy Raymond founded the lingerie shop in San Francisco in the 1970s. He eventually sold his five-store chain to The Limited, Inc. in 1982 for $3 million. Intimate Brands acquired Victoria's Secret in 1995, but both are still in the Limited family—over 80 percent of Intimate Brands is owned by the Limited.

In addition to purchasing Victoria's Secret's brand equity and hundreds of retail shops, Intimate Brands acquired the lingerie-maker's calling card—the Victoria's Secret catalog. Started in 1978, the catalog generates close to $1 billion in annual revenue. More important, it is one of the most anticipated and read pieces of direct mail in America. Over 426 million catalogs are mailed each year to women—and men. It features tantalizing shots of supermodels in lingerie, bras and panties, swimwear, and casual clothing marketed by the company. Although the clothing line is women's-only, a survey revealed that over 88 percent of male Stanford University MBA students reported reading the catalog on a regular basis.[41] I seriously doubt they were reading the catalog in their marketing classes.

It's an understatement to say that the Victoria's Secret brand image is one of glamorous sexuality. The company cultivates its sexy image with supermodels and the seductive tonality of its marketing. Victoria's Secret commercials feature supermodels Claudia Schiffer, Tyra Banks, Laetitia Casta, Stephanie Seymour, and, more recently, Gisele Bundchen, with tight camera shots that show off their Miracle Bra-enhanced bodies. The camera roves over the women's torsos as if it's devouring them. The models exude a sexy confidence as they move with the purpose of being watched. Although the brand's identity is sexy, writer Sandra Dolbow says that Vic-

Figure 6.7: Victoria's Secret supermodel Gisele Bundchen (2002). Courtesy of Victoria's Secret.

Figure 6.8: Victoria's Secret fragrance. Courtesy of Victoria's Secret.

toria's Secret is striving to distance itself from what she calls "sluttish sex appeal." Ed Razek, Intimate Brands' president of brand and creative services, told *Brandweek*: "The marketing has moved dramatically over the past five years. Our message now is... aspiration, sex and glamour."[42]

Add a dash of "erotic" to Razek's description, and you may have a more accurate sense of the brand's essence. Its marketing efforts contain a hot-blooded blend of sophistication and salaciousness. Consider the company's recent "Desire" bra campaign. In these commercials, Victoria's Secret models Stephanie Seymour, Heidi Klum, and others offer their definitions of "desire." The ads, filmed in black-and-white, feature close-ups of the models' faces and breasts, while they purr and giggle about what desire means to them: "wanting something you can't have," and "wanting something so badly, it hurts." Their explanations could just as easily be interpreted as the sexual frustration experienced by men viewing the commercials.

A carnal four-page magazine layout in 2002 features lingerie-clad supermodel Gisele Bundchen (see fig. 6.7). Dressed in black, she wears a strapless bra, thigh-high hose with garter belts, panties, and black stiletto heels. She's standing in a large window that reaches from floor to ceiling, perhaps in a Hollywood Hills mansion, overlooking the twinkling citylights at dusk. Gisele strikes three different prurient poses that emphasize her tanned, gorgeous body. In one pose her long hair dangles across her face. In another, she looks down while mussing her hair with both hands. In each shot her exceptionally long legs are spread apart. She's serious, not playful. If there is sophistication in this layout, it's the art direction, a beautiful deep blue hue, and the model herself. Is the ad "aspirational?" For men, perhaps (as well as inspirational).

A more subdued, yet revealing, "Dream Angel" print ad featured model Daniela Pestova. The supermodel is completely naked except for a huge pair of snow-white angel wings (see fig. 6.8). Kneeling, and with arms folded to contain her breasts, she is tastefully covered. Despite being unclothed, Pestova portrays a classy elegance. It might be her angelic look. With slightly parted lips and a deep stare at the camera, however, she begins to ride the line between refined and salacious.

In its quest to sexualize its brand image, the company occasionally pushes the limits of acceptability too far. In 1996, for example, CBS executives rejected a Victoria's Secret commercial featuring Claudia Schiffer dancing seductively in her underwear. A revised version was allowed to run after 9:00 P.M. Similarly, a full-page, black-and-white Victoria's Secret ad promoting the 1999 Web-cast fashion show was too much for the *Wall Street Journal*. The ad featured a skimpily dressed Tyra Banks. Although the ad was run by *USA Today*, an alternate version with another model was finally accepted by the *Journal*.

Super Bowl

In 1999 Victoria's Secret scored a promotional touchdown with its Super Bowl commercial and Web-based fashion show. Tied to Valentine's Day, the spot contained footage of Casta, Banks, and others models walking down the catwalk in their intimates. The footage was from the previous year's fashion show, but that didn't seem to matter. Most notable about the spot was "the jiggle." As the women walked, presumably in high heels, their breasts—very noticeably—jiggled. There is no other way to describe it. Eyes across America were suddenly glued to the television screen. Collectively, men could be heard saying, "Did you see that?" Collectively, women erased their men's smirks with swift elbow jabs. *Adweek* critic Debra Goldman called the spot "30 seconds of lace-trimmed jiggle."[43] Barbara Lippert said it was the "Bud Bowl of Breasts."[44]

For a Super Bowl ad, the commercial was unique because it contained no voice-over—it didn't need to. Text was interwoven with images of the models as they flashed on the screen. "The Broncos won't be there." "The Falcons won't be there." "You won't care." Cut to a model on the catwalk, followed by edits of three other models. "Victoria's Secret Fashion Show." "Live in 72 hours." "Only on the World Wide Web." The result was online traffic being tied up for hours! Over one million people—mainly men, I suspect—checked out the Victoria's Secret Web site within an hour of the commercial. Traffic was five times normal, and sales more than tripled. According to Razek, "a million people left their sets and turned on their computers and went to our site. That's the largest collective behavior shift in the history of entertainment programming."[45] Lippert put her spin on the event: "From the hubbub surrounding the Victoria's Secret Super Bowl TV and Internet event, you'd think no one had ever seen a set of hooters before."[46]

In terms of awareness and impact, the ad was compared to the Orwellian

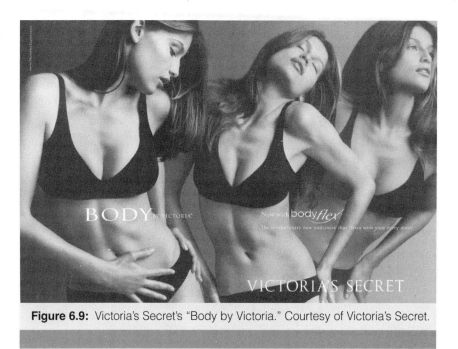

Figure 6.9: Victoria's Secret's "Body by Victoria." Courtesy of Victoria's Secret.

Macintosh spot aired during the Super Bowl several years before. Not only did the Victoria's Secret spot get a lot of attention, it drew people to the Web site—too many. The streaming fashion show was so successful, the servers couldn't handle all the traffic. Most were treated to bandwidth woes consisting of choppy video, poor image quality, and intermittent sound. On many computer-screens the image was too small to see clearly. But Victoria's Secret was prepared the next time. When the company Webcast its next fashion show, its Internet partners made sure viewers were accommodated. Consumers could even buy online as they watched the show.

Prime-Time Special

Victoria's Secret scored another marketing coup with its hour-long network special. Its landmark "Victoria's Secret Fashion Show" was broadcast during primetime on ABC in November 2001, just in time for the holiday season. Victoria's Secret reached an agreement with ABC that approximated a barter arrangement.[47] Victoria's Secret paid for the production costs and ABC split the program's advertising slots with the lingerie-marketer.

Victoria's Secret was masterful at creating a promotional buzz leading up to the broadcast. The company promoted the special in six magazines, as well outdoor advertising and direct mail. Its models also appeared on ABC shows. For example, Victoria's Secret models were contestants on *Who Wants to be a Millionaire* and they also made appearances on *The View* and *Politically Incorrect with Bill Maher*. As a special tie-in, the supermodels were integrated into an episode of *Spin City*. The plot revolved around the show's characters attempting to get tickets to the fashion show.[48]

Not everyone was impressed with the show, however. NOW president Kim Gandy was especially critical. Regarding ABC, she said it was "a sad attempt to lift its ratings with Miracle Bras."[49] ABC executive, Andrea Wong, responded by saying, "To us, this was pure, escapist entertainment."[50] Although the show drew over 12.3 million adults, which was slightly better than usual for ABC, the program ranked behind both NBC and CBS during the time-slot. For Victoria's Secret, however, the program was a success. Beyond the publicity and notoriety surrounding the program, sales in Victoria's Secret's stores increased 9 percent.[51]

In response to criticism Victoria's Secret received about its advertising, Razek told *Adweek*: "We're not using lingerie to sell trucks. We're not using lingerie to sell tortilla chips or beer. If anybody has a right to use lingerie to sell lingerie, it's us. It would be criminal if we didn't."[52] It's obvious many women agree with Razek. Not only do they reward Victoria's Secret's marketing efforts with their dollars, they see the company's brand image as right on the mark. Several female financial analysts gave their take on Victoria's Secret's image in a recent *Barron's* article. "Fashion-driven romance, modern sexuality," said one. "This is a place for lingerie—and lingerie that is sexy in a positive way, not in a trashy way," said another.[53] These perceptions reflect how many women perceive the Victoria's Secret brand and the products that carry its name.

Currently, Victoria's Secret is a leader in the intimate apparel category. With a 15 percent market share, Victoria's Secret is currently a leader in the $12-billion intimate apparel category. It's been very successful and scored several promotional knockouts—all by maintaining a consistent image that is sexy and noticeable. But their approach begs the question, "How far can they go?" It seems as if the models have taken off as much as possible. An annual poll finds that undergraduates consistently rank Victoria's Secret ads as some of the most sexual ads in the media landscape.[54] Can the brand continue to push the boundary of sexuality in advertising? My guess is that as long as people want to feel sexy and be attractive to others, Victoria's Secret will be right there for many years to come.

VASSARETTE

While Victoria's Secret and Wonderbra were stealing the limelight with their sexualized marketing strategies, another intimate apparel brand subtly utilized some of the same tactics to quietly become the number one selling bra brand in America.

Vassarette, the self-proclaimed "Victoria's Secret of the mass channel," has positioned its intimate apparel lines as sexy, yet comfortable, lingerie. The message is difficult to ignore with the sensual imagery and feel in Vassarette's advertising, product packaging, Web site, and in-store displays. As a result of its marketing strategy and ability to successfully tap into an expanding market for fashionable discount underwear, Vassarette's stretch satin underwire bra is currently the top-selling bra in the country across all retail channels.[55] When Atlanta-based VF Corporation, formerly Vanity Fair, bought Vassarette in 1990, the brand wasn't sexy or a sales leader.

VF is a world leader in apparel manufacturing and marketing of jeans, intimates, swimwear, and children's wear. When it purchased Vassarette, VF owned several intimates brands, such as Vanity Fair, Lily of France, and Bestform, but wanted to round out its holdings. VF's Vanity Fair brand was an upscale innerwear brand sold primarily through department stores. Vassarette was purchased to help VF increase its sales in mass market channels, such as discount retailers Wal-Mart and Kmart. Market trends were such that bra and panty sales in department stores were decreasing while mass channel sales were increasing. About the same time, Victoria's Secret and Wonderbra advertising efforts were increasing women's demand for fashionable intimate apparel. VF foresaw these trends and repositioned Vassarette to capitalize on them. Tom Wyatt, president of then Vanity Fair Intimates, told *Apparel Industry Magazine*, "Vassarette provided us with that opportunity because it was a department store label that had lost some positioning, yet had strong brand equity."[56]

Figure 6.10: "Man Eater." Vassarette. Courtesy of Vassarette, The Martin Agency.

Vassarette conducted extensive research into women's identities, aspirations, and lifestyles to determine needs and wants regarding product offerings and how to best communicate to women about products. As a result, Vassarette identified young women and women with full figures as profitable consumer segments. Both groups want fashion choices, including colors and styles. "They want to be sexy and comfortable without looking like a grandmother," Sharon Dickson, Vassarette merchandising director, told *Discount Store News* in 1997.[57]

John Smithers, Vassarette's director of business planning, described the company's target market to *Discount Store News* in 1998, "Vassarette customers tend to be between the ages of 18 and 34. They want sexy, comfortable lingerie, and that's what we sell—regardless of size. We don't separate figure types in our national ads. For us, it's more important to convey an attitude."[58]

Vassarette responded with a full range of sizes, designs, and color assortments. Color options included flower prints and plaids, silhouettes, and coordinated bra/panty sets as well as its Technoshine line in 2000. In addition, Vassarette and its marketing partners positioned the company's products to reflect a sensual brand. The slogan, "Sexy comfortable lingerie," appears in advertising, packaging, and on the brand's Web site. Vassarette marketing director Terri Polk explained the company's marketing strategy to *Discount Merchandiser* in 1999, "There's a range of 'sexy' we try to play up. Everything is sexy—the core, the essence. The look we want is sexy but obtainable. It's not like she [a female shopper] has the biggest boobs and smallest waist."[59]

Vassarette's Web site provides to consumers an explanation for why the brand is sexy. "The Art of Being Sexy" describes how Vassarette bras and panties allow women to express themselves confidently, and that its bras also let you the women: "revel in the power of your own seduction. You are the pursuer. You are confident and in control.... We don't claim to be sexy because it's the latest fad or it's where everyone else is headed. We've not changed. We claim to be sexy because that is what we stand for. That is what we are all about. Sexy, comfortable lingerie."[60]

Vassarette chose to herald its new positioning in 1997 in its first major consumer advertising campaign handled by the Martin Agency, Richmond, Virginia. Whereas most mass apparel suppliers make decisions about positioning and media placement in-house, VF chose to use Martin Agency's expertise. Art director Mark Wenneker, creative director Mike Hughes, and writer Jeff Ross emphasized the key attributes Vassarette wanted to emphasize—sexiness, comfort, and style. In addition, the agency produced a distinctive print campaign consisting of four-color magazine ads, fully emphasizing color and sensuality. The ads appeared in the women's magazines *Cosmopolitan*, *Mademoiselle*, and *Vogue*, and magazines with a high proportion of female readers such as *People*. Vassarette invested over $5 million in advertising in 1999.

The print ads emphasized features of the bras while associating Vassarette with sensual images. Some ads are two-page spreads and others are single pages. All ads bleed off the page and the edges of the ad look like brown paper with rough edges. Heavy, black, sans-serif letters emphasize a particular color theme. A solitary model, clad only in the theme-colored bra and panties, is featured in each ad. What is most interesting is the way the models are photographed and retouched. Taking retouching to another level, and in true mixed-media form, photographer Toni

Figure 6.11: "Who Needs Luck?" Vassarette. Courtesy of Vassarette, The Martin Agency.

Meneguzzo took pictures of the models with a Polaroid camera.[61] He then photocopied and painted the prints by hand. As a result, the ads—and models—are truly distinctive. Not only do the ads stand out, but they visually enhance the brand.

Each ad emphasized a different "innerwear" color. For example, the headline of a 1998 ad, printed in bold, sans-serif letters, read "COLOR: MINT" with the note "FOR AFTER DINNER." The image features an attractive model clad in a lime green matching bra and panty set. Similar to the color of the fabric, the background is also green. To emphasize attributes of comfort, the ad lists two features: "Ribbed fabric stretches and locks for support," and "Plush-backed elastic edges lay flat against your skin." On strategy, the ad obviously emphasized comfortable beauty. The implicit message in the ad is, "You can be sexy, maybe even someone's after-dinner mint, if you wear our comfortable, sexy lingerie."

Overall, Vassarette has been successful by uplifting its image through sensual positioning. Vassarette used sexy fashion images to shift consumer perceptions of its bras from a functional, utilitarian brand, to a top-selling, fashion-oriented brand. This change was achieved with distinctive advertising images that consistently reinforced the sensual image, both verbally and visually. In addition, the company made a concerted effort to stay current with fashion trends in the fast-growing intimates segment with colors, matching sets, and support styles. More important, they have done so without alienating the millions of women who don't look like the models in ads for competitors like Victoria's Secret, Calvin Klein, and Polo/Ralph Lauren. Vassarette truly may be the Victoria's Secret of the mass discount retailer chain.

CONCLUSION

As intimates and underwear taboos have fallen by the wayside, the once "unmentionables" are sold in increasingly erotic ways. In a sense, it hardly seems as if there is anything "unmentionable" left to say—or show—about innerwear. As illustrated in this chapter, several brands have eroticized their advertising by different means for a variety of reasons.

Some brands have sought to sexualize the brand through mere association. In Calvin Klein ads, stylish imagery of perfectly lithe bodies in the designer's underwear serves as the sexual stimulus. No words are necessary. Through constant repetition the underwear becomes loaded with sexual meaning. When Calvin Klein briefs were introduced 1983, they were very similar to Jockey's classic brief, with some slight variations. The most important difference between the two brands was perceptional; Klein's briefs were perceived as "sexier." Because of this difference, consumers were willing to pay more for a pair of Calvin Kleins—almost three times more—than for brands that tout their products as basics.

Sexy ads also help brands stand out from the crowd. According to one Playtex executive, the reason the company concentrated its advertising in television was that magazines were chock-full of competition. "If you look in many of the women's and fashion books, there's just bra ad after bra ad."[62] In addition, new brands trying to carve a niche for themselves strive to get noticed with a sex-tinted promotion strategy. They use it because it has been shown to work. Guess, Tommy Hilfiger, and Polo/Ralph Lauren have all used sex to get attention and to garner small, but profitable, niches.

Another approach is simply to say that "our intimates are sexy." Wonderbra playfully did just that with its witty double entendres. To a lesser extent, Vassarette emphasizes that its lingerie is comfortable and sexy. But it's important to deliver on those promises. Stephen Phillips, Bali Company's vice president of marketing for department and specialty stores, told *Apparel Industry Magazine*, "The challenge is in creating [brand] equity by communicating to consumers what the brand stands for and what they can expect in performance and quality."[63] Comfort can easily be assessed by consumers, but what about "sex appeal?" Personal field studies may suffice. The two young women who emailed their anecdotal Wonderbra stories conducted their own "product test" with stunning results.

The decision to "go sexy" isn't entirely based on gut instinct anymore. More mass apparel suppliers are making marketing decisions using increasingly sophisticated methods. According to Debby Stankevich, editor of *Discount Merchandiser*, more apparel houses are relying on advertising agencies and syndicated data services to make the best use of advertising and consumer research.[64] As a result, innerwear marketers are more savvy about knowing what consumers want and feeding it back to them. Do consumers want sexy intimates because that's what they see in ads, or is it simply consumer desire? A little of both, perhaps.

7
Designer Desire
Jeans

In August 1980 Brooke Shields, then just fifteen, uttered the legendary line, "You know what comes between me and my Calvins? Nothing." She spoke those words in what may be the most famous—certainly the most referred to—designer jeans commercial of all time. Written by Doon Arbus and filmed by Richard Avedon, the spot, titled *Feminist II*, was weighted with sexuality. Shield's remark was an unmistakable double entendre when framed with a camera shot that took thirteen seconds to slowly move along the length of her inseam before including her face.

The Shields spots (there were six of them) rocketed Calvin Klein's popularity as a designer into the stratosphere. According to one source, "The Brooke Shields jeans campaign exploded into the public's consciousness with the force of a tsunami."[1] News reports, industry buzz, and consumer interest added to the hype. In January 1982 Calvin Klein and a jeans-clad Brooke Shields made the cover of *People* magazine: "Brooke and Calvin—Her bottoms-up commercials have made Klein the best-known name in U.S. fashion."

Not everyone approved of the spots, however. They drew complaints from viewers and media critics, causing television stations to relegate the spots to late-night time slots or stop running them altogether. *Advertising Age*'s Bob Garfield was especially critical. He characterized the Klein spots as "pantiless jailbait," saying that for Calvin Klein "there's no more shock value to exploit and no more dignity to lose."[2]

Regardless of the criticism (more of that was to come), the ads were a success and helped to cement Calvin Klein's sensual brand image. In addition, the ads boosted not only Klein's already briskly selling designer jeans, but the bottom line of other designers during the jeans frenzy of the late 1970s and early 1980s. Klein's spots, and many others at the time, were emblematic of fashion and designer brands that were able to infuse fashion advertising with increased sexual content.

JEANS AND STYLIZED SEX

In addition to Klein's ads, designer jeans ads ushered in their own brand of provocative advertising with what Barbara Lippert labeled "Cinema derriere." She credits the first Jordache jeans commercial, aired in 1979, with the origin of the butt shot. "The mother of the genre, [the Jordache spot] introduced the sort of tacky, cheesy, rear-end bending jeans ad approach that became the rage in the early 1980s."[3] Lippert was describing ads that zoomed in on the models' backsides where the designer label could usually be found. It was a formula that worked well for Jordache, Guess, and other jean designers.

Advertising became sexier as more designers entered a crowded market. Designers tried to surpass each other in an attempt to corner the market on sex appeal, to be perceived as the most erotic. The result was that fashion advertising became more unabashedly sexual than ever before. "Fashion advertising has been injected with a brazen new elitism, sexism, and objectification of the flesh," wrote Andrew Sullivan in 1988. "Abuse of women, homosexual erotica, and the milder forms of sadomasochism are now commonplace marketing techniques directed at the average American household."[4] Sullivan was describing designer ads with women in coerced situations, ads with young women appearing ready to perform fellatio on middle-aged men, and ads with Aryan-inspired bodies.

More recently, readers may have spotted seamen making out in Diesel ads, sex with a robot in Bruno Magli ads, and naked men in Versace ads. They might also notice "lesbian chic" images—ads with a hint of

Figure 7.1: Jordache introduced "Cinema derriere" to jeans marketing. Courtesy of Jordache Enterprises.

Figure 7.2: Sergio Valente. Sergio Valente, © Louis Sanchis/A+C Anthology.

Figure 7.3: Zana-di. Courtesy of Zana-di Jeans © 2002.

homoeroticism between women and common for brands associated with haute couture (fashion, accessories, and fragrances). These images function to grab attention and position a brand as avant-garde by associating taboo or edgy sexuality with the brand—important qualities for differentiation among some fashion brands.

Fashion brands also imitate each other's promotion efforts, especially if a competitor's rousing ad strategy appears to be working. Lippert characterized the dominant venereal formula for jeans in the early 1990s: "In creating ads to sell denim to the under-25 crowd, this usually results in (a) hiring a hot photographer to shoot a portfolio of shockingly provocative black-and-white pictures that (b) show an odd number of pouty young models having art-directed sex on location."[5] Sometimes the formula works and sometimes it doesn't. Consumers can fail to respond if models are too unobtainable or don't ring true. That's not the case for the bulk of the campaigns described here. They represent some of the most effective contemporary sex-tinged fashion campaigns in terms of style and consumer response.

CALVIN KLEIN CAMPAIGNS

"Quite frankly, when advertising gets publicity it's like free advertising, and there's nothing wrong with that," remarked Calvin Klein in a 1992 interview.[6] Klein was responding to a question about the buzz generated by his recent 116-page outsert in *Vanity Fair*—a pictorial expose of a day (and night) in the life of a faux rock band. The hype centered on shots that contained nudity and homoeroticism, but Klein could just as easily have been talking about his jeans billboard in 1978, Brooke Shields's commercials in 1980, his Obsession fragrance campaign in 1985, or his jeans campaign in 1995. Publicity is what Klein evokes with advertising known for riding roughshod over boundaries of acceptable sexual content.

Since their humble beginnings in 1968, Klein and his partner Barry Schwartz have built a fashion powerhouse. "The Calvin Klein brand name has become one of the most recognized symbols of American fashion," wrote business writer Sara Pendergast.[7] Beginning with an upscale line of coats, the team has designed and marketed a broad range of products, including several lines of women's and men's clothing, a stable of fragrances, underwear, eyewear, and swimwear. The company's flagship remains, however, its ready-to-wear collection of women's clothing. Products bearing the Calvin Klein name produce annual retail revenue of over $5 billion.

Few designers have influenced the look of fashion advertising more than Calvin Klein. Historically, the organization's advertising is produced in-house with Klein either directing or influencing advertising efforts. Some of the biggest names in fashion marketing have worked on Klein's campaigns, including Doon Arbus, Richard Avedon, Steven Meisel, Herb Ritts, Sam Shahid, and Bruce Weber. Together they have created artful images of beautiful models clothed (or not clothed) in Klein attire. Often filmed in black-and-white, the ads grace the pages of magazines, billboards, television screens, and product packages. More important, the image creators infused Klein's advertising with a distinctive brand of sex that has extended the boundaries of acceptability. So provocative, so distinctive, and so consistent have these images been, that sex and Calvin Klein-the-brand (and designer) have virtually become one and the same. And as the supreme compliment, their work has spawned many imitators who've mimicked their approach, sometimes flooding the fashion advertising landscape with Calvin Klein-esque ads.

Klein achieved his sex-tinged reputation with some of the most memorable and controversial ads in recent history. Two years after introducing his line of designer jeans in 1976, Klein generated a great deal of attention with a provocative billboard in Times Square. The board featured a salacious shot of model Patti Hansen posing doggy-style in her Calvin Klein jeans. She was pictured on hands and knees, hair flung back, with "her derriere sticking receptively up in the air," the Calvin Klein label visible on her hip. The image was shot by Saks Fifth Avenue photographer Charles Tracy, who said that after a couple of cocktails, it just happened: "All of a sudden she got on all fours and threw her head back and I said, 'That's it!' "[8]

Klein's jeans were already selling briskly. Priced at fifty dollars a pair, Klein was selling thousands of pairs each day. But the image on the billboard grabbed attention and caused sales figures to climb. "The jeans went right through the roof," remarked Stanley Kohlenberg, president of Calvin Klein Cosmetics. "It was the most amazing explosion I ever saw in my life, with Patti Hansen's tushy sticking out all over Broadway.'"[9] In 1979 Calvin Klein jean sales topped $60 million, with some of that success attributed to the Hansen billboard. The billboard remained above Times Square for four years.

Two years later Richard Avedon cast Brooke Shields in the memorable series of Calvin Klein jeans commercials referred to earlier. Shields spoke lovingly about her "Calvins," playfully extolling their virtues. It was Klein's first foray into television advertising. "In the jeans area [TV advertising] has been so saturated, so boring, and so tasteless, I didn't want to become part of it," Klein said initially.[10] However, his alluring campaign turned out to be not only controversial but extremely successful.

Klein's campaign with Brooke Shields was remarkable because its spots oozed with sexuality and the lines were pregnant with sexual innuendo. For instance, in one of the spots, titled *Teenager*, Shields teases, "I've got seven Calvins in my closet, and if they could talk, I'd be ruined." When she wasn't saying anything, Shields exuded sensuality. Some of it was Shields's natural beauty and school-girl appeal. Direction also played a role. Avedon guided her performances, coaching her intonation and timing.

In the spot titled *Giggler*, Shields falls backward, giggling, as she tries to recite a poem: "Help, I'm going to split my Calvins!" In another spot (*Bookworm*), Shields declares that "reading is to the mind … what Calvins are to the body." "Whenever I get some money, I buy Calvins. And if there's any left, I pay the rent," Shields confesses in *Fashion Freak*. In *Flirt*, Shields said that her mother warned her about boys who only want her for her "Calvins."[11]

In addition to the lines and the way Shields cooed them, the spots were shot suggestively. "The lens lovingly explored Brooke's body, in various limber and suggestive poses," observed Gaines and Churcher.[12] Avedon made a radical departure from "Cinema derrière." Without a lot of bouncing booty, the ads were tastefully shot with top-level production to achieve a high fashion look. Avedon said he wanted the spots to imbue "the Calvin Klein image to jeans and not a jeans image to Calvin Klein."[13] Klein invested a mountain of money in the campaign; Shields was paid $500,000, Arbus reportedly received $100,000, and over $5 million of airtime was purchased.[14] In comparison, the original Jordache jeans spot was produced for $15,000.

Viewer complaints increased during the latter half of 1980. Two spots causing the most concern were *Feminist II* and *Teenager*, but four of the spots were deemed inappropriate by the CBS Los Angeles affiliate. Other stations were refusing to run the spots. News media picked up on the story, creating a lot of discussion. Klein also was criticized by feminists. Gloria Steinam and Women Against Pornography condemned the ads for "sexualizing a very young model as a matured, experienced seductress... [the] ad campaign... consists of an aboveground representation of child pornography."[15] "People said we were taking advantage of a fifteen-year-old, which was not the truth," said Klein.[16]

Everyone could agree on the results of the campaign, however: sales of Calvin Klein jeans reached 2 million pairs a month. Because of these sexy strategies, designer jeans were a "must have," and Klein's jeans became the undisputed leader. "Marketed as chic, sexy status symbols, designer jeans became a staple in the closet of the fashion-conscious consumer, who was buying not so much a pair of blue jeans as 'Liz Claibornes' or 'Calvin Kleins,'" wrote business writer Barbara Brady.[17]

To revitalize jean sales, Klein ran a brazen, 116-page magazine outsert (bagged with the magazine) attached to issues of the 1991 October issue of *Vanity Fair*. The ads, as noted earlier, depicted a day in the life of a rock band with provocative, gender-bending roles, homoeroticism, and partial nudity that nevertheless left little to the imagination. The outsert was distributed to 250,000 of Vanity Fair's 850,000 subscribers. At $1 million to produce and distribute—the equivalent of a 29-page spread—the outsert was the most expensive ever to run at that time.

Black-and-white Bruce Weber shots photographed in San Francisco's Warfield Theater made up the spread. *Time* called it "a jumbled pastiche of naked bodies, black leather jackets, Harleys and tattoos, with cameo roles by a crying baby and a urinal. Biker chicks straddle their 'hogs' and rough up their men. Rippling hunks wield electric guitars like chain saws, grab one another, sometimes themselves. Oh yes, there are even a few incidental photographs of jeans, most of which are being wrestled off taut bodies or used as wet loincloth."[18] On page 54 a totally nude Carre Otis is kissing a shirt-less male jeans-clad model. She's holding onto the fence with hands above her head. Page 58 contained the most discussed image. Shot in the shower, a nude Mark Schlenberg clutches a pair of wet CK jeans between his legs.

Stuart Elliot of the *New York Times* counted the instances of nudity: two nude male posteriors, four nude female posteriors, twenty-seven bare-chested men, two topless women, and one urinal shot.[19] In short, the ad was controversial. Many people said they just didn't get what it was all about. Klein told *Advertising Age*: "I've thought maybe I went way too far with those photographs, but I thought it was something very special."[20] He also said he wasn't disappointed with the outsert although sales did not increase as expected. *Family Circle* publisher Valerie Salembier wasn't very forgiving. She called the outsert a "gigantic failure" that caused lost revenue and heads to roll: "Perhaps the enormous loss of revenue led Klein to an epiphany that led him to get into the market's head and hearts, instead of their pants."[21] As some measure of success, however, Calvin Klein's print campaigns were rated by consumers as the most outstanding and memorable in 1991.[22]

If imitation is the best form of flattery, Klein received a compliment from another jeans maker a year later. Request Jeans ran a forty-eight-page supplement distributed with the October 1992 *Details* magazine. The pictorial related the story of two glamorous models in a Western motif. Similar to Calvin Klein's outsert, it was shot in black-and-white and contained provocative images. Request's ad campaign motivated Barbara Lippert to observe: "Add cleavage, a vaguely threatening storyline suggesting imminent violence, bi- and/or homosexuality, and somebody relieving himself, and voila, you have yourself an ad campaign."[23]

Calvin Klein's most recent controversy, a back-to-school jeans campaign in 1995, promoted the most vociferous reaction to date. The jeans campaign was viewed by many as containing pedophilic themes rather than mainstream sexuality. The television spots were gritty and had a home movie camera feel. An older man with a gruff voice asked young men and women to take off their clothes or to dance around. One observer described the setting as a "seedy, wood-paneled, purple shag carpeted basement."[24] The man's compliments pertaining to people's bodies created an uneasy tension, both in the commercials and with viewers. The ads were unmistakably sexual, but too real and too disturbing.

The campaign was abruptly pulled, but not until after a massive onslaught of criticism in the press. After canceling his remaining ads, Klein issued an full-page apology in the *New York Times*. His apologia didn't stop the initiation of hearings by the FBI and Justice Department to determine if his models were underage. The probe was dropped in November with no cause for further action.

Despite the uproar, sales of Klein's CK jeans soared, with net sales in 1995 increasing to $462 million. The jeans were in such demand that over $200 million in orders went unfilled.[25] Although adults were appalled, the controversy caught the fancy of teens who were "striving to define themselves as rebellious, hip, and defiant."[26] Some in the industry said they could see through Klein's strategy. "When he's seeming to be provocative and outrageous to most people, he's right on strategy for young people," said Brian Sitts, a group creative director at J. Walter Thompson. "He's perpetuating this image that everything with the Calvin Klein name on it is hip and contemporary."[27]

Since the beginning, Calvin Klein's advertising has evolved and varied, but primarily revolved around sex. Entangled limbs, nudity, flirtation with the taboo, and sexual attitudes exemplify his advertising. In so doing, he has single-handedly pushed the boundaries of what is acceptable with regard to usage of sex in advertising. Not only does Klein's advertising attract attention and stir controversy, but his products, especially clothing and fragrance, have resonated with fashion-conscious consumers, helping them envision themselves as more sexually attractive, both to themselves and others, while creating wealth for himself.

GUESS?

Guess's advertising campaigns, launched during the designer jeans craze, propelled it to the top as a global designer jeans label. The company instituted a signature black-and-white ad style, featuring tight-fitting jeans worn by some of the sexiest models in the business. Its magazine ads boosted the careers of then newcomer models Claudia Schiffer and Anna Nicole Smith, while contributing to a sensual Guess brand image. Since 1981, the Marciano brothers and Guess, the company they created, have continued to exert an influence on casual designer fashion and fashion advertising.

Guess *is* the Marciano brothers. Three of the original four brothers— Maurice, Paul, and Armand—run the publicly owned company, wielding what some have described as a powerful influence.[28] Born in Algeria and raised in southern France, the brothers got their start in the fashion business

Figure 7.4: Guess Jeans. Guess? Inc., Creative Director: Paul Marciano, Photographer: Pablo Alfaro.

by designing and marketing jeans and other denim designs. Their meteoric rise began in December 1981 when the brothers convinced a buyer at Bloomingdale's to display two dozen pairs of Guess jeans; all the jeans were sold in a few hours.[29] With intense advertising, the Marciano brothers capitalized on the designer trend to create a highly profitable fashion fiefdom with revenue growth from $6 million in 1982 to over $800 million in 2000.

Paul, the youngest of the four brothers, has been responsible for the Guess brand image since the beginning. He is the company's creative director as well as its co-chairman and co-CEO. Most ads are produced in-house under his direction. Since 1982, the company's advertising has been known for its early use of black-and-white or sepia-tone photography. Guess advertising is also known for its use of beautiful models—Claudia Schiffer, Laetitia Casta, Carre Otis, Naomi Campbell, Eva Herzigova, and Anna Nicole Smith, to name only a few—photographed in a high fashion, yet lascivious style. Celebrities such as Drew Barrymore and Tom Skerritt have also made appearances in several Guess campaigns. Guess ads are primarily print based, running in a range of men's and women's lifestyle magazines. For example, the $25 million ad budget in 1997 covered over 200 ad pages in February and March alone.[30]

The first Guess ads shot by Wayne Maser appeared in 1985.[31] They featured what has been referred to as a glamorous lifestyle among a sensual set of beautiful people. One of the first Guess campaigns, called "Austin," made its debut in 1986. The layout featured shots of models outdoors with a Texas western flavor. They included classic photography of women and men looking good, showing cleavage and men's chests. The models wore tight-fitting country-wear—lots of denim, belts with big buckles, boots, and fringe. As jeans sales took off, the Marciano's capitalized on the Guess name. The company licensed and marketed signature watches, footwear, and fragrance, as well as children's, athletic, and eyewear. All were supported with in-store promotions and print advertising campaigns.

Claudia Schiffer first appeared in a Guess ad campaign in Fall 1989. Photographed by Ellen von Unwerth and shot in Nashville, Tennessee, this campaign also contained a country-western feel. The ads featured Schiffer hanging around with male model Ron Schwartz in a record store. The shots emphasized Schiffer's Guess clothing as well as her midriff and chest. In one layout, Schiffer's denim sleeveless shirt is unbuttoned revealing her black

Figure 7.5: Guess. Guess? Inc., Creative Director: Paul Marciano, Photographer: Dewey Nicks.

bustier and deep cleavage. With her long blonde hair, svelte figure, and beautiful smile, Schiffer was an immediate sensation. She was the embodiment of the "Guess Girl," and young women across the country would attempt to emulate Schiffer by wearing Guess clothing and accessories.

The same year, Paul Marciano returned to Europe to feature model Carre Otis in an shoot set in the Italian countryside. Otis was mostly shot in outdoor locations: a barnyard, a haystack, a beach, an outdoor café. In several shots, she is accompanied by a dark, muscular Italian beau. In one provocative shot, Otis is photographed in short-shorts and a tee-shirt while sitting on the back of a motorbike. The man she is holding onto has a hand on the back of her denim shorts, and she has her bare legs over his faded jeans. These images lent Guess a sensual European image.

Anna Nicole Smith, famous for her modeling work for Guess and Playboy—but more recently for inheritance lawsuits and her reality television program, was featured in a Guess glamour-shoot in Miami in Spring 1993. Reminiscent of 1950s movie star glamour photography, the campaign was shot by Daniela Federici. The busty Smith posed like Marilyn Monroe, at times looking European with dark eye makeup. Shots featured Smith stretching out a long leg as she steps out of a car. In other shots she lies on her stomach propping herself up on her elbows. Smith became the new "Guess Girl," modeling in several campaigns for Guess (see fig. 7.6). Coinciding with her supermodel stardom with Guess, Smith appeared as a cover girl and centerfold in *Playboy*, and was named the 1993 "Playmate of the Year."

According to *Adweek*, Guess's first serious advertising venture on network television was in 1994. The television campaign consisted of three sixty-second spots that told a story if aired consecutively. "The campaign, extravagantly executed in Europe with feature film production talent," observed *Adweek*'s Kathy Tyrer, "evokes the mystery and glamour associated with Guess's earliest advertising."[32] Shot in sepia tones, the story is set in the European cities of Budapest, Geneva, and Barcelona. Pursued by a group of mysterious men, the woman eludes apprehension through narrow escapes. But the ultimate conclusion, do they catch her or does she get away, is unclear. "As has been true of most Guess ads, it's hard to tell that the actors wear Guess clothing, shoes and eyewear, all secondary to the mysterious action in the spot," said Tyrer.[33] The first ad broke during the 1994 MTV Music Awards.

Figure 7.6: Anna Nicole Smith in a 1992 Guess ad. Guess? Inc., Creative Director: Paul Marciano, Photographer: Daniela Federici.

Figure 7.7: Guess's extension into "Innerwear." Guess? Inc.,
Creative Director: Paul Marciano, Photographer: Daniela Federici.

Figure 7.8: Guess (1994). Guess? Inc., Creative Director: Paul Marciano, Photographer: Ellen von Unwerth.

Another electronic venture, the short film "Cheat," won Guess several Clio awards in 1996. Marking a return to television commercials for Guess, the ninety-second spot was shot in a film-noir style.[34] The only indication that the ad was for Guess was its logo, aired at the end of the spot. The film (it was shot in 35mm film) told the story of a private detective (Harry Dean Stanton) hired by a woman (Traci Lords) to ensure her fiancée's fidelity before she marries him. The detective hires one of his "girls" (Juliette Lewis) to be the temptress. The unsuspecting fiancée fails the test, due in part to the irresistible appeal of the setup girl clothed in hot Guess attire. In the ad, Stanton comments that his girls "know how to dress." At the end of the commercial he confides, "My girls look so good that people ask me, is it fair? And I have to tell them, quite frankly, no." The not-so-subtle message of the commercial was that girls who wear Guess are overpowering. The ad ran on cable and network television, as well as in thirty-four hundred U.S. movie theaters.

Aside from also going public in 1996, Guess initiated an Internet presence with its Web site guess.com. *Brandweek* writer Elaine Underwood described a noticeable element on the site: "Master image-maker Guess knows what fuels apparel sales: provocative ads. So it's no surprise its new Web site exploits that heritage."[35] Underwood was describing the availability of past campaigns and "behind the scenes" links on the site. E-commerce on the site was launched in 1999.

As with past advertising, recent Guess ads rarely feature any words other than the Guess logo and a word or two describing a particular product: for example, ads for women's tops feature teasing mid-shots of models in stretch tops. In one ad, a female model looks at the reader with her arms placed behind her back to emphasize her breasts. The words say, "GUESS. Stretch." A surprisingly similar ad features model Laetitia Casta wearing a leather choker and the words, "GUESS. Jewelry."

Guess jeans and the company's provocative advertising established Guess's brand identity from the beginning. Paul Marciano's art direction contributed to a brand image that was erotic, sexy, and glamorous. The beautiful models had a European look and the photography emphasized the models' exquisiteness in Guess clothes. Images were photographed to emphasize shapely figures: namely breasts, faces, abdomens, and legs. Guess designs are tight-fitting, playful, and oriented toward a youthful market. As a result, Guess was a "must-have" label for young, hip Americans.

In recent years, Guess continues to benefit from a very strong brand image created by its annual investment in multi-million-dollar advertising. Paul Marciano told *Brandweek* in 1996 that "People immediately associate Guess with Claudia Schiffer and we have not advertised Claudia for over six years."[36] Paul Marciano also discovered through focus group consumer research that respondents still underestimate the volume of Guess men's fashion business because of the female-focused campaigns. "The word, 'Guess Girl' comes back over and over, yet our business is 50% men," observed Marciano.[37]

Aside from running several ads with lesbian chic imagery, Guess ignited controversy in 1996 with a series of ads labeled "heroin chic." The images feature a young female looking drugged out. She's clothed in skimpy Guess attire but sans the glamour and elegance of signature Guess advertising. With dark circles under her eyes, she appears disheveled and undernourished. She is young—too young—and shown slouched in a movie theater and other locales. Kirk Davidson, a marketing professor and author of *Selling Sin*, observed "This ad is pornography, pure and simple, worthy of *Penthouse* or *Hustler*."[38] Davidson argued that Guess was sending the wrong message to young women.

By the mid-1990s Calvin Klein's jeans label—CK Jeans—represented 40 percent of the designer jean market, a segment once dominated by Guess. Guess's share of the market was estimated at 20 percent. However, despite an increasingly competitive market, and controversy about labor law violations, Guess continues to survive.[39] In 2000 an analyst remarked that, "The brand still has strong appeal."[40] And today it continues to appeal to fashion-conscious youth by associating sexuality and fashion in its advertising campaigns.

LEVI'S "OPT. FOR THE ORIGINAL" CAMPAIGN

Sales of Levi's, once the world's most popular jeans brand, declined precipitously in the late 1990s. The Levi's brand, as well as the look and style of its jeans, was losing favor with young consumers. Between 1996 and 2000 the apparel maker's revenue fell 35 percent—a loss of billions of dollars. In an attempt to woo back teens, the company initiated its "opt. for the orig-

Figure 7.9: Young men in a Guess Jeans ad (1999). Guess? Inc., Creative Director: Paul Marciano, Photographer: Pablo Alfaro.

inal" campaign; consisting of three of the sexiest commercials in Levi's history. The threesome included an invisible naked couple, a sex-inspired artist, and a resourceful supermodel. The commercials, produced by TBWM Chiat/Day, were popular among young viewers but not with critics. *Advertising Age*'s Bob Garfield called the campaign desperate, and likened the turnaround strategy to, "Watching people hump."[41]

Levi Strauss is the "original" jean maker. Produced for over 150 years, Levi's are known as "the pants that won the West." California's gold seekers and farmers wore the button-fly, straight-leg style jean for its ruggedness and durability.[42] Although Levi's was to jeans what Kleenex is to tissue, the company never sold more than $2 million internationally until the 1950s. The jean earned a reputation for style as its popularity increased on college campuses, and being worn by James Dean and Marlon Brando—in their white T-shirts—added a rebellious mystique. As Americans enjoyed more leisure time and "dressing down" became a trend, Levi Strauss steadily grew to become the largest apparel company in the world.

Demand for Levi's began to fluctuate, however, as fashion tastes shifted and competitors such as Calvin Klein, Jordache, and Guess stole market share in the 1980s and early 1990s. In 1995 sales of Levi's 501 style jeans experienced a renaissance, due in part to an award-winning campaign designed by Foote, Cone & Belding, San Francisco, Levi's longtime advertising agency. The "501 Reasons" campaign increased brand awareness and sales to record levels, earning the agency in 1996 *Advertising Age's* agency-of-the-year honors.

The campaign's success was remarkable considering that baggy, relaxed-fit jeans had increased in popularity. Young skateboarders and aging yuppies wanted styles other than straight-leg, tight-fitting jeans. Late to introduce roomier alternatives, Levi's share was gobbled up by an increasing array of competitors catering to those segments. The slow start proved costly; after sales peaked at $7.1 billion in 1996, overall sales plunged to $4.6 billion by 2000.

Another reason for Levi's fall was its brand image. Levi's, once the dominant standard of jeans wear, wasn't considered cool anymore. After the success of the Levi's "501 Reasons" campaign, the company began selling its jeans in "mid-tier" department stores such as Sears and J.C. Penney. According to industry watchers, image-conscious teens were reluctant to be associated with clothing available in those distribution retailers.[43] As a result, hip young people—important opinion leaders for setting and maintaining style trends—left the brand. According to *Brandweek's* Sandra Dolbow, "Levi's biggest challenge has been recapturing the brand's cultural relevance with teens."[44]

A recent market study by Zandl Group revealed that Levi's still maintains relevance to the youth market, but not at its once dominant level.[45] Levi's ranked at the top—tied with Tommy Hilfiger—with high schoolers; 9 percent said it was the brand of jeans they were most likely to purchase. Levi's was also top (12 percent) among college students. A long line of competitors followed closely behind Levi's in the preference list, however.

Unhappy with declining sales and market share, Levi's was determined to stop the slide. Nick Coe, director of merchandising for Levi's, told *Brandweek* it takes two things to make a fashion turnaround—product innovation and advertising. "Our whole goal is to rejuvenate and reinvent this iconic brand through communication and great product development."[46]

Product development was accomplished with the introduction of two new styles, the L2 and Engineered Jeans.

"Communication" meant new advertising campaigns. "Opt. for the original," introduced in 1999, wasn't the first. A string of previous campaigns had failed to resonate with consumers. But the "opt. for the original" campaign promised to be different. It was initiated with three commercials, two that aired August 1999—in the all-important back-to-school push—with the third commercial airing the following spring. The theme of this campaign, unlike previous campaigns, was light-heartedly built around sex. The commercials were laced with sexual situations, and nudity of a sort.

Labeled "Invisible Couple," the first commercial was a sensually romantic vignette featuring an invisible couple wearing Levi's. The spot begins with an invisible young man watching a football game on television, only to be interrupted by his equally invisible, but tight-fitting-Levi's-clad girlfriend. It's soon clear she has only one thing on her mind. Entwined in various contortions, the young woman leads them from the entryway to the kitchen to the couch as they groove to Marvin Gaye's "Let's Get It On."

The audience can only imagine the unseen girlfriend as she stands up and unbuttons her red sweater, throwing it striptease-style on what would be her boyfriend's head. She then wiggles out of her tight-fitting Levi's jeans to reveal her lack of underwear. Viewers see only her shoes as she heads to the bedroom. Running, tripping, and frantically stripping, the young man follows her only to be interrupted again by the doorbell. "Mom," he says, as he opens the door.

The commercial is notable for what it doesn't show. You can't see her, but the curvaceous girlfriend is the camera's star. Because the model is invisible, the camera can rove over her body in a way that would not be possible if she could be seen. In that way the spot can emphasize the tight fit of Levi's jeans and tops while allowing viewers' imaginations to fill in the gaps. The woman is clearly the aggressor, as she leads her boyfriend around, both straddling him and stripping for him. The couple's interaction also contributes to the spot's steaminess.

The second commercial in the campaign also features a dominating female. The spot centers around Lola, an artist who uses men to create her works of "jeans" art. The music coos, "What Lola wants, Lola gets..." And what Lola wants is young Levi's-clad men on her studio floor. In a scene reminiscent of Farrah Fawcett's foray into body-painting, Lola and a young hunk thrash about in foreplay that culminates with the man laying on his back as she paints his jeans. Cut to a scene in an art gallery where two men, admiring canvases of painted jeans, nod to each other knowingly. Call it a labor of love, all involved seem satisfied. Garfield commented that "she is exhibiting her work, and her entire sexual history."[47]

In the third commercial, Victoria's Secret supermodel Daniela Pestova makes a stunning appearance. Her goal is to create a pair of cutoffs, and her technique is ingenious if a bit old-fashioned. She slips out of her jeans and throws them on a railroad track. Her problem is solved when the train cuts the legs off her jeans. Bob Garfield commented in *Advertising Age* that the ad "is total retro-cheesecake, but the Levi's do look mighty fine."[48]

The three spots in the "opt. for the original" campaign reflect what executives say teens and young adults are looking for—sex and rebellion. Lee Clow, chairman and chief creative officer for TBWA Worldwide, told *Advertising Age* that "Levi's is about being sexy and rebellious."[49] Not everyone has agreed with TBWA's execution of the strategy, however. Bob Garfield, panning the campaign, described it as a last-ditch effort to increase sales, one in which sex was the last resort. He mused, "the two introductory ads [Invisible Couple and Lola] are far too busy depicting coitus, and pre-coitus, in various ways between various shapes and forms." According to Garfield, the themes of the ads had little to do with supporting the tagline. "What Levi's has done" he commented, "is...opt. for original. sin."[50]

Although the campaign received criticism, the ads did register in the minds of young adults. A study reported in the advertising trade magazine *Agency* revealed that college students considered the "opt. for the original" ads likeable and very sexy.[51] The "Invisible Couple" ad was identified by more students answering the survey than ads for Victoria's Secret and Calvin Klein ads. College students—a large part of the target market that consists of teens and young adults in their twenties—is an important group for Levi's to reach: "Our top challenge is to attract the youth generation back to the Levi's brand and stabilize our share with that group," explained Levi's brand marketing director Sean Dee to *Brandweek.*[52]

As naked as the strategy was, sex may have worked. After all, a playful, sex-tinged campaign also proved successful for another Levi's brand. In 1995

Figure 7.10: Bisou-Bisou Jeans. Courtesy of Bisou-Bisou.

Foote, Cone & Belding created the Dockers' "Nice Pants" campaign to reverse a sales trend.[53] Dockers, a line of casual fitting khaki-style pants, was losing share in 1994 after tremendous success ever since the brand's introduction in 1986. The series of commercials featured attractive men with various people commenting on their "Nice Pants." In a popular ad, a man and woman exchange looks on a subway train. After he gets bumped off the train she mouths "Nice Pants" through the window as the train pulls away. Sales, as well as young men's preferences for Dockers, rose to record levels in 1997.

CONCLUSION

As long as people wrap themselves in clothes and seek to draw the attention of desirable others, fashion will revolve around sexual attraction. But what good is a pair of jeans if no one is aware they exist? For that reason, manufacturers use advertising to promote their brands' alluring abilities. Many seek to imbue their brand with erotic properties, creating sexual meaning for the label through advertising. They do so with provocative imagery consisting of beautiful people in scintillating dress, poses, and lustful embraces. If designers can package their designs with enough sexual energy—and it resonates with consumers—a self-fulfilling prophecy develops. The jeans become sexy because they are advertised in a sexual manner.

Nowhere were these processes more evident than in jeans advertising in the 1980s and 1990s. Request, Diesel, Calvin Klein, Jordache, Guess, and others took sex in advertising to a new level, using ever increasing sexual imagery to steal market share from each other, as well as from the dominant brand, Levi's. Advertising was costly, but it proved a worthwhile investment as jeans marketers reaped much higher prices and profit margins. A pair of designer jeans, emblems of sensuality, could sell for fifty dollars or more, compared to 501s in the twenty- to thirty-dollar range.

Sexual marketing strategies can sustain brands, at least for a while. Of the two designer brands we explored, Calvin Klein is still a major force, earning over $5 billion. Guess still earned over $675 million in 2001, but the brand has lost its dominant position. One reason for the difference between the two designer brands is that Guess's cornerstone was its jeans. As the market waned and competitors entered the arena—often using similar imagery—Guess had to share more of the marketplace with imitators. Klein, on the other hand, had his name on jeans while maintaining his other lines.

Sexual imagery also became a way to differentiate jeans, essentially a parity product. Sex was used for different reasons for different styles. Klein's look maintained a high-brow, though highly controversial, image, at least until recently. Guess advertising had a more European flair that could be characterized as naughty, with peek-a-boo shots of female models in sexual situations with middle-aged men. Levi's, on the other hand, normally doesn't depend on blatant sexuality to sell its jeans. Attractive models are its mainstay, but the "opt. for the original" campaign combined sex and humor, integrating both into the storyline. Overall, many contemporary ads for jeans, designer clothing and accessories, and popular fashion use sexual imagery to create brand images that are tauntingly sensual.

8

Arousing Aspirations
Lifestyle Apparel
and High-Fashion

"Speaking of nakedness, there was never a pitch more naked than Abercrombie's: the non-display of its products, in deference to sheer biological determinism."[1]

That observation was recently made by William F. Buckley, conservative stalwart and founder of the *National Review*, after looking through *A&F Quarterly*. Buckley happened across the 300-page publication—part magazine, part catalog—while shopping for a pair of pants. His curiosity was piqued as he noticed a subscription card at the counter saying that ID was required to purchase the "magalog." Looking through one, he discovered page after page of nude and seminude young men and women: "A few pages on, the young man is entirely naked ... Below the waist there is nothing at all, except, of course, her naked body ... A few pages later the young man is naked again ... A few pages later we have five beautiful blondes in full summer wear, draped about a Byronic young man ... a loose towel over his crotch."[2]

Blatant display of bodies, many without the company's clothes, caused Buckley to wonder just exactly what it was that Abercrombie is selling: "clothiers live and die from the sale of clothes. But the current A&F catalogue goes far in suggesting that young men and women are better off wearing no clothes."[3]

Of course Abercrombie sells clothing, but it does so by creating an image and packaging that image as a "lifestyle." Lifestyle marketing appeals to those who aspire to be more than they are. It appeals to those who desire to look like the models in the advertising, do the same things they do, and exude the same attitudes. Perhaps consumers aspire to have more popularity or friendship, or the ability to attract good-looking others. These needs are especially important to young consumers, Abercrombie's target market. "[Abercrombie has] found a way to package, market, and sell popularity," remarked *Fortune*'s Lauren Goldstein.[4] Abercrombie and other youth marketers use lifestyle images to lure those seeking group membership or the establishment of identities.

The models are real but the advertised lifestyles are not. The image is carefully constructed by creative directors and marketers—it's their conception of a dream they believe will resonate with a segment of the population large enough to be profitable. If consumers want to buy into it, they can; the product is simply positioned as a tool to complete the formula. Sex is often an important part of the image, because it gets the advertising noticed and associates the brand with a sensual tone. Sam Shahid recently told *Advertising Age* that he used seminude/nude models in a campaign for Perry Ellis because it helped to build a fashion-forward image for the brand.[5] His explanation was code for giving the brand a more sensual image. Young consumers seeking to appear more sensual—especially those who are dating or looking for a partner—can buy into that lifestyle. That is how Abercrombie sells its clothing.

What follows is a description of several apparel companies that successfully use "lifestyles" in which sex—nudity and physically attractive models—is a primary ingredient, and the product is secondary. Abercrombie, Tommy Hilfiger, and Polo/Ralph Lauren create these sex-tinged images to sell apparel to fashion-conscious youth. Some of the same factors work for high-fashion designers such as Gucci, Versace, and Christian Dior, who use the product as a prop in a sex-charged drama. Often, these artfully staged images play at the edges of mainstream sexuality with what some would consider a pornographic style including same-sex eroticism, sadomasochism, and fetishism.

ABERCROMBIE & FITCH

Let's look at Abercrombie & Fitch in more detail. Employing a strategy of "cool" with its youthful casual clothing, and hyping it with nudity and a sexy "just between us boys" marketing approach, the company has success-fully tapped the fickle fourteen- to thirty-year-old crowd in a short time. The company courts eighteen- to twenty-two-year-old college students

Figure 8.1: This is the cover of the 2002 Holiday issue of the *A&F Quarterly*. Readers must be at least 18 years old to buy or subscribe to the 350-page "magalog." Courtesy of Abercrombie & Fitch.

with its controversial "magalog" featuring Bruce Weber shots of seminude and nude buff models. *Time* described the book as "frolicking models draped in nearly as much eroticism (hetero and homo) as they are in sweaters."[6] Through assessing and shaping young people's tastes, and feeding it back to them with sensual lifestyle images, Abercrombie's success is nothing short of spectacular.

Abercrombie's CEO, Michael Jeffries, has taken his company, headquartered in Reynoldsburg, Ohio, from rags-and-debt to riches. Founded in 1892, Abercrombie & Fitch was traditionally an upper-crust sporting-goods and apparel store frequented by the likes of Teddy Roosevelt and Ernest Hemingway. *Fortune's* Lauren Goldstein described it as a "high-wasp travel emporium...selling conservative men's wear."[7] The once-bankrupt company was languishing when it was bought by the Limited in 1988 for $47 million.

When Jeffries took over in 1993, Abercrombie was losing $6 million on sales of $85 million. In 2001 profits stand at $168 million on revenue of $1.35 billion, with a market value in excess of $2.5 billion. Paralleling its revenue increases, the company's mall-based retail stores have grown from 36 stores in 1993 to over 491 in 2002.

The transformation has been fast. Just a few years ago my father-in-law popped into an Abercrombie's expecting to find some stodgy sportswear. Immediately assaulted by blaring music and "a bunch of kids running around the place," he did an about-face, heading right back out the door. The "kids" were college-age students, an important Abercrombie target. According to Jeffries, the target market has radically switched from "70s to death" to the other end of the age spectrum, teens and young adults ages eighteen to twenty-two. Clothing is described as upscale casual and includes sweaters, khakis, shirts, and what *Newsweek* called "a lot of rugged and military styles."[8] Abercrombie's price point is positioned between its family members, The Gap and the more expensive Banana Republic.

Abercrombie uses aggressive marketing tactics to keep up with teen tastes. It hires fraternity and sorority kids to wear Abercrombie with the stricture that they "look cool and have fun." It positions good-looking models outside its doors to attract girls. "Cool, great-looking guys attract cool, great-looking girls, who attract...Get it?" explained Jeffries.[9] *Time* observed that "A & F shrewdly understands that teens want to belong, and has captured their dollars by making sure they want to belong to the beautiful, exclusive world that the Abercrombie image projects."[10]

Regarding image, Abercrombie is to fashion what *Maxim* is to magazines. Both are extremely profitable, enjoying exponential sales increases, and both use skin to appeal to teens and young adults. Jeffries, with Sam Shahid and Bruce Weber, two fashion veterans who have created provocative images for Perry Ellis, Calvin Klein, and Banana Republic, are credited with Abercrombie's image. Shahid was creative director of Klein's in-house agency from 1981 to 1992. Not surprisingly, many of the models in Abercrombie ads could pass as younger brothers of Calvin Klein's Obsession models—statuesque, white, and muscular. Young women in the ads are slender and shapely. The signature shot is of shirtless models with pants pulled down below their hips. Many ads feature young men pulling up their shirts to reveal washboard stomachs and low-riding boxers, swimwear, or shorts.

As previously mentioned, the cornerstone of Abercrombie's marketing is its magalog, the *A&F Quarterly*, a combination catalog/magazine. According to *Time*, "Its quarterly 'magalog' has become a youth manual."[11] Mailed to over 350,000 youths, the magalog boasts 350 pages (just 100 pages when it was introduced in 1997). A year's subscription is twelve dollars; individual issues are six dollars.

The *Quarterly*, meant to be humorous and fun, takes a decidedly sexual tone. Its images are chock-full of nude and seminude female and male models in lifestyle shots. *Newsweek* described it as "stuffed with photos by Weber...Everyone's frolicking about in Abercrombie garb or nothing at all."[12] Titles are "XXX" and "The Pleasure Principle." Because the magalog is meant to parallel the "college experience," it contains articles about drinking games, scoring in your dorm room, and where to ski nude. Recently, it featured sex tips from porn star Jenna Jameson. Regarding the references to sex, Jeffries doesn't deny it. "It's within the context of friends, family and caring for one another. It's not promiscuous sex."[13]

Other promotional efforts include limited advertising, in-store displays, and a catalog suitable for all ages. Abercrombie's advertising budget in 1998 was $1.6 million, small compared to tens of millions of dollars for competitors Polo and Tommy Hilfiger. Advertising is concentrated in print. Buys have included *Rolling Stone*, *Vanity Fair*, and *Out*. Many of the ads are shot in black-and-white, which gives Abercrombie an upscale look. The company ventured into television in 1999 with a commercial about wrestling—"what men do in boys' basketball season." Women found the spot appealing. *Adweek's* Barbara Lippert described it as "a scene as carnal and voluptuous as a cinematic love act or perfume commercial."[14] She was describing shirt-less young men with "glistening chests in all their pec-titude."

The company's ads have been described as homoerotic, primarily because of the ubiquitous shots of muscle-bound young men referred to by Lippert. According to Shahid, homoerotic interpretation is strictly in the mind of the viewer. Intimations were evoked in 1996 with an eight-page spread in *Vanity Fair* shot by Weber. It featured two men, John Wayne's son and grandson, on a boat having a good time. Any homoerotic tones were coincidental, said Shahid. "It's sexy and romantic in a fun way. I've heard that people thought it looked like they were a couple, but it was never meant to be that way."[15] The company does openly court gays, however, as several of its media buys include *Out*.

Not surprisingly, the sex hasn't gone unnoticed. Abercrombie is catching a lot of heat for its magalog. Perhaps parents—some of them elected officials—shocked by Calvin Klein's 1995 debacle, have mobilized, determined to protect their children from sex-marketers. For example, Michigan's attorney general Jennifer Granholm insisted on Abercrombie asking for identification to enforce the eighteen-year-old age limit. Former lieutenant governor of Illinois, Corinne Wood, mother of three teens and a preteen, publicly objected to the sexual content in the magalog. In a letter to Jeffries, she objected to the company's "irresponsible promotion of gra-tuitous sexual behavior and promiscuity through the use of pictures of young models in compromising and sexually suggestive positions." She continued, "Often these pictures do not include any of the clothing your company so eagerly seeks to sell."[16] Woods has organized boycotts and a grassroots campaign. A protestor outside an Abercrombie store said, "It's like saying sex is OK to 12- and 13-year-olds."[17]

Recently, Abercrombie sales have slowed, though growth is still in double digits. Any slowdown can be attributed to fickle tastes, not Aber-crombie's sexy strategy—the magalogs are still as popular as ever. Protests from parents only serve to make Abercrombie more hip with rebellious teens. At any rate, it's a successful pitch that gave life to a dying apparel marketer.

Figure 8.2: These Wilke-Rodriguez ads gained attention in 1992. Courtesy of Wilke-Rodriguez.

Figure 8.3: Wilke-Rodriguez (1992). Courtesy of Wilke-Rodriguez.

TOMMY HILFIGER

Another fashion designer appealing to the youth market is Tommy Hilfiger. His lifestyle ads appear in men's and women's general-interest magazines such as *Details*, *Esquire*, *Maxim*, *Cosmopolitan*, and *Glamour*. Hilfiger ads are colorful, with images of his clothes and plenty of skin tone, and include models like Rebecca Romijn-Stamos and others who are popular with young adults.

Hilfiger, his company based in Hong Kong, started his designer line of clothing in 1985 after leaving Jordache. Approaching the $1 billion revenue mark, his company has found much of its success with the youth market. According to business writer Daryl Mallett, "The Hilfiger name became a part of the youth-oriented pop culture."[18] Recently, his brand ranked as a Top 12 teen brand. His signature red, white, and blue logo is prominently displayed on his sportswear, which has been labeled a distinctive regatta-style line of clothing.

Regarding Hilfiger's advertising, Robin Kamen made the observation in 1994 that Hilfiger took a much more tame approach to its underwear advertising than other sexy marketers: "Hilfiger softened the in-your-face sensuality of the Calvin Klein ads to appeal to men...Hilfiger takes a playful tone."[19] Kamen was describing ads that featured young adults on the beach, having fun, in their "Tommies" as they are frequently called. Models splash, run, and grab each other. There always seemed to be group shot where the models line up, facing the camera, in a "I'm having fun on summer vacation" look. Their Tommy waistbands are invariably protruding from their shorts, or they are simply wearing Tommy boxers.

More recently Hilfiger's ads have taken a more sexual tone, especially for his swimwear and underwear lines. A 2002 swimwear ad features a beautiful young female model clad in her plaid Tommy two-piece. Looking right at the viewer with piecing blue eyes, she exudes a look more accurately described as lustful than playful. Another swimwear ad, run several years ago, pictured a topless Romijn-Stamos on a lava beach. The ad is playful; she's wearing a big smile, but with legs spread wide; other, more libidinous interpretations are valid.

Two Hilfiger underwear ads are notable. One is a whopping two-page spread of a young man's Tommy briefs shot from his navel to just under his

Figure 8.4: "You want me to do what?" French Connection, UK. FCUK "Jumbled Words" Campaign. Spring 2000.

pouch. It is a shot that could almost be labeled "actual size." Forget images that show the rest of the model; this ad is a close-up of the product in use. The other ad, for intimates, shows a female model. Clad only in her intimates, she's photographed stretched out across the back seat of a car. The red-tartan plaid bra and panties stand in full relief to her fair skin and the white upholstery of the bench seat. The shot is slightly reminiscent of Calvin Klein's controversial campaign in 1995. The image is enticing, and that's exactly the problem. The woman is young enough to make older viewers uncomfortable. But older viewers aren't the target market. Neither were they Calvin Klein's.

POLO/RALPH LAUREN

A young, long-haired brunette is stretched across two pages of April 2002's *InStyle*, her pink sundress hiked up to her panty-line. Penelope Cruz dons a *very* sheer top on the inside cover of *Bazaar*. And a bikini-clad Anne Heche look-alike presses the flesh with a muscular Italian beau. Recognize this advertiser? Perhaps it will be clear if I mention Tyson Beckford's pectorals or a male model on an army cot baring his derrière.

When asked, most people describe Ralph Lauren's models as preppy, oxford-wearing patricians hanging out at country clubs, polo fields, and English country homes. Not anymore. What people find surprising is that Polo increasingly markets its products with sexy images so it can appeal to a younger market and stave off sex-charged competitors like Abercrombie & Fitch and Tommy Hilfiger.

Beginning with a line of ties in 1967, Lauren chose the name Polo Fashions because it conveyed the image he wanted to express in his designs—affluence, style, and exclusivity. For more than thirty years, that image established Polo as a leader in the design and marketing of aspirational lifestyle products. Still personally directed by its founder, the company believes Polo/Ralph Lauren "is an original idea, built on the universal and enduring appeal of the American lifestyle," and that its products "seem always to be the perfect expression of how people want to live."[20]

Originally known for its signature fragrance and oxford shirts, the company is now a mega-brand with over twenty product lines and ten international licensing partners. In 2001 the company's brand value was estimated at $1.91 billion, ranking it eighty-fifth among the top one hundred *global* brands.[21]

Lauren's advertising reflected the image he sought to portray. The quintessential Ralph Lauren ad depicted polo players within the image of a green Polo cologne bottle. Ad images exuded affluence and privilege; props and settings often included expensive automobiles, country clubs, and English-style manors. Models looked like Aryan gods or the idle rich dressed in khakis, oxfords, and conservative attire.

Somewhat surprising for a fashion designer in the 1980s, Polo ads were devoid of any sexual imagery. At a time when competitors were making big profits with scintillating images in ads for jeans and fragrances, Lauren eschewed erotic appeals. That appears to have changed, however. Perusal of Lauren's recent ads feature many images of young men and women in revealing displays. *Adweek*'s Barbara Lippert offered her assessment of a recent Polo men's underwear ad: "It's highly stylized to look trashy—the hair and the tattoo, mostly—but what makes the picture so different is the focus: the eye goes naturally to the largest expanse of skin in the picture, the sensual arc of the small of his back. (Partly and artfully covered bodies are much more erotic or, in this case, homoerotic, than nude ones)."[22] Lippert wasn't the only one to notice the evolution of Lauren's lifestyle image. As far back as 1995, *Time*'s Margaret Carlson observed, "Even Ralph Lauren who previously confined himself to Aryan youth on sailboats...has succumbed this fall to the aggressively sexual."[23]

A recent study shows that these observations aren't aberrations. In research at an advertising conference, a presentation revealed that Polo's ads are increasingly sexual.[24] For his master's thesis, Tray LaCaze analyzed all Polo advertising in *GQ* from 1980 to 2000. He found that in 1992 models began showing more skin and were photographed in more sexual ways—wanton stares, hiked-up skirts, hunky men and curvy women in underwear posed in body-accentuating ways. For the first ten years Polo/Ralph Lauren advertising was exclusively demure, but sexual clothing—skimpy dresses, underwear, and towels—accounted for 60 percent of ads in 2000. "Stick your nose in *GQ* this month and find yourself smack in the middle of a taut male torso spread across two full pages, pictured only from the region of his belly button to the region of his Polo briefs," wrote Carlson.[25]

Why might a carefully cultivated brand move away from its quintessential image of affluence and sophistication to that of sexualized urbanite youth characterized by muscles, tattoos, and mussed hair? Competition, perhaps. Over the past few years, fashion brands such as Abercrombie & Fitch, DKNY, Tommy Hilfiger, and Perry Ellis have built brands with attention-getting nudity and sexual imagery. Similarly, other competitors like Levi's, Banana Republic, and The Gap—just to mention a few—include sex in their advertising mix.

The shift also coincides with new product introductions. The change may simply be a reflection of Polo's brand extensions. Underwear, intimates, and swimwear lend themselves to a skin-enriched image strategy, and fragrance lends itself to, well, romance.

Courting youth is yet another reason. Over the past decade, Polo models have become younger and more racially diverse. Well-heeled models who once watched polo matches, yachting, or equestrian activities now sport long hair, beards or stubble, and tattoos, and hang out in lofts and tents. Lauren may have discovered that stuffy, affluent images have little appeal to today's young adults. According to *Business Week*'s Ellen Nueborne and Katherine Kerwin, "This is the first generation [Y] to come along that's big enough to hurt a boomer brand simply by giving it the cold shoulder—and big enough to launch rival brands with enough heft to threaten the status quo."[26]

Ralph Lauren's redefinition appears to be paying off. Polo products still command a premium (high prices) as its advertising reflects a more youthful look—all the while maintaining the aspirational lifestyle. More important, Polo continues to show quarterly profit increases amid aggressive marketing by upstarts like Abercrombie. In Polo's case, the transforming of advertising images from polo matches and country clubs to that of sexy, rough-cut youths worked.

TOP-SHELF SEX: HIGH-FASHION BRANDS

Gucci

Lesbian-eroticism, a penis, and belt collars. All three have made appearances in Gucci advertising since 1994—with great effect. The once-declining luxury goods brand has been invigorated by Gucci Group's management team, consisting of CEO Domenico De Sole and Creative Director Tom Ford. Their work has not only boosted Gucci's brand image but has placed Gucci in a leadership role in the high-fashion market.

Founded by Guccio Gucci in 1923, the brand came to symbolize wealth, prestige, and luxurious Italian style. Over time, neglect and too many licensing agreements diluted the brand's image. The Gucci family sold out in 1993, and De Sole and Ford were set in place a year later. According to *Advertising Age*'s Faye Rice, De Sole and Ford "transformed the company from a tattered leather-goods company to a dazzling cutting-edge clothing and accessories icon," rescuing Gucci from bankruptcy and "fashion purgatory."[27] Record revenues topped $1.5 billion in 2002, with growth averaging 15 percent since 1997. Stellar growth was reported in several of the brand's signature collections of handbags, watches, and ready-to-wear fashion. The growth is stunning when compared to 1994 revenues of $264 million.

How do you turn a brand around? Management did it by cleaning up the brand: greater control over licensing agreements, innovative design, new introductions, and a groundbreaking advertising strategy. Directly responsible for the brand's positioning, Ford annually invests close to $100 million in marketing communications to maintain a consistent, global image.

Ford shapes his brand's image with what Faye Rice calls "gutsy, hard-edged glamour presented by haughty unisex models."[28] Her assessment is evident in a multi-page layout simulating stills from a grainy porn-video, shot to look like it's on television. The ad features several stylized erotic images pieced together in an intentionally confusing menagerie. The images include an extreme close-up of a female model's open mouth painted with bright red lipstick. Another page shows a man's lips about to kiss a woman's foot that is heeled in a glittering-red stiletto slide. The grand finale is a faux sado ménage à trois scene with the man, eyes closed, surrounded by two women dressed in black leather.

Can Gucci's ads go too far? By some accounts, yes. In August 2000 Wick Allison, publisher of Dallas's *D Magazine*, trashed 70,000 copies of his September issue just as it was being delivered to subscribers. Looking through the magazine, Allison noticed two ads he considered "obscene." Although Allison never pointed the finger, it's widely believed one was a

Figure 8.5: Bisou-Bisou. Courtesy of Bisou-Bisou.

Gucci ad.[29] Shot by Alexei Hay, the ad features a woman on all fours in front of a man whose pants are noticeably tight. The ad, set in an arid location, is reminiscent of a movie scene in which a survivor crawls out of the desert in search for water. The woman is slender, attractive, and clad in a revealing Gucci mini-dress. The shirtless man is visible only from the chest down. Near her head is the unmistakable and clearly visible outline of the man's penis. Although it was rejected by *D Magazine*, the ad ran in high fashion magazines such as *Vogue* and *Glamour.*

These are just two examples of Ford's promotional strategy, a strategy that has earned respect from top advertising professionals. "Gucci has gone from staid to current and hip," Linda Sawyer, managing partner of Deutsch, NY, told *Advertising Age*. "As a fashion leader, its ads are innovative and have succeeded in moving the needle."[30] She was referring to Gucci's leadership status among other high-fashion brands. The strategy is working thus far.

Versace

Versace is another fashion house known to position its brand with sexy imagery. Versace ads are somewhat unique in that they also feature sensual men. Some are feminized muscle-boys. A 1995 ad features men who are not only feminized, but glamorized and beautified—no toughies here. Two young Italian look-alikes in top hats, open blazers with no shirts, and tight snakeskin pants with bows on the cuffs, stand on a portico, perhaps at the Versace Mansion.

A classic multi-page layout from the mid-1990s features a totally naked Helena Christensen shooting pool. Her male counterpart, also in the buff, is ironing a shirt, presumably his own. Another young man is shown taking a bath in a tiled tub. Cradling a bar of soap on his shoulder, he stares ponderously at the floor, as does his mannequin-esque male servant.

The look of women in Versace ads is continually evolving. Several models, including Claudia Schiffer, appeared nude in Home Collection ads in the early 1990s. In one, a bare Schiffer holds a beautiful Versace comforter over her front section while exposing her rear profile. Ads in 1995 running in *Vogue* and *Vanity Fair* contained a layout featuring Madonna in Versace dresses. In one ad—with her bosom falling out of a Versace bodice—she's playing backgammon with a pooch. In another, she's eaten the proverbial poisoned apple and is lying head first down a flight of stone stairs—eyes open. Since then, other female models have often appeared drugged out and exceedingly thin, though always with hiked-up skirts and heavy makeup. Often, their tops have necklines that reach to their navels.

In a 2000 campaign shot by Steven Meisel, the models have what *Adweek*'s Barbara Lippert describes as: "Sharon Tate in *Valley of the Dolls* meets atrophied Trophy Wife."[31] Lippert has a way of putting things. The ads have a '70s retro feel, with tanned female models sporting big blond hair and vacant stares.

Christian Dior's Lesbian Chic

Rub two female models together in a fashion ad and what do you have? Lesbian-chic—or, after much overuse, lesbian-obsolete. Not so in 2000, when Christian Dior not only tweaked the same-sex taboo, but broke it wide open. Dior's attention-getting campaign featured supermodels Brazilian Gisele Bundchen and Rhea Durham entwined in steamy positions as they showcased Dior fashion and accessories—and perspiration. The ads ran in American women's fashion magazines in both 2000 and 2001.

Although lesbian-eroticism had become a standard device in designers' advertising arsenal (it's here to stay), Dior's campaign was notable for its blatant homoeroticism. As with most attempts at mainstream advertising of lesbian imagery, it's obvious that the two models are "straight." They both fit one of the stereotypical supermodel beauty ideals—thin, Euro-American, physically attractive, with long legs and long arms. But the imagery in the Dior ads thrust the women together in a series of tight poses. The execution is an unmistakable attempt to make these women appear as if they're engaging in a hot sexual merger. Past same-sex scenes in other designer ads are G-rated—only hinting at the prospect of a sexual encounter—compared to Dior's.

In a particularly humid ad, the two women are pressed against each other, breast to breast. Both are perspiring profusely. Their hair is tangled and they are holding each other tightly. Their eyes are closed and their facial expressions clearly signify heightened physical arousal. They may even be close to coming.

Figure 8.6: Guess Jeans. Guess? Inc., Creative Director: Paul Marciano,
Photographer: Pablo Alfaro.

The ads in the campaign look as if they were all shot at the same session. The background is sky blue. All that changes is the women's positions, accessories, and denim outfits. The women wear Dior halter tops, cutoffs, and short skirts. They have denim Dior handbags draped over their shoulders. They wear gold Dior necklaces, and don yellow and red Dior sunglasses. Jane Thompson, a writer for the *National Post*, provided her own description of the campaign, "With lips parted, a leg lifted, eyes opened in a *Basic Instinct* dare to readers not to get turned on, they look as if they're doing more than admiring each other's outfits."[32]

These images are part of a rage comprised of playful lesbian tease ads for designer brands. Other houses using same-sex eroticism include Prada, Louis Vuitton, Guess, Dolce & Gabbana, Gucci, Kenneth Cole, and Burberry, among others. A recent ad for Hard Rock Hotel and Casino ran in a 1999 issue of *Rolling Stone*. The illustrated ad depicted two straight women hugging and kissing, much to the delight of men in the ad. What was the unspoken message? "Want to see some of this? Come to the Hard Rock."

When you consider Dior's French designer roots, the ads may reflect a European influence. Christian Dior is part of the world's leading luxury goods group, LVMH Moet Hennessy Louis Vuitton. The ads were run by Christian Dior Couture, Dior's fashion line. The lesbian-chic trend reflects designers' desire to associate their products with the avant-garde and sexually taboo, since image and perception are often the only features that distinguish designer goods.[33] The trend toward lesbian imagery may simply boil down to trying to stand out in an increasingly competitive designer market that results in page after page of fashion ads. Those that find a way to stand out get noticed.

CONCLUSION

Recently I was sitting in a café-bakery close to campus just as the semester was about to begin. The place was packed with young Greek coeds getting ready for rush. Young men were wearing shorts, tee-shirts, and polo-style shirts; many young women were wearing the same thing but a few were wearing crop tops and halters. With a few exceptions all were clad in Abercrombie & Fitch and Tommy Hilfiger. An outsider's conclusion: These kids have bought into the advertised lifestyle.

Today young people choose which look they want to buy into. For the three apparel brands discussed here, sex is integrated into the "lifestyle," but with subtle variations. Abercrombie's lifestyle is youthful and uninhibited, with rebellion limited to stripping and streaking: beaches, having fun, just good-looking guys and girls having a good time. The magalogs have plenty of scintillating skin shots and the text is also sexually tinged—how-to-score guides and tips from porn queens. The magalog is a toned down *Playboy* for teens with clothing suggestions. It's a lifestyle that has resonated with teens and young adults, helping to reinvigorate a declining apparel brand.

Tommy uses sex to sell its lifestyle with a similar approach. Models are young and good looking, but different from Abercrombie's. Hilfiger models are typically wearing more of the designer's clothing, unless it is an underwear or swimwear ad. For several years, the ads have cultivated a lifestyle with music concerts and admiring girls. Polo uses sex to help it respond to its competitors, as well as to repackage some of its lines to appeal to youth. Polo's lifestyle is young but affluent, characterized by rich kids hanging out by the pool: classier youths who could be described as gorgeous girls and guys, but not as muscular as Abercrombie's. Polo doesn't use the outdoor approach used by Abercrombie or the group photo look of Hilfiger. Many ads, for all three brands, contain nudity, provocative poses, and models who stare at the camera with subtle sexual invitations.

Like many other apparel brands, these marketers appeal to youth— teens and young adults—because it works. A recent Market Facts survey found that 44 percent of eighteen- to twenty-four-year-olds said they would be more likely to buy clothing if it was advertised with sexy images.[34] Ads for Abercrombie & Fitch, Tommy Hilfiger, and even Polo/Ralph Lauren demonstrate that those designers are aware of the power of sex to attract young customers who are eager to be attractive to others. This has translated into much financial success.

Many sexual ads for top designers are more stylized than those for Abercrombie, Hilfiger, and Polo. The ads sometimes transcend voyeurism, intentionally symbolizing haughty decadence and playfulness. At the very least, they titillate by playing at the edges of mainstream sexuality. One trend manifesting lately is homoeroticism: not so much among men but among women. Initially same-sex eroticism showed up in fashion ads that appeared only in women's magazines, but has spread to men's magazines where it has a more prurient intent.

Is lesbian chic sexual for women? Yes and no. Some recent academic research shows that women perceive the ad as sexual, as having sexual meaning, but it's not sexually arousing.[35] They view it as a message that the designer is trying to pass along, "That our designs are edgy, taboo, risqué." What function does lesbian chic play in advertising, especially when targeted to straight women? It's obviously attention-getting, but for brands whose value is entirely wrapped up in its name, brand image is important. What separates them is not material, workmanship, or the look, but the label. These sexually charged images are meant to communicate that their brand is chic and at the cutting edge. The study also revealed that women view the same-sex displays as liberating. The message they perceived was, "You can do what you want with whomever you want—not just men." They did not see the ads as advocating lesbianism, rather as co-opting the status quo to make a point.

9

Aromatic
Aphrodisiacs
Fragrance

"Hello?"

"You snore."

"And you steal all the covers. What time did you leave?"

"Six-thirty. You looked like a toppled Greek statue lying there. Only some tourist had swiped your fig leaf. I was tempted to wake you up."

"I miss you already."

"You're going to miss something else. Have you looked in the bathroom yet?"

"Why?"

"I took your bottle of Paco Rabanne cologne."

"What on earth are you going to do with it . . . give it to a secret lover you've got stashed away in San Francisco?"

"I'm going to take some and rub it on my body when I go to bed tonight. And then I'm going to remember every little thing about you . . . and last night."

"Do you know what your voice is doing to me?

"You aren't the only one with imagination. I've got to go;

they're calling my flight. I'll be back Tuesday. Can I bring you anything?"
   "My Paco Rabanne. And a fig leaf."

Paco Rabanne—A cologne for men. What is remembered is up to you.

Not convinced about the power of product placement? Paco Rabanne had no hesitations. The company discovered a way to inventively insert its own product—Paco Rabanne cologne—into a series of sexually laden tête-à-têtes. The dialogue belonged to a two-page spread revealing the inside of an artist's flat (see fig. 9.1). Against the far wall a man sits up in bed, sheets to his hips, talking on the phone; an empty bottle of wine sits near the foot of his bed. The dialogue flows down the page on the right side of the picture.

Additional vignettes include a lonely writer in Pawgansett, a musician with a towel wrapped around his waist promising the caller another bedtime story, and a man on his boat making arrangements for a rendezvous. All flirted with their lovers over the telephone, and all plots revolved around a missing (or empty) bottle of Paco Rabanne.

The ads created a mini-sensation when they first appeared in the early 1980s. Readers had fun guessing what the other person looked like. Some even speculated about the caller's gender—notice that the text is ambiguous, and there *is* that reference about "a secret lover . . . stashed away in San Francisco." An academic study even investigated another Paco Rabanne ad to see how readers interpreted the motive of a female caller— was she a slut, in control, out of control, rich?

Sexual content in fragrance advertising is manifest in the usual ways: as models showing skin—chests and breasts, open shirts, tight-fitting clothing—and as dalliances involving touching, kissing, embracing, and voyeurism. These outward forms of sexual content are often woven into the explicit and implicit sexual promises discussed in chapter 1: promises to make the wearer more sexually attractive, more likely to engage in sexual behavior, or simply "feel" more sexy for one's own enjoyment.

The Paco Rabanne campaign didn't contain nudity (much anyway), and it didn't come right out and say, "This is what attracts her to you . . . or you to him." But, like most fragrance advertising, the campaign did create

Figure 9.1: Paco Rabanne (1985). "Artist's Studio." Domestic Advertising Collection, J. Walter Thompson Company Archives, Hartman Center for Sales, Advertising & Marketing History, Rare Book, Manuscript, & Special Collections Library, Duke University, Durham, North Carolina; Paco Rabanne, 20 East 55th Street, New York, NY 10022.

a sensual mood, and moods are essential in fragrance advertising. "A fragrance doesn't do anything. It doesn't stop wetness. It doesn't unclog your drain. To create a fantasy for the consumer is what fragrance is all about. And sex and romance are a big part of where people's fantasies tend to run," confessed Robert Green, vice president of advertising for Calvin Klein Cosmetics, to the *New York Times*.[1]

One thing is certain: fragrance marketers play to people's fantasies. A study in 1970 conducted by marketing analyst Suzanne Grayson revealed that sex was the central positioning strategy for 49 percent of the fragrances on the market.[2] The second highest positioning strategy was outdoor/sports at 14 percent. In Grayson's analysis, sexual themes ranged from raw sex to romance with the fragrance positioned as an aphrodisiac— an aromatic potion that evoked intimate feelings or provoked behavioral expression of those feelings. According to Richard Roth, an account executive for Prince Matchabelli, "Fragrance will always be sold with a desirability motif."[3] Roth's prediction, made in 1980, has proved accurate as desirability, attraction, and passion remained central themes in fragrance positioning through today. What did change, however, was the content and expression of the desire motif over time. For one, as the Paco Rabanne repartee demonstrates, women became equal partners in "the chase."

FRAGRANCE ADVERTISING IN THE 1970s

The 1970s were viewed by some in the industry as a cooling-off period, when blatant sexual come-ons—at least those targeted to women—came to be considered passé and in bad taste. Some industry experts predicted that as sex roles evolved, with women entering the workforce and pushing for equality, sexual appeals casting the woman as a sex object would decrease. Grayson's study seemed to confirm these observations. While sex was the largest positioning strategy in 1970, by 1979 only 28 percent of fragrances used a sex-only strategy. Sex was still present in many ads, but it was combined with other strategies such as youth, status, sports, and fantasy, which of course could have a underlying sexual theme. The tenor of women's fragrances changed from the theme of turning on men to turning on the self—being in control and self-sufficient.

Two women's fragrances, described in more detail in the following sections, exemplify this transition. Introduced in 1975, Aviance used the "desirable quarry" approach. The perfume's message was: use this to turn on your men. Effective then, this type of approach was soon deemed as "not what women respond to." By the end of the 1970s, appeals could still contain sex but those with women in control would prove most effective. Fantasy was deemed a exemplary approach: "In fantasy, a lover may be part of the picture, but he is not needed, isn't integral. Most importantly, sexual fantasy represents the woman in control."[4] Chanel's 1979 ad featured fantasy as well as a subtle sexual reference.

Targeting men? That's a different story. Use whatever strategy works, and Jovan chose one that was brazenly sexual. Its ads made outright promises, or pledges, rather, about the sexual outcomes of using its colognes. The campaign proved very successful, leaving one to wonder if men will ever learn.

Aviance's "Night" Campaign

Despite having a scent described by its own marketing director as "not that appealing," Aviance perfume proved to be a smash for Prince Matchabelli.[5] Mark Larcy, now the president of Parfums de Coeur, was the marketing director who put together a successful campaign designed to play to the insecurities and desires of stay-at-home wives in the mid-1970s. The "I'm going to have an Aviance night" campaign sought to "... reassure the traditional housewife that she was still alluring, still exciting, and still able to be wild and carefree with the man she loved," wrote brand historian Anita Louise Coryell.[6]

Debuting in September 1975, the campaign's original commercial was built around the proverbial "lingerie-clad wife meets husband at the door" motif. The spot features a woman transforming herself from housewife to lover—with Aviance as the latchkey. The housewife "throws off her unsightly cleaning clothes, including her bandana wrapped around her hair, dons an alluring negligee, coifs her hair, puts on makeup, and sprays herself with Aviance. She greets her husband at the door with a fetching look, and he gives her the once-over. His eyes light up with approval," wrote Coryell.[7] Anticipation may have been on his mind. The spot's jingle was especially catchy: "I've been sweet and I've been good, I've had a whole full day of motherhood, but I'm gonna have an Aviance night."

Short-lived, the spots ran intermittently for four months in 1975. The print campaign consisted of a four-color, full-page shot of the husband leaning against the doorway, as seen through the bare legs of what is assumed to be his horizontally positioned wife (see fig. 9.2). She raises the knee of one of her legs to create a triangle that frames the scene.

The ads were designed to appeal to an emergent segment of the population—women who were staying home in an era when more feminist-minded women were entering the workforce. In-depth research commissioned by Larcy found what he described as, "The stay-at-homes visualized their husbands at work with voluptuous, liberated women."[8] In addition, research revealed that women used fragrance to assist with role transformation. It helped them move from mother and wife to a sexual partner, or what Larcy described as "their better sexy self."[9] Aviance was positioned as the fragrance that would assist in that transformation.

Figure 9.2: Aviance Night Musk (1985). Domestic Advertising Collection, J. Walter Thompson Company Archives, Hartman Center for Sales, Advertising & Marketing History, Rare Book, Manuscript, & Special Collections Library, Duke University, Durham, North Carolina; Parfums de Coeur.

Despite subsequent criticism about the way the woman in the ad is objectified—her only worth to her man is as a sexual plaything—women played an integral role in the campaign's development. The research effort was led by a female sociologist who was able to tap not only the insecurities, but the predilections and aspirations of women in the focus groups. In addition, the ad was produced by the female-agency Advertising to Women, the only agency to understand the product's positioning, said Larcy. Even the jingle was created by the agency's president, Lois Geraci Ernst.

In spite of its unappealing "strong, slightly musky scent," the spot resonated with women. Aviance sold over $7 million its first year and the ad was selected by *Advertising Age* as one of the best commercials in 1975. In the 1980s, sexualized women would continue to be a mainstay in fragrance advertising, but women were just as apt to objectify as to be objectified.

Chanel "Share[s] the Fantasy"

Chanel first aired its "Share the Fantasy" or "Pool" commercial in 1979. The sensual spot was conspicuous for its *lack* of sexual explicitness and bold propositions. Showcasing a woman's fantasy, the commercial was praised for requiring viewers to fill in the "missing images."

Selling for over $250 an ounce, Chanel No. 5 has been one of the world's top-selling perfumes since its introduction on May 5, 1921. An enduring symbol of French designer Coco Chanel's influence, the package has remained virtually unchanged since she first tested the fragrance in the vial labeled "Chanel No. 5." According to brand researcher William Baue, the 1979 commercial for Chanel No. 5 "became a defining moment for the French fragrance and company's fashion advertising."[10] The campaign was part of an overall effort to boost the House of Chanel image, which had diminished after Coco Chanel's death in 1971. The campaign was an important step for the company to help it reposition itself for the future.

The commercial began with dramatic yet sensuous retro music and a shot of the enticing blue water in a swimming pool. A woman, facing away from the camera, lies on her back at the edge of the pool. The shadow of an airplane passes over her, followed by a woman's European-accented voice-over, "I am made of blue sky and golden light, and I will feel this way forever." A tall, dark man in a black Euro-style swimsuit dives in the water from the other side of the pool. Swimming underwater, he rises up in front of her—then disappears. "Share the Fantasy" was the tagline for the commercial, but only in the American version. It wasn't needed in France where Chanel's brand identity is at icon status.

Directed by Ridley Scott, a British film director whose later credits include *Alien*, *Blade Runner*, and *Thelma & Louise*, the spot was produced in-house under the guidance of Chanel's longtime artistic director Jacques Helleu.[11] A beautiful spot with rich colors, it was truly an indulgent yet tranquil fantasy—sure to lower heart rates in its brief thirty seconds.

The spot's lack of carnality and blatant sexual referents diverged from other fragrance advertising at the time. "Focusing on fantasy allowed Chanel to harness the power of sexuality without crossing the border into distaste," observed brand researcher William Baue.[12] The subtle approach was a wise strategy considering that the target audience was older women: "Our advertising is sexy, but never sleazy. If anything, we tend to pull back, rather than go too far, which is opposite of the rest of the business," remarked Lyle Saunders, a Chanel executive, to *Adweek*.[13] "Pool" was one of five spots produced for the long-running campaign; the spot ran from 1979 until at least 1985, perhaps longer. Although the company doesn't release its sales figures, Chanel ratcheted up its prestigious image, and Chanel No. 5 never lost its status as one of the top best-selling perfumes in the world.

Jovan's Advice: "Get Your Share" ... of?

Jovan, Inc., a small fragrance marketer, spiced up consumer advertising and the fragrance industry in the mid-1970s. Executives at the company used blatant sex appeals to boldly introduce a line of musk-oil-based colognes and perfumes. Headlines proclaimed, "Sex Appeal. Now you don't have to be born with it," and "Drop for drop, Jovan Musk Oil has brought more men and women together than any other fragrance in history." The approach earned the company and its three executives accolades, and sales soared from $1.5 million in 1971 to $77 million by 1978.[14] Eleven years after it was founded, a British conglomerate bought Jovan for $85 million. With no previous experience in the fragrance industry, Jovan's founding executives implemented a sexual marketing strategy that proved to be a very smart venture.

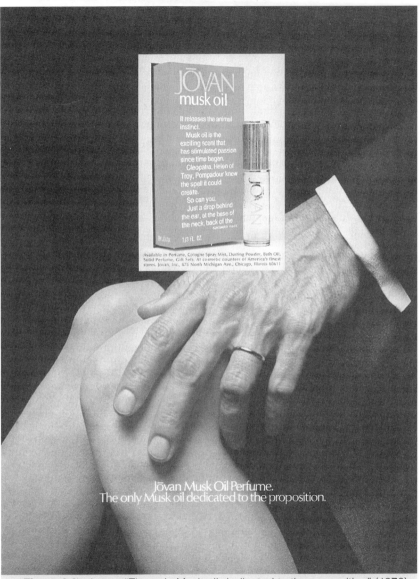

Figure 9.3: Jovan: "The only Musk oil dedicated to the proposition" (1976). Domestic Advertising Collection, J. Walter Thompson Company Archives, Hartman Center for Sales, Advertising & Marketing History, Rare Book, Manuscript, & Special Collections Library, Duke University, Durham, North Carolina.

Bernard Mitchell and Barry Shipp were looking to get into a new line of business in 1968 when they founded Jovan with a mink oil bath product. The company's name was chosen for two reasons: Jovan sounded French, and the name was similar to the company's two primary competitors, Revlon and Avon.[15] Richard Meyer, a Chicago ad executive, soon joined Jovan to write the ads and creatively manage the fragrance campaigns. Meyer eventually became president of the company.

The company's success was linked to its Jovan Musk Oil, introduced in 1972. Musk, a synthetic version of an animal pheromone, was marketed for its ability to enhance sexual attraction—though musk's magnetism is debatable. The product's genesis was happenstance. Shipp was passing through Greenwich Village when he saw lines of young people buying small bottles of full-strength musk from street venders.[16] Shipp carried the idea back to Jovan, and soon the company was producing a fragrance based largely on musk. Until then, musk had been used only in small amounts as a fragrance additive.

The company's success was tied to several factors, one of which was its sexual marketing strategy. All promotional activities appeared to position the fragrance as a sexual entrée. For example, consumers were told that Jovan products would help them attract members of the opposite sex, and increase their odds for steamy liaisons. Many Jovan ads contained the subtle argument that people were having sex, and if the reader wasn't satisfied with his or her "share," Jovan could be of service. Sex and intimacy were the prizes, and Jovan was positioned as the purchase that helped consumers achieve those ends. Consider a Jovan Musk Oil headline in 1977: "In a world filled with blatant propositions, brash overtures, bold invitations, and brazen proposals.... Get your share."

A 1975 retail ad for Jovan Sex Appeal aftershave/cologne for men, contained the headline, "Sex Appeal for Sale. Come in and get yours." The tagline read, "Jovan Sex Appeal. Now you don't have to be born with it." The only image in the ad, besides the headline, was an illustration of boxed Jovan bottles. The packaging was unique because it *was* the ad's copy. The anti-packaging, this brown bag approach, fit the spirit of the '70s. What did Sex Appeal smell like? Just read the box: "[a] provocative blend of exotic spices and smoldering woods interwoven with animal musk tones." The description begs the question, what exactly is an animal musk tone? And what species were they referring to—dog or wild jungle beast? It didn't matter; consumers were buying Jovan by the truckload.

The Fragrance Foundation also liked the ads. In 1975 it voted Jovan's Musk Oil promotion the "most exciting and creative national advertisement campaign." Jovan's CEO, Bernie Mitchell, also earned an industry award. He was voted "the year's most outstanding person."[17]

Often, the packaged fragrance was the only illustration. These ads contained attention-getting headlines that relied on double entendre, references to sex, and explicit promises. Copy in the ads served to elaborate on the suggestive reference in the headline. Consider a 1977 ad appearing in *Jet* magazine. It contained the headline, "And, it's legal." The copy went on to read: "The provocative scent that instinctively calms and yet arouses your basic animal desires. And hers.... A no nonsense scent all your own. With lingering powers that will last as long as you do. And then some.... It may not put more women into your life. But it will probably put more life into your women. Because it's the message lotion. Get it on!"

Other ads contained images of nudity and sexually suggestive behavior. For example, another full-page ad appearing in *Jet* contained a small image of an apparently naked Black couple in a passionate embrace. He's kissing her neck. Her head is tilted back and her eyes are closed, seemingly in rapture. The headline read, "Drop for drop, Jovan Musk Oil has brought more men and women together than any other fragrance in history."

A seductive ad targeted to women ran in issues of magazines in 1976 (see fig. 9.3). The headline read, "Jovan Musk Oil Perfume. The only Musk oil dedicated to the proposition." The image was an extreme close-up shot of a man's hand lightly resting on a woman's knee. The man is wearing a wedding ring, but who knows for sure if it's his wife's leg he's touching—it was the '70s after all. The packaging on the box reads: "It releases the animal instinct. Musk oil is the exciting scent that has stimulated passion since time began. Cleopatra, Helen of Troy, Pompadour knew the spell it could create. So can you." Similarly styled ads promoted men's cologne. For example, an ad scheduled to run in *Jet* contained Black models in a similarly posed shot.

The headline in a 1976 ad, targeted toward women, contained a blatant double entendre typical of Jovan ads, "Someone you know wants it" (see fig. 9.4). Another ad for a different women's fragrance, Belle de Jovan per-

Figure 9.4: Jovan: "Someone you know wants it" (1976). Domestic Advertising Collection, J. Walter Thompson Company Archives, Hartman Center for Sales, Advertising & Marketing History, Rare Book, Manuscript, & Special Collections Library, Duke University, Durham, North Carolina.

fume, contained an image reminiscent of a 1930s romantic appeal. In the hazy image, a man is kissing a woman's neck. The headline reads, "Introducing Belle de Jovan Perfume. Open. Apply. Experience. Savor. Whisper. Touch. Caress. Stroke. Kiss…" There is little doubt about the lustful allusion in this ad. As a call to action, the ad's tagline reads, "Wear it for him. Before someone else does."

A 1977 Jovan ad designed to appeal to men read: "11 great Jovan aftershave/colognes. If one doesn't get her, another will." The scene evokes thoughts of a singles' bar. The man is sitting at a bar with a drink, looking at the viewer. A smiling woman closes her eyes as she whiffs his cologne. The obvious meaning is that men will attract women if they wear one (the correct one, mind you) of Jovan's colognes.

Jovan carried its sexual expression one step further when it sponsored a limerick contest in 1979. The company invested $500,000 in television and magazine advertising to promote the contest. Readers submitted new last lines for limericks published in the ads. Winners were eligible for cash prizes and trips to Club Med. In the ad, the limerick was scrawled on a wall in the men's room. Other scrawls in the ad attempted to make the scene believable. For instance, there were hearts with initials in them, a Kilroy-esque symbol, and a phone number for "Arlene." The limerick read as follows:

There was a young man named McNair, Whose cologne did defile the air. Women with him were brusk, Until he tried Jovan Musk, And now he gets more than his share.

"More" was bold and underlined. A limerick aimed at women told of a boring young maiden who "pleasantly found of the action around, She now gets her share and much more." These limericks helped to reinforce Jovan's "get some" strategy.

Until Jovan's brazen advertising approach, fragrance ads had been mysterious and subtle about the seductive powers of their perfumes. According to an *Advertising Age* writer, "Perhaps it is because the company's blatant claims about enhancing the sensual characteristics of a woman's basic animal instincts exploit what the more decorous fragrance marketers have only been hinting at for years."[18] Another writer observed that Jovan had ignored the "mystic marketing approach beloved by established fragrance houses"—much to its own success.[19]

Jovan's success was also tied to its distribution strategy. Unlike most advertised fragrances, Jovan mass marketed its products like packaged goods instead of upscale, image-conscious products. Compared to most colognes and perfumes, Jovan was very competitively priced. For example, smaller bottles were priced at $1.50 and displayed near the checkout at mass merchandisers, drugstores, and department stores.[20] In 1976, for example, Jovan was available in over twenty-two thousand outlets. Using a convenience-goods-marketing technique (extensive distribution and low price point), Jovan ramped up sales. One ad headline unabashedly proclaimed, "Sex Appeal by Jovan. Now at Walgreens."

Jovan also created demand for a "wardrobe" of fragrances. Instead of purchasing one Jovan fragrance, consumers were encouraged to use different fragrances throughout the day. Depending on your activities (or goals), there were lighter scents for work and play. In 1977, for example, there were eleven product lines—scents, as Jovan preferred to refer to them—for men.[21] A line of "light colognes" for women was promoted in an interesting ad. A woman is shown sitting between two men who are obviously interested in her. All of them are wearing sports attire (e.g. tennis shorts, tank tops) and she's signaling "time out" with her hands. "Sometimes you'd rather keep it light," read the headline. What was the message? If you want to smell nice but keep the boys at bay, wear a lighter musk. In 1981 Jovan introduced Andron (for men and women), a pheromone-based fragrance. True to form, Andron's pheromone mixture was touted as a signal for sex.

As previously mentioned, an innovative technique used by Jovan was to print sales copy directly on the box. This approach was referred to as the "talking package" because copy on the box described the contents.[22] For example, a magazine ad for Jovan's Sex Appeal in 1975 featured images of a teal box with silver and white lettering. Aside from the headline, "Now you don't have to be born with it," the ad's copy was what was printed on the packaging. "This provocative, stimulating blend of rare spices and herbs was created by man for the sole purpose of attracting woman. At will." The copy also proclaims that men can never have enough "sex appeal." This particular ad ran in *Viva*, *Cosmopolitan*, and *Oui*. Ads for Sex Appeal for Women fragrance appeared in *Harper's Bazaar*, *Mademoiselle*, *Glamour*, *Essence*, and *People*.

Jovan is the story of a sexual positioning strategy that paid off hand-somely. In Jovan's advertising, packaging, and promotions, sex was always at the core. True, perceptions did exist at the time that musk, Jovan's primary ingredient, was a sexual attractant, but Meyer and Jovan's agencies exploited the belief for all it was worth. Unlike other fragrance ads up to that time, Jovan's advertising contained unabashed sexual claims that Jovan users would become sexual magnets.

More important, Jovan's appeals resonated with consumers. In 1976, Jovan was third in market share for men's fragrances and tenth for women's lines. Although market share for men's fragrances was a fifth of the market for women's fragrances, Jovan exploited a male market that was just begin-ning to take interest in personal care. As a result of its success, Jovan was bought for $85 million by British conglomerate Beecham. With over 97 percent of the purchase price going to Jovan's three top executives, it's fair to say that they "got their share."[23]

FRAGRANCE ADVERTISING IN THE 1980s

If there was a theme in 1980s fragrance advertising, it was that women and men were equals in the sexual pursuit. *Forbes* writer Joshua Levine com-mented in 1990, "Advertisements today frequently picture women as sexual aggressors or at least equal sparring partners, rather than available sex objects."[24] He could have been describing any number of fragrance ads targeted to both women and men. Perhaps it was the Paco Rabanne ads described earlier, in which the women are just as deft as the men at trading playful one-liners.

Revlon's Charlie created a stir with a subtle gender-bending pat on the backside in 1987. Successful since its introduction in 1973, writer Robert Crooke described the Charlie campaign as "geared to a theme of energy and female self-sufficiency that borders on brazenness."[25] Shelley Hack, soon to join *Charlie's Angels*, was the original model. The brazenness was put into action when a Charlie model reached down and gave her male col-league a pat that lives in infamy. Was the gesture sexual or merely playful? According to Mal MacDougall, the man who wrote the ad, "It was meant as an asexual gesture, the same kind of thing a quarterback does to a lineman."[26] Not everyone was convinced; the *New York Times* refused to run the ads, saying they were sexist and in poor taste.

Women's newfound sexual assertiveness was evident in many ads at the time. A 1985 ad for Anne Klein perfume shows a couple disrobing in a sequence of twelve snapshots. The woman begins the action by pulling off the man's tie—no headline for the ad was necessary. A woman pins a man against the side of a giant fragrance bottle in a Coty Musk cologne ad. Pulling his shirt off, she presses up against him, a leg thrust between his: "It must be the Musk." In "The Joy of Sax" ad for Saxon aftershave, a woman is shown stroking a man's face: "Your partner will respond to the difference."

Another trend influenced the look of fragrance advertising in the 1980s. Referring to the influence of AIDS, *Adweek*'s Dottie Enrico made the following observation in 1987: "Today we're seeing plenty of sex in ads, but much of it is being couched in the more cautious context of obviously monogamous relationships."[27] Enrico was referring to a dampening of unabashed sexual interaction in advertising. Reflecting the country's mood, the headline for a Coty Emeraude perfume ad read: "I love only one man. I wear only one fragrance."

Revlon struck the right balance with Charlie, but hit resistance with its Intimate perfume television spot in 1987. Hot (and cold) and steamy, the spot contained what some referred to as a *9½ Weeks*-inspired ice-cube scene. In the ad, a man sensually runs an ice cube down a woman's cheek and neck. The ad had to be reworked before it was allowed to run on network television. "It's chilling—both literally and figuratively," remarked market researcher Judith Langer, of Langer and Associates. "I think it went too far for a lot of people."[28] Although the couple was "partnered," the ad was deemed too risqué at a time when, as Levine noted, "fear of AIDS has given overt sexual imagery menacing overtones."[29] The print version of the campaign contained the headline, "An Intimate Party," and tagline, "The Uninhibited Fragrance." Revlon's Intimate wasn't the only fragrance spot that had to be reworked. Networks refused to clear a broadcast version of the Paco Rabanne dialogue ad until the male model donned a wedding ring. "I think we're seeing less of the swinging single in advertising because of the current health situation," advertising executive Lynne Seid told *Adweek*.[30]

Despite the dampening of erotic imagery, nudity—especially in Calvin Klein fragrance ads—set new boundaries. Although Obsession was not introduced until 1985, Calvin Klein campaigns dominated fragrance advertising in the 1980s, not in sheer number, but in tone.

Obsession and Eternity

Similar to the introductions of his jeans and underwear lines, Calvin Klein, in 1985, employed a dose of advertising shock-therapy to introduce his Obsession fragrance. Three years later he introduced Eternity. Both campaigns dealt with sexual relations, but the similarity stopped there: Obsession was characterized by what *Inside Print*'s Maureen Goldstein described as "a smorgasbord of nude men and women," and Eternity ads exuded timeless romance and familial love.[31]

Some even speculate that the sexual tenor of Klein's fragrance ads mirrored his personal life. Obsession, with its images of tangled nudes, was introduced after Klein's divorce, a time in which he admittedly engaged in a promiscuous "anything goes" behavior. "Obsession was about insanity, not just my own personal insanity," said Klein. "It was society's obsession with work and love."[32] By the time Eternity was introduced in 1988, Klein had remarried and settled in with his new wife. The campaign exuded romance with images of family and walks on the beach. Both launches were hugely successful and both influenced the look of fragrance advertising, Obsession more so than Eternity.

Launched in 1985, Obsession quickly broke fragrance first-year-sales records. Domestic sales reached $30 million the first year, $74 million in 1986, and over $100 million in 1987.[33] Much of that success is attributed to Obsession's provocative campaign. Shot by Bruce Weber, Obsession ads dealt at some level with carnality and fleshy obsessions. The initial print campaign contained two distinct looks that were summarized succinctly by *Adweek*'s Barbara Lippert as "a continuing series featuring group sex in darkened rooms or four male and two female rumps under the Mexican sun."[34]

The "rumps" style of Obsession ads featured a parade of nudes in statuesque poses "draped over a Nuremberg-style obelisk," observed Andrew Sullivan in the *National Review*.[35] The men are displayed in positions that accentuate their musculature, whether it's their pectorals, washboard stomachs, biceps, or glutes. The women are slender, photographed from behind or in profile. Sullivan likened the scene to a neo-fascist, "It's-1934-in-

Bavaria," image. The models don't interact but merely adorn the ad, creating an aloof but sensual image for Klein's Obsession. "None of these models cares about anything, nor do they represent anything recognizably humane. Their bodies are as objectified as the obelisk they stand on," observed Sullivan.[36]

The "group sex" style of Obsession ads is what most observers talk about. The ads featured tangled limbs and nude bodies. Often it was difficult to determine what body parts belonged to which body. In an early ad, shot by Weber in Acapulco, a nude woman appears to be sitting between two nude men, though it's not entirely clear. Explained Klein, "It's a passionate and sensuous photograph which says if a woman wears Obsession, men will be totally obsessed."[37] For the men's fragrance, a two-page spread contained three nude women draped over each other. The emphasis is not on their faces—only one is partially visible—but on their buttocks, hips, arms, thighs, and breasts. The ads were printed in sepia tones or black-and-white, occasionally in dark blue, and only the image of the bottle and the brand name "Obsession" appeared in color. Another characteristic of these ads was what looked like thin lines haphazardly strewn across the page. *Artforum*'s Glenn O'Brien referred to the lines as "weird werewolf like scratches."[38] The lines were meant to give the ad an aged feel, as if it was ripped out of a magazine and stored in a pocket.

The television campaign(s) was very different from the print campaign. Airing only in major markets, at least three different series of commercials were produced. All dealt at some level with obsessive love and fixation. David Lynch, the film director, directed the first series of spots. Models quoted passages about love and romance that were written by authors such as F. Scott Fitzgerald, Ernest Hemingway, and D. H. Lawrence. In one spot, a young man recites a short passage while thinking about a woman—the object of his fixation. Another set of commercials, produced by Avedon and Arbus, was less idyllic. It featured vignettes involving staged action—generational obsessive love, a surreal courtroom scene—and the line, "Between love and madness lies Obsession." Each commercial ended with the uncharacteristic Calvin Klein tagline, "Ah-h-h ...the smell of it." In the *New York Tribune*, critic Robert Stricklin likened the second set of spots to "esoteric, portentous drivel."[39]

If Obsession was about nudity and madness, Eternity was about growing up. Launched nationally in September 1988, Klein claimed the fragrance and campaign reflected his new life. According to business writer Sara Pendergast, "The campaign for Eternity reflected the return to traditional, monogamous relationships, mirroring Klein's marriage to Kelly Rector and his retreat to a more sedate, private life."[40] The campaign also reflected a culture grappling with HIV/AIDS and other sex-related issues. Irresponsible sexual behavior was viewed as overly indulgent and dangerous. Klein explained the genesis for Eternity: "I'm thinking about love, and I'm thinking about... what Obsession represents... [and] that kind of advertising is the exact opposite of what I want to do now. I want something completely different, something softer, something much more romantic, much subtler... I'm projecting where America will be, what people will be thinking in the next five years. So I tried to think, What's happened after the sexual revolution? After all, with AIDS, with people now being afraid of having sex with a lot of people, [people are] thinking about romance and thinking about commitment."[41]

Print ads shot by Weber featured black-and-white lifestyle images of a beautiful couple, clad in white clothes and wedding rings, with a young boy riding on the man's shoulders. Christy Turlington—who appears in many Calvin Klein ads—was chosen as the Eternity model. Less appreciated was a series of ten commercials produced for the campaign by Richard Avedon. It featured a love-tortured couple, Turlington and Chris Lambert, over the course of their relationship. Describing the television campaign, Klein biographers Steven Gaines and Sharon Churcher write, "They take the viewer through the trials and tribulations of romance—fighting, reconciling, parenthood—each commercial color-tinted according to its mood; cool blue, warm red, steely white. In each, love triumphs eternal."[42] Over $4 million was budgeted for the television campaign.

Obsession ads were a success, with fashion-conscious adults willing to pay handsomely for the prestige fragrance. With its brazen imagery, the campaign dominated print advertising in the late 1980s—it was the most memorable print campaign for four years running.[43] Eternity was remarkable for its romantic tone that appealed to consumers looking for a less salacious scent. By 1991, international wholesale volume of Calvin Klein fragrances reached $300 million.[44]

FRAGRANCE ADVERTISING IN THE 1990S AND BEYOND

It's clear today that some of the fragrance marketing trends established in the 1980s continued to flourish in the years to come. Not only was there more skin, but beefcake had become a main course in fragrance advertising. *Forbes's* Josh Levine commented that "while girl-watching seems here to stay, guy-watching is also."[45] The theme of sexual attraction—the fragrance's ability to draw people closer, to turn them on, or to enhance the odds of sexual outcomes—is alive and doing well. A more recent development, however, is the use of sex to sell fragrance to a younger market, targeting teens and twenty-somethings with sexy and irreverent ads. Campaigns in 1999 and 2000 for Lucky You and Candie's fragrances employed blatant sexual themes laced with teasing shots and double entendres.

Of Bodies and Breasts

Nudity, both female and male, continues to be a staple in fragrance marketing, giving credence to an advertising industry report published in *Advertising Age* in 1993 that predicted more nudity in advertising.[46] *Brandweek* featured a similar report in 1994 as one of "10 Trends to Watch."[47] *Artforum's* Glenn O'Brien believed it was a 1989 Obsession ad that brazenly broke through the boundary of female frontal nudity above the waist. O'Brien referred to a two-page spread in the February issue of *Elle* as "the first real full-frontal big-time mainstream topless ad ... [that] breaks the bust barrier with its fierce, shameless nipples."[48] If it was the first, it was soon followed by other full-frontal above-the-waist views of Kate Moss in mid-1990s Obsession ads and a Nike campaign in the late 1990s. Breasts had made an appearance in mainstream ads as early as 1981, however. A topless model appeared in a series of one-third-page ads for Jolen cosmetic crème bleach. The ads ran in many women's magazines without complaint.[49]

Overall, the presence of women's nipples is still extremely rare in mainstream advertising, and the pubic region is never shown. More common are shots of topless women covering their breasts with their arms, or posed in such a way that only a profile of the breast is visible (see figs. 9.5 and 9.6). In a 1994 Oleg Cassini ad, a nude woman lies on her stomach propping herself up on her elbows. Cradling the large fragrance bottle in

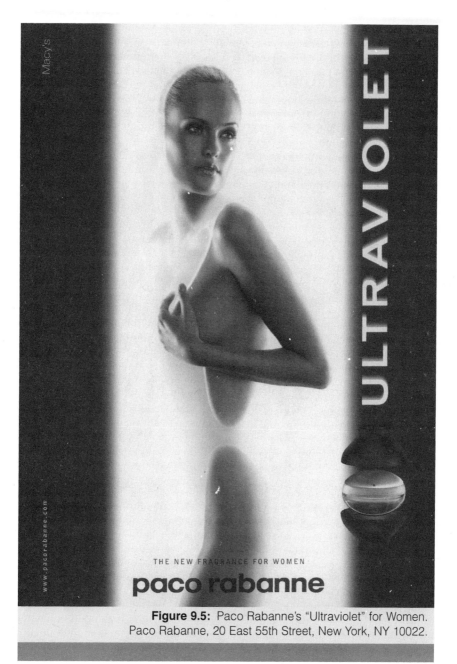

Figure 9.5: Paco Rabanne's "Ultraviolet" for Women. Paco Rabanne, 20 East 55th Street, New York, NY 10022.

Figure 9.6: Navy (2000). New Dana Perfumes.

her hands, her breasts dangle between her arms. Yves Saint Laurent's Opium recently featured a completely nude—and very pale—woman lying on back, her hands cupping her breasts. Ads for Christian Dior's Eau Svelte, a fragrance and firming spray, appeared in women's magazines in the mid-1990s. A nude woman's profile stretched across the page at an angle, one hand resting on her back, the other holding a pink, gauzy scarf across her nipples. The crease of the underside of her breast—deemed too taboo for most magazines in the early 1980s—is not only clearly visible but the ad's focal point. Similar ads containing female nudity are simply too numerous to mention.

Not That Kind of Six-Pack

If women's nipples are rarely shown, the opposite is true for men. If fragrance advertising changed at all, it was with the ubiquitous addition of men's bodies—especially their abdomens—in the 1990s. Beefcake, or what *Adweek*'s Stuart Emmrich referred to as "himbo," was stretched out across the pages of men's, women's, and general-interest lifestyle magazines throughout the decade.[50] "One outcome of the [women's] movement seemed to be that it 'liberated' women to turn the tables and enjoy viewing men as sex objects," remarked Barbara Lippert.[51] Not any chest would do, however: ads required men with muscular, but hairless, bodies.

If any one advertiser flooded the market with images of men's chests in the 1990s, it was a series of ads for Davidoff's Cool Water for men. The ads ran in Europe for three years before being introduced in America, partly because they didn't think America was ready for the feminized beefcake.[52] Totally wet, a tanned man lies on his back seemingly asleep, with arms folded so his hands are behind his head and the surf bubbling around him. "Cool Water" and the blue bottle are superimposed in one corner. A similar image was used to promote the company's Zino fragrance. Lying on white sheets, eyes closed, is a muscular male model visible from his nipples to the top of his head. "Zino. The Fragrance of Desire." Meant to appeal to both men and women, the ad ran in *Vanity Fair, Esquire, Sports Illustrated*, and *Glamour*.

Similar images for other men's fragrances soon followed. Paco Rabanne's XS men's fragrance appeared in a 1994 issue of *Vanity Fair*. While some might call the ad subliminal, it clearly crosses the line into the conscious. The shot is a sepia-toned close-up of a man's abdomen, shot from his pectorals to his big silver belt buckle (see fig. 9.7). Light reflects off the perspiration on his chest. Resting on his stomach, just above his buckle, the man's hand is wrapped around an angled bottle of XS. The lid is popped open, the dispenser clearly resembling the tip of a penis. Even the most ardent subliminal nonbelievers could not fail to miss the resemblance. Other than the brand name, the line "Sensation. To EXcesS" alludes to the ad's intended message.

Yet another "himbo" abdomen shot, this time for Joseph Abboud, ran in the mid-1990s. Shot from the belly button to top of the pecs—the formula requires at least one nipple—the model holds the fragrance bottle close to his body. Other ads with abdomens include Jovan's Bodytonic, featuring a shirtless man being doused with water, and the headline, "They're like sports drinks for your skin." A Stetson cowboy, denim shirt unbuttoned to reveal his hairless chest and big rodeo belt buckle, smugly looks away from the camera: "The attraction is legendary."

Not to be outdone, Ralph Lauren showcased the male body in his ads for Polo Sport. In a classic shot, Tyson Beckford is shown from head to navel—emphasis on his muscular chest and arms—with a large blue bottle of Sport behind him. In a two-page spread, Beckford's arm is extended across the ad, a black medicine ball in his hand. In a nod to diversity, and especially to objectivity, several Sport ads featured muscular male body parts. One ad displayed a muscular arm with a boxing glove on one end, and a damp gray tee shirt with the sleeve cut off on the other. An ad promoting a Polo Sport beach towel giveaway contains a well-defined male, a lone towel around his hips.

Men didn't have to be alone to be shot gratuitously. Raw Vanilla's "In the Raw" ad, which ran in men's magazines in 1995, contained two images of a shirtless young man: in one, he's standing in water to his hips, slicking his hair back as he strikes a Charles Atlas pose; in the second image, he's kissing a woman but the emphasis is clearly on him (see fig. 9.8). Similarly, an ad shot by Herb Ritts for the introduction of Guy Laroche's Horizon For Men clearly emphasizes a man's lithe body, placing the woman's secondary. In the single-page shot, they're both in the water. He's embracing her with one arm and her head is resting against his chest. The smooth arc of his muscular back and arm is clearly visible.

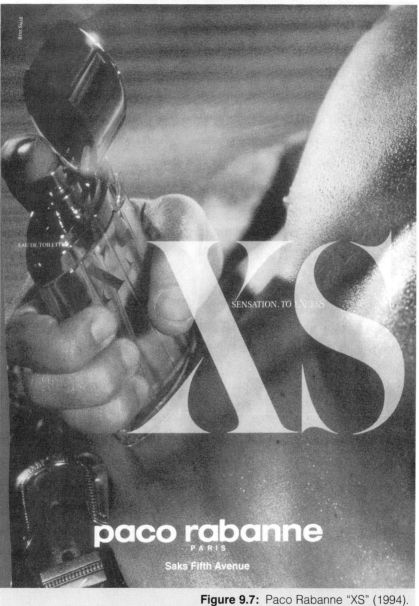

Figure 9.7: Paco Rabanne "XS" (1994).
Paco Rabanne, 20 East 55th Street, New York, NY 10022.

Men's torsos continue to flourish, most recently in ads for Lagerfeld's Jako for men, Giorgio Armani's Acqua Di Gio, Gucci's Envy, and Givenchy Parfums' Michael. Debuting in 2002, Michael proved the male torso is not dead. The campaign, created by Baron & Baron Advertising for fashion designer Michael Kors, featured close-ups of muscular male torsos shot from mid-hip, or just above the pubic bone, to—you guessed it—the nipple. These fragrance ads give staying power to Emmrich's observation in 1991 that "a perfectly formed (and usually unclad) male torso is... replacing a woman's curves as a prime selling tool."[53] More accurately, beefcake merely supplements the use of women's bodies, thereby enhancing advertisers' repertoire of carnality-based sales devices.

Sexual Attractant: Romps, Dalliances, and Romance

Aramis ads, running in the mid-1990s, featured a topless woman, elbows on her knees and hands in her disheveled hair, looking intently at the camera. "I'm all ears," she said. Coupled with the ad's tagline, "Aramis talks," the ad's promise is that a whiff of Aramis will stop a woman in her tracks. If this kind of sexual appeal went out of style after the sexually charged 1960s and 1970s, it was back with a vengeance in the 1990s.

Often fragrance ads featured couples together in sensual or heated embraces, accompanied by copy that made the intended meaning unmistakable. A Stetson couple in a tender embrace come with the tagline, "Easy to wear, hard to resist." Throughout the 1990s, Gravity's fragrance for men promoted the promise of sexual attraction: "Gravity... The force that pulls you closer." Ads featured a couple—in a magnetic embrace—about to consummate the gravitational pull on their bodies.

Sometimes more than a couple is involved. In 1999 Liz Claiborne marketed its Curve fragrance with a shot that hinted at group sex. The ad featured a trio of flirty women with two men mixed in for good measure. All are clothed and all are sitting on top of each other in a booth at a nightclub (see fig. 9.9). One woman reaches across the crowd to playfully touch one of the men's shirts. It could all be fun and games, but when coupled with the headline, "See where it takes you," possibilities emerge. Although the image is sufficiently vague, the model's sexual interest would be clear to a nonverbal specialist.

Figure 9.8: Beefcake and "Raw Vanilla."

In a short-lived but provocative print campaign, Bernini of Beverly Hills combined several elements of heated sexuality to sell its men's fragrance. The full-page ads appeared in 1995 issues of men's and women's magazines, including *GQ* and *Vogue*. One ad featured a young woman in bed, lying on her side, a sheet positioned to cover her nipples, but little else, and the headline: "Sometimes she recalled his scent so vividly, she would lie there, aroused by her own imaginings." A second ad contained a close-up shot of a woman pulling down the spaghetti strap of her low-cut black dress, accompanied by the headline: "Possessed by his scent, she planned to seduce him." Yet a third ad featured a thong-clad, long-haired blonde, her back to the camera, brushing her hair. "His scent lingered in her hair, adding an unbearable pleasure to her morning ritual." Created by The Advertising Consortium in Los Angeles, the agency's president, Kim Miyade, characterized the campaign as classic "sexy, suggestive." Although the campaign was successful, she said it was dropped because it was too superficial for the audience: "The point is, our audience is not the guy who drives a Ferrari and wears alligator shoes," she said, "he's much deeper than that."[54]

Aside from Polo Sport's emphasis on healthy bodies, Ralph Lauren (and licensee Cosmair) introduced two new fragrance lines with sensual and romantic tones in the 1990s. The first, Lauren's Safari for women, was launched in 1990 to accompany Lauren's safari clothing line. Print ads emphasized a romantic safari with two beautiful male and female models donning open shirts and bikini tops. The young couple lounged around a safari tent with Ralph Lauren Home Collection décor, complete with a live lion cub. It's estimated that the women's line brought in $25 million its first year, and the men's line more than $28 million in the first six months.[55]

Similarly, a pair of young nostalgic urban types—beautiful, of course —helped to launch Lauren's Romance fragrance in 1998. Photographed by Bruce Weber, the campaign consisted of black-and-white imagery of real-life couple Tanga and Cedric. The images show the couple embracing, kissing, and riding a bicycle. In some scenes he carries her, her legs wrapped around him, as they dance. Commenting about the image, Barbara Lippert said, "She has him locked ... [but] the sexiest thing about it is the way he looks at her mouth."[56] In another shot, Cedric is on his knees, mouth pressed against Tanga's abdomen, as she looks down at him. In a 2000 two-page layout, the couple is bathing naked in a claw-foot tub

Figure 9.9: Curve. Courtesy of Liz Claiborne Cosmetics.

placed in the middle of a field under a big tree. She's in the tub, legs hanging over the side, while he pours water on them with a pitcher. The ads clearly are intended to capture the romantic moments of a young—supermodel—couple. To accentuate the point, mother and son duo Carly Simon and Ben Taylor sing "My Romance" from Rodgers and Hart in the television commercials.[57]

Between Love and Madness Lies—Escape

Escape, backed by a $40 million advertising launch in 1991, is Calvin Klein's third major fragrance line. Meant to reflect escape from the rat race, as well as an embrace of romance and commitment, Klein described Escape as "about Kelly and myself, what we do and how we live."[58] On a libidinal scale, however, its positioning registered somewhere between Eternity's serenity and Obsession's carnality.

Escape advertising is exemplified by its attractive couples in several different settings throughout the years. Shana Zadrick and Scott King were featured in the $30 million launch of the men's line in 1993. The two appear in a trio of heated television spots that were truly captivating. Filmed in black-and-white by Weber and Irving Penn, none of the commercials contained words except for the product ID at the end. With rising action, complemented with an entrancing score, the couple ends each voyeuristic encounter in a passionate embrace. In one libidinal spot, King disrobes on a diving board as Zadrick stares at him, eyes transfixed. The camera explores both their bodies as the music builds. The climax is when he lifts her out of the water for a hot kiss. Another spot resulted in a beach embrace similar to the beach scene in *From Here to Eternity*. Robert Green, vice president of advertising for Calvin Klein Cosmetics, told the *New York Times* that the Escape campaign was "definitely romantic" and "very erotic," but "not a wanton orgy-like thing like at the launch of Obsession."[59]

Obsession ads experienced a transformation in the early 1990s. Instead of a panoply of nudes, viewers had to settle for one—Kate Moss. "The new Obsession ads will continue to stand for sex, but sex between two people instead of a ménage à trois or quatre," Robin Burns, a Calvin Klein Cosmetics executive, told *Advertising Age*.[60] In artful, black-and-white television commercials, the camera roves over Moss as she plays the object of the

Figure 9:10: Carolina Herrera for Men (1997).
Carolina Herrera, 501 Seventh Ave., New York, NY 10018.

camera's obsession in a white-stuccoed coastal village. The print ads were spin-offs from the television spots. In several ads in the early 1990s she appeared bare-breasted or lying naked on a couch. Occasionally, Moss wore a black dress. With few exceptions, Moss looked deeply into the camera as if to make a meaningful connection with the viewer.

After the Escape launch, ads for Calvin Klein's six fragrances flooded magazines with a sensual-range of glossy images. Klein's decision to continue with his sexualized fragrance strategy paid off. By 1994, Calvin Klein fragrances represented 10.4 percent of the $4.8 billion domestic fragrance market.[61] Klein has introduced several fragrances since Escape—cK one, Contradiction, and Crave—each with its distinctive sexual tone. For example, ads in 2002 for Crave feature a buff, long-haired young man and the line "Get it on." The model's CK jeans are unzipped to reveal his Calvin Klein underwear—true cross promotion. Although some of the models have changed, ads for Escape, Obsession, and Eternity continue to appear in America's magazines.

GOING YOUNG

Lucky You

Launched in 2000, Lucky You is marketed to emphasize the alluring power of fragrance to young adults ages eighteen to thirty-four. Positioned as an attractant with a 1950s flair, the fragrance launch was supported by a $20 million print and television campaign, Web support, and a radio ad.[62] The television spot consists of an attractive man walking into a '50s-style diner. The jukebox flips on a song from the era and suddenly actress Jaime Pressly, popular with teens, appears to give him an appraising look. They walk out of the diner together as another girl walks in. Pressly tosses her a fragrance bottle, telling her to "Get Lucky." Despite the obvious reference to one-night stands and casual sex—they just met in a diner—the agency's president, Frank Ginsberg, said, "It's not about one-night stands and experimentation."[63] Another agency executive, Tom James, said the ad is meant to appeal to people who "are looking for something more stable, like romance and bedrock relationships."

Figure 9.11: Latest rendition of the classic Tabu campaign (1995). "Tabu," New Dana Perfumes

The print version of the campaign features Pressly pulling the lapel of a leather-jacketed "James Dean/Elvis Presley" type. He's fully dressed, but she's in hot pants and a low-cut, V-necked blouse. A handwritten note in the corner of the ad reads, "Get Lucky! XXXOOO." Despite assertions to the contrary, the tagline is a double entendre with an obvious sexual interpretation.

Candie's and its "Anywhere You Dare" Campaign

What do celebrity-actors Alyssa Milano, Carmen Electra, and Jodie Lyn O'Keefe have in common with former NBA star Dennis Rodman and pop-music sensation Mark McGrath? All are popular with young people and all recently appeared in a series of irreverent ads to promote Candie's men's and women's fragrances. Designed to reach teens and twenty-somethings, the "Anywhere You Dare" campaign displays the seminude celebrities in playfully suggestive situations—like squirting fragrance into boxer shorts. Other accoutrements include a medicine chest full of condoms, voyeuristic paparazzi, a phallic rocket, and a rocking bed.

The campaign is not out of character for Candie's Inc. The design and apparel company has a variable past when it comes sales, the popularity of its shoes, and advertising. Candie's story is the tale of a fashion marketer who tried to distance his company from its early sexy-chic marketing success only to return to it to revitalize languishing sales. The return was marked by a 1997 ad featuring former Playboy centerfold Jenny McCarthy sitting on the toilet.

Candie's lifeblood is its shoes. Headed by Neil Cole, Candie's is an offshoot of the original Cole family shoe design and import business. Even Neil's brother, Kenneth Cole, got his start designing and marketing shoes in the family business. Introduced in 1978, Candie's Slide—a slip-on with thin high heels—was very successful. Over 14 million pairs of Candie's shoes were sold in the first three years, and by 1984 the company recorded $180 million in annual sales. Part of the success is attributed to commercials showing envious young women after each other's Candie's. *Forbes* writer Luisa Kroll described the campaign as consisting of "television commercials starring half-naked coeds chasing each other around college dormitories."[64] The popularity of the shoes waned however, and by 1991 revenues at Candie's hovered around $29 million. Unpopular product introductions and an "uncool" image resulted in poor sales among the company's essential fourteen- to thirty-year-old female target market.[65]

Cole attempted to insulate the company from volatile fashion shifts by introducing a line of low-cost sneakers and hiking boots. In 1996 Cole described his new strategy to *Forbes*, "We've traded the flash and trash of the Eighties for a Nineties look. I'm no longer interested in fads that are here today, gone tomorrow."[66] Unfortunately for Cole, teens weren't interested in Candie's "nineties" look, and shoe sales were barely able to keep the company profitable. Instead of looking forward, Cole should have looked behind him. Retro fashion trends proved to be Candie's savior as sales of Candie's original Slides began to pick up. To capitalize on the trend, Candie's hired Jenny McCarthy, a sexy spokesperson popular with the teen market. The former *Playboy* centerfold and popular star of MTV's program "Singled Out" added a sexy and irreverent in-your-face persona to the brand.

In 1997 McCarthy was featured in an ad viewed by many as not only in poor taste but offensive. McCarthy was shown sitting on a toilet, newspaper in hand and panties around her Candie's slides. Another ad featuring McCarthy espoused the tagline "Just Screw It," a knock-off of Nike's "Just Do It" slogan. Despite criticism—or because of it—the ads drew attention and young women started buying the colorful Candie's shoes. Sales rose to $85 million in 1997, double the 1996 sales.

Seeking to capitalize on increasing sales, the company extended its product line with licensing deals, including a Candie's fragrance. In 1999 the company initiated its "Anywhere you dare" campaign featuring another sexy celebrity, Alyssa Milano—a regular in programs popular with the teen and young adult market, including *Who's the Boss*, *Melrose Place*, and *Charmed*. According to Cole, "Alyssa is not only one of the sexiest and most popular stars on television today, but also an icon to our generation Y customer."[67] The $20-million campaign introduced fragrances and toiletries to take advantage of Candie's popular brand image among teens.

A sexy commercial featured plenty of playful camera shots of condoms and Milano's body as she stretches out on a bed, waiting as her boxers-clad male friend searches frantically for something in the condom-filled drawers. Throughout his search, the camera cuts intermittently to shots that explore Milano's body as she writhes longingly to Roy Orbison's "Candy Man." The viewer soon discovers the young man has been looking for his Candie's cologne, which he sprays on himself—including a quick spray in his boxer shorts. The last scene is a close-up of the fragrance bottles rocking back and forth on the sheets of the bed as the voice-over intones "Anywhere you dare. Candie's fragrances for men and women."

The commercial was popular among young people. According to one survey of college students, the ad was one of the five sexiest ads in 2000.[68] Commercials aired on programs popular with teens, and print ads appeared in *Details*, *Rolling Stone*, *Vogue*, and *YM*. Considering the plethora of condoms in its commercials, it's not surprising that Candie's entered a joint promotion deal with a leading condom marketer. In 2000 Candie's teamed up with Lifestyles condoms to promote a "special" gift for Valentine's Day.[69] The gift pack was available from Candie's and Lifestyles' Web sites. For ten dollars the pack contained two trial-sized his and her fragrances, four Lifestyles condoms, and four individually wrapped chocolates.

Another provocative set of ads in 1999 featured interracial couple Dennis Rodman and Carmen Electra. One of the ads showed Electra, draped over Rodman's bare leg, pulling down the front of his boxers shorts with the intent of spraying him with Candie's. In another ad, the apparently naked couple, covered in violet satin sheets, lay together in bed. She's looking at him, he's looking at the camera, and paparazzi are looking at them. A curtain behind the bed is pulled back to reveal several men outside with cameras frantically photographing the then-married couple.

Candie's introduced another controversial campaign in 2000. These ads featured two popular celebrities: Mark McGrath, lead singer for the music group Sugar Ray, and Jodi Lyn O'Keefe, an up-and-coming television and movie actor. The celebrities were chosen for their appeal to young women. Analysis of chat on the company's Web site revealed that young women were talking about the kinds of things you'd expect young girls to talk about. According to Cole, "One point that is made over and over again is that our customer talks about boys, music and fashion so what better way to reach them than with Mark McGrath."[70]

One McGrath-O'Keefe ad gained national attention for its questionable content and its portrayal of women. In the ad, McGrath is shown sitting at a computer keyboard. O'Keefe is sitting on top of the computer monitor, legs spread, with a bottle of Candie's pressed against her cheek. The monitor's screen shows the image of a rocket blasting off—its trajectory headed right between O'Keefe's legs. The ad won the dubious distinction for the year's Grand Ugly Award in 2000 by the Advertising Women of New York, a professional group of advertising women. McGrath didn't have a problem with the ad, however: "The campaign is very risqué and I think that's what makes the Candie's ads so much fun."[71] Appearing on television and magazines, the ad maintained Candie's reputation for gritty but playful offensiveness.

Perhaps to redress perceived past wrongs, Candie's parlayed its provocative image to launch a foundation to combat teen pregnancy. Founded in 2001, The Candie's Foundation seeks to educate teens about the penalties of premarital sex by running PSAs promoting abstinence. One spot features Jenny McCarthy interrupting a teen couple engaged in foreplay. The PSA ran on MTV and other networks popular with the target market. Given Candie's preoccupation with condoms, sexual imagery, and innuendo in its ads, it appears to be a way for Candie's to continue teasing teens with its provocative campaigns while deflecting criticism. And at least they're using condoms.

After peaking at $114 million in 1999, Candie's sales leveled off at $90 million in both 2000 and 2001. The company planned to open seventy-five outlet stores by 2007, but with an economic downturn the company's retail expansion efforts remain to be seen. All things being equal, it appears that Candie's campaigns have boosted its image and stabilized sales to teens and young adults.

CONCLUSION

Does sex sell fragrance? These examples prove that it can. Sexual content doesn't guarantee success, but the attention it garners and the belief that sex is an outcome of using the product doesn't hurt. Other themes are present, but the degree of sex appeal is an important point of product differentiation. "The problem fragrance advertisers have is that there is no surefire product advantage, other than an imagined one," said Stuart Pittman, an advertising consultant.[72] As long as consumers want to be attractive to others—or to themselves—fragrances positioned as attraction facilitators will be in demand.

A more interesting question is: Why aren't all fragrances marketed with sexual imagery successful? Perhaps the approach is unbelievable or the models don't ring true? For older audiences, maybe a rich, indulgent lifestyle sells over blatant sex. Often the marketing budget is insufficient to target a large enough audience. Most likely, the look is already in use by another fragrance. Consider the three men's colognes using male torsos in the 1990s: Cool Water, Joseph Hubbard, and XS. The six-pack was the same but it was packaged differently, from flagrantly sexual to artful. The Michael fragrance introduced in 2002 uses the same six-pack, but raises it to a highly stylistic level. Usually sexual imagery is at the other end of the spectrum—blatant and salacious. Speaking about Calvin Klein's Obsession campaign and the imitators it spawned, *Adweek*'s Barbara Lippert observed: "Unfortunately, few of Klein's imitators maintained the same high level of photography and design."[73]

If sex isn't working, another strategy is to expand into untapped—or innocent—markets. Candie's and Lucky You are intentionally targeting teens and young adults with sexual ads. It is a shrewd strategy; sex is foremost in the minds (and bodies) of many adolescents, and research shows that teens respond to sexy ads. More important, the teen fragrance market is substantial. According to a report in *American Demographics*, teenage girls spend over $700 million on fragrances for themselves and over $420 million as gifts for their boyfriends.[74] Can there be any doubt that Candie's wants a piece of that action, especially when its ads feature teen celebrities and its buys include *Seventeen, Teen People*, MTV, and USA and WB networks?

It's a safe, if not obvious, conclusion that sex-themed ads will continue to occupy a prominent role in fragrance marketing. Talking about fragrances, industry observer Robert Crooke said, "The very nature of this product has dictated that certain advertising themes will remain constant."[75] The tone may vary—as it has with nudity, equality between the sexes, and beefcake imagery—but sex in fragrance advertising will remain a constant.

10
Prurient Potions
Beer, Spirits, Soft Drinks, and Coffee

The camera cuts to the mouth of a captivating blonde as she bites into a sliver of lemon. Juices flow. Eyes closed, she presses an ice cube across her parted pouty lips. She turns abruptly, reaching to grab a man's head with both hands. Pulling him close, she gives him a sensuous, open-mouthed kiss. But the camera pulls back to reveal that the young man, engaging in a humorous lip-sync, is alone. He's only been kissing air. Voice-over: "Yeah, it's kind of like that." The spot is an inventive demonstration of the potency of Sierra Mist's lemon-lime flavor.

Open to a young couple "parking" in a convertible (see fig. 10.1). The girl asks, "When we kiss, do you ever, you know, fantasize that I'm somebody else?" He looks at her, then takes a ponderous sip of his drink. Looking back, she quickly morphs into a hot brunette in a tight, low-cut dress. "No!" he responds, shaking the vision from his head. Satisfied, the girl takes a sip of her drink. When she looks back at him, he suddenly morphs into the seductress, this time running a tantalizing tongue over her lips as she winks at the girl. "Whoa!" the girl exclaims with a smile. "Get A Jolt," reads the screen—a spot for Jolt Cola.

Both soft drink ads contain sexual content, and both won national advertising awards in 2001. More important, both ads demonstrate that soft

Figure 10.1: Jolt "Fantasy" commercial. Courtesy of Wet Planet Beverages.

drink marketers have stolen a page from the beer-marketing playbook. Sierra Mist and Jolt aren't the only examples of sexy soft drink promotions. Cindy Crawford, Lucky Vanous, and, more recently, Britney Spears and Christina Aguilara have been giving soft drink advertising a sexy edge. Beer advertising, notorious for its sexual content, took a puritanical tone in 1992 as its bikini-clad models went into hibernation following Old Milwaukee's Swedish Bikini Team debacle. Libido is making a comeback, however, as beer brands attempt to regain share and add excitement to their brands. Spirit marketers, too, are becoming more brazen in print and television ads with salacious imagery and innuendo.

Aside from obvious differences between alcohol content, taste, and usage, alcoholic beverages and soft drinks share an important commonality—negligible differences between brands within product categories. As a result, beverage marketers invest massive amounts of money to differentiate drink brands in the minds of consumers. Advertising assists by creating meaningful differences between brands through celebrities, popular songs, humor, sex, and memorable imagery. Advertising helps to cultivate brand images that are energetic, fun, youthful, exciting, and prestigious. There are many instances of sex in advertising used for these purposes—more so for alcohol than soft drinks, and even once for an instant coffee brand.

SUDS APPEAL

From 1975 to the early 1990s, much beer advertising contained titillating shots of busty women in bikinis and slinky dresses. These women weren't always alone—they danced with men on beaches, in bars, and at other locations. One reason for the cheesecake is simple: men are the primary consumers of beer. According to Coors executive Janet Rowe, the primary market for most brands is men ages twenty-one to thirty-four, with the twenty-one to twenty-four age group especially important. "If you're trying to interest men in that age bracket," said Rowe, "obviously one of the ways is with women. I don't think women in beer advertising will ever go away."[1] Women are part of a fairly simple male vocabulary: sex, cars, drinking, and sports. A creative director for a major beer account recently summarized, to another writer, what he thought represented his brand's identity: sexiness, men and women hooking up, confidence, and a bit of mystery.[2]

Pretty women adorning beer advertising isn't a new trend. In early beer advertising beautiful women were a staple. If you remember the Portner Ale posters described in chapter 2, you'll recall that over one hundred years ago images of naked women hung on the walls in bars and taverns. In the 1950s many beer ads were still adorned with women. Rheingold print ads focused on taste in the ads' text, but the primary visual was a pretty girl, typically a Miss Rheingold. For instance, a 1957 two-page spread for Rheingold contained images of six Miss Rheingold contestants. Readers were encouraged to pick their favorite and "vote for her in any Rheingold store or tavern." Schafer, Pabst, and Ballantine Ale also mentioned taste but packaged their ads with leggy ladies and bright-eyed beauties in swimsuits and tight pants. Similarly, Budweiser ads showed close-ups of pretty women sipping big heads in frosty glasses, and the tagline "Where there's life … there's Bud."

As society became used to more sexually charged ads, the ads became spicier. This usually resulted in women wearing less. (Can you wear less than the standard two-piece?) Images were sexualized with shots of their breasts, legs, and behinds. Story lines revolved around guys getting these girls with beer or because of beer, or of woman becoming interested in men, with beer as a visible prop. Settings became beach locales in ads for Coors, California Wine Coolers, and many others. These ads served to titillate while reinforcing the association between the brand and sexual outcomes. A Busch campaign in 1989 of sexy men and women on the beach contained a double entendre tagline, "Looking For A Busch." A Michelob campaign associated itself with the attraction between men and women, and nightlife with its "The Night Belongs to Michelob" campaign in late 1980s. Joanne Lipman of the *Wall Street Journal* called the campaign a "steamy celebration of pickup bars" with shots "in which the camera lingered over young women's curves."[3]

Consider that a major campaign featured sexy, spandex-clad women fawning over a dog. Spuds MacKenzie was Bud Light's most popular spokes-dog from 1987 to 1989, but Spuds rarely traveled alone. "To ensure against the uncertainty of Spuds's appeal, Anheuser-Busch's ad agency … surrounded Spuds with the Spudettes, a veritable harem of young women who titillated Bud Light's target market," noted one source.[4] Arthur Kover, professor emeritus at Fordham University, said, "You've got this animal that's sort of ugly and sort of cute. Yet he's surrounded by these sexy women. It's like every postpubescent male's dream."[5] Advertising continued to heat up as competition between breweries increased, each scrapping for half a share point … until 1991, a year that did more to dampen beer advertising's sexual appetite than any other.

The Swedish Bikini Team: "It doesn't get any *worse* than this."

Have you ever been in a situation where people are telling jokes—engaged in joke-telling one-upmanship—when someone jumps in and tells one that falls flat? Perhaps someone snickered, but the faux pas silenced the group? That is the reaction that Stroh Brewery Company received in 1991 when they told *their* joke—the Swedish Bikini Team. The ads, meant to one-up the beer industry by spoofing its sexist ads, were not very funny to women. The campaign spiraled into a public relations fiasco that tagged Stroh and its Bikini Team as icons of exploitive beers-and-babes advertising.

According to those close to the campaign, the 1991 Old Milwaukee (owned by Stroh) campaign was a joke, a parody of other blatantly sexist beer advertising. Looking back at Old Milwaukee's long-running campaigns, no gratuitous bikini shots appeared until 1991. For years images revolved around a group of guys (sometimes women) enjoying the great outdoors. Sitting around the campfire, fishing, and spending time together; they exemplified the slogan coined in 1973: "It doesn't get any better than this."

The brand, targeted to a blue-collar segment, was a leader in the low-price beer category. Since Old Milwaukee had gone national in 1975, it had grown from a regional beer to the fifth-largest-selling brand by 1985. Sales dipped, however, as Miller Brewing, Anheuser-Busch, and Coors fought for market share. To make matters worse, research was showing that men under twenty-five—an important segment—weren't responding to the campaign's theme.

Airing in May 1991, the new campaign was designed to humorously extend the long-running campaign. As the goofy buddies were camping in the outdoors (the spots were filmed in Malibu Canyon State Park), one of the trio says, "Guys, it doesn't get any better than this." A voice-over says, "Walt Smith was wrong… because when Muskrat Mike discovered gold… it got… somewhat better. And when the Swedish Bikini Team came downstream it got… a little better. Then when reinforcements of Old Milwaukee arrived… it most certainly got better." Viewers see Muskrat Mike lifting a fist-sized nugget of gold from the stream, the Swedish Bikini Team roaring down the stream in an inflatable boat, and six-packs of Old Milwaukee parachuting from the sky. In the next scene the women gyrate to the music of a rock band; cuts of dancing are intermixed with several breast shots. Grinning, the guys can't believe their luck—things can get better, especially when Old Milwaukee arrives. "Old Milwaukee and Old Milwaukee Light. It just doesn't get any better than this." In other versions of the commercial the Swedish Bikini Team parachutes in, the beer arrives in an Old Milwaukee truck, lobsters fall from the sky, and a live rock band appears from nowhere.

All good fun—except for the platinum blondes in skimpy swimsuits. The Bikini Team consisted of five models/actors based in Los Angeles. All were beautiful and buxom—the epitome of models in beer ads. It was meant to play off other beer commercials in which bikini-clad women arrive at the beach to liven up the party. Some involved in the campaign were surprised to discover that people thought the Bikini Team was real. For the record, there really was no such thing as a national bikini team from Sweden.

"This campaign takes advantage of the brand equity we have," Mark Steinberg, brand director for Old Milwaukee, told *Adweek*. "But we wanted to bring a little more fun and fantasy to it."[6] The concept was formulated in a brainstorming session by Patrick Scullin and Marcus Kemp, both vice presidents and creative directors at Hal Riney. The two said they wanted to have some fun with the campaign by taking the established tagline a step further to appeal to guys in the under-twenty-five segment.[7] According to Scullin: "[The] Swedish Bikini Team was a three word joke. A truly pretentious notion.... They were a send-up for beer commercial babes.... They were a running joke, the only constant in the campaign. The campaign itself was a spoof of all beer advertising, even Old Milwaukee's."[8]

As the campaign was about to break, Steinberg told *Adweek*, in words that were are now ominous, why Stroh put $20 to 25 million into the media buy: "Since [the campaign] is new, we want to make sure consumers see it and talk about it."[9] It generated talk, all right. The Bikini Team was a joke that might have gone under most people's radar screens except for a sexual harassment lawsuit filed six months after the first ad appeared on national television. The suit alleged, among other things, that the campaign contributed to sexual harassment for female Stroh employees. The suit drew national attention, especially after the Clarence Thomas-Anita Hill hearings. Women were in no mood for a sexist joke at their expense.

The sexual harassment suit, filed by attorney Lori Peterson, contended that the campaign contributed to an harassment-charged work-place "by fostering an anti-female attitude through its advertisements."[10] "These ads tell Stroh's male employees that women are stupid, panting playthings," Peterson told *Time*.[11] The suit was originally filed by four women, each seeking a minimum $350,000 in damages. The suit named thirty-two male employees accused of activities including: slapping the women's buttocks, rating the women's bodies by number, and following the women home, among other accusations.[12] Peterson said she made the link between the company's advertising and sexual harassment when she asked her clients to bring in examples of Stroh promotional materials posted in the plant. Many of the posters and ads were images of buxom women in provocative poses. "I thought, they are harassing them with the company's own advertising," Peterson told the *ABA Journal*.[13] Stroh reached an out-of-court settlement in 1993 with eight former female employees for an undisclosed sum.

Events continued to spin out of control. Two months after the suit was filed, the Bikini Team appeared on the cover of *Playboy*. The magazine contained a nude layout of the women, and *Playboy* set up a 900 number so callers could hear their voices on a recorded message for three dollars per minute. The *Playboy* layout, although it was arranged by the models themselves, hurt Stroh's image further. Considering the negative publicity, the campaign was a disaster. There were some positive effects on sales, however. Although beer sales were down industry-wide, sales of Old Milwaukee dropped 6.3 percent compared to Stroh's overall drop of 8.6 percent. Sales to young men showed some positive movement, but the Bikini Team ads were shelved at the end of 1991 and no sexy ads ran in 1992. The agency eventually lost the account.

Bikini Fallout

Old Milwaukee's ads were followed by a string of events that called brewing marketers to task. In November 1991, Surgeon General Antonia C. Novello publicly asked alcoholic beverage marketers to curtail "ads that focus on bikini-clad women and athletic men frolicking on beaches or playing sports to the sounds of the latest rock music, saying that they 'unabashedly' target young people," reported Jodi Duckett in an article that appeared in the *Portland Oregonian*.[14] There were even grumblings in Washington about banning beer advertising from television.

In October 1991, a scathing *Advertising Age* editorial scolded the breweries: "For years, many beer companies have used blatantly sexist advertising to titillate male beer drinkers. And leading brewers say they see no reason to change. They are wrong."[15] The editorial went on to say the only purpose of these ads is "to delight macho men who drink macho beer with their macho buddies." Some brewers denied that their ads were at all sexist. In January 1992 a spokesperson for Miller Brewing Co. said, "We have been and continue to feel very positive about how beer drinkers, both men and women, are portrayed [in our ads]. They're sociable, fun, and are presented in a realistic manner."[16]

Although most brewery executives denied being influenced by the Stroh fiasco, changes took place almost immediately. According to *Marketing News*'s Cyndee Miller, Stroh's pulled an ad that showed three bikini-clad derrieres for its Augsburger brand.[17] Joanne Lipman of the *Wall Street Journal* said, "Michelob and Budweiser, too, have deliberately retreated from sexist images of women in their ads. Budweiser last fall led the way with a campaign featuring an electric-guitar-playing granny; that campaign bumped one in which young men's fantasies came to life, and in which bikini-clad babes naturally played a major role."[18] In 1992 August Busch IV, Budweiser brand manager and son of the head of Anheuser-Busch, said that his company was moving away from "typical beer advertising" to advertising in which women "will have equal roles and be treated in an equal manner."[19]

Change didn't happen overnight, however. In 1992 packs of seductively dressed young women, Miller's Cold Patrol Six Pack, promoted MGD Light in local Pennsylvania taverns.[20] Six young women were hired to wear mini-skirts, revealing tops, and bikinis as they chatted with male patrons, talking up the plusses of Miller beer. William Pappano, general manager of Banko Beverage, said, "It does sell beer. People don't understand that sometimes. Sometimes we forget realities. We become a society so concerned with political correctness."[21]

Beer advertising's celibacy from the early 1990s to 2000 is mostly characterized by humor, edginess, and lifestyle advertising. Viewers saw, and continue to see, ads with an emphasis on humor and animation—note

Budweiser's ants and lizards. Playing on edgy humor, one ad tells the story of a man who betrays his buddy to a bear so he doesn't have to share the beer. If sex is present, it's often partnered with humor, with men as the butt of the joke. Consider an ad titled "Centerfold" produced by Dieste & Partners. A young man sits on the couch drinking a Bud Light while looking at a girlie magazine. Setting the open magazine on the coffee table he spills beer on it. Concerned about wasting his Bud Light, he's licking the page as his wife and her female friend walk in. "Carlo!" exclaims his wife, while the other woman shakes her head. He can't get a break when they walk in on him again as he's drying the page by rubbing it across his chest—"Carlo!"

Miller Genuine Draft's "Opportunity"

Looking back at past beer advertising, a television/film director said in 2000, "...five to seven years ago, there was a lot of sexy beer stuff going on. For the past few years, I'd been wondering when someone was going to make the leap backward towards trying something sexy again."[22] The director was Tarsem Singh, known for directing the award-winning R.E.M. "Losing My Religion" video in 1991, and the motion picture "The Cell" in 2000. He was, using his own words, the person who would take the "leap backward" with a cheeky campaign for Miller Genuine Draft in 2000.

Miller Genuine Draft initiated a series of spots in 2000 that contained couples, nudity, and innuendo, all couched in good fun. The campaign was designed to build on its "Never miss a genuine opportunity" theme, by showing people ingeniously making the most of opportunities at odd moments.[23] The campaign took a decidedly sexual approach because sex appealed to beer drinkers, and nonsexual humorous beer ads had saturated the airwaves. According to Tarsem, "Over the past year...all the comedy [in beer advertising] had become so universal that you couldn't tell one funny [ad] from another."[24]

These Miller spots are known not only for their sex appeal, but for their lack of spoken dialogue between the actors. For example, one of the spots garnering attention features a young woman stripping down to her intimates as she does laundry. About this time, a young man walks into the room with his basket. She's a bit uncomfortable, especially since she's trying to stuff her overloaded washing machine. Assessing her problem, he offers her a Miller while gesturing that he has room in his machine. The man's eyes widen as he watches her bra disappear in his tub.

"Love Thy Neighbor" is another spot that created a buzz. A young couple is playing Jenga but their game is disturbed by pulsing music coming from next door. Looking from the balcony, the man discovers the music is originating from a party. Going to the adjoining wall (in the bedroom), he watches as a pair of barrettes bounce to the beat on the bedside table. Getting an idea, he grabs two Miller Genuine Drafts from the refrigerator and motions for his girlfriend to join him in the bedroom. He sets a bottle cap on the bedside table. Watching it bounce, she fails to guess his intention. This time he puts a bottle cap on the bed. Watching it bounce a couple of times, she finally looks up at him with knowing eyes and a smirk.

The spot was meant to be sexy but also communicate an equality between the two actors. "We went for more of a sensual, sexy feel. We wanted to keep the playing field very equal," said Bob Merlotti, J. Walther Thompson group creative director and writer of "Love Thy Neighbor." "If there are spots like this that tend to be sexual, the thing to do is not go into bimboland. If it's the kind of girl you would play scrabble with and also love to have sex with, then you can usually put in a lot more innuendos," commented Tarsem.[25]

In another spot ("On the Lam"), a young man is sitting on the edge of a hotel bed watching a newsflash on television. A recent crime spree has been committed by someone who he recognizes when her face is flashed on the screen. He then does a double take as his female companion walks out of the bathroom. She's the same woman as the person on the screen, though now she's clad in her underwear. "Never miss a genuine opportunity," reads the tagline.

Initially, JWT had considered a different approach to the campaign, but humor was so prevalent among beer advertisers that a brand like MGD, without a massive media budget, would have a difficult time competing. According to Merlotti, "We were trying to go for sophisticated humor, but we found out that you get lumped in with all the beer stuff that's on the air—Bud Light, Miller Lite, and so on. Not that that's bad, but it's well-mined territory and they own it. A brand like MGD just doesn't have the media weight to compete there."[26]

One critic wasn't buying it. *Advertising Age*'s Bob Garfield called the campaign "a desperate attempt to regain traction somewhere—anywhere" by "shamelessly and vulgarly pandering to the crudest common denominator."[27] He likened the series of spots to "a series of subadolescent sex fantasies." Not everyone was as critical, however. "Love Thy Neighbor" was selected as "Spot of the Week" by *Shoot* magazine. *Shoot*'s writer, Kathy DeSalvo, said the "Love Thy Neighbor" spot is sexy but manages to do so "without resorting to juvenile, lowbrow comedy." She also said the spot "strikes the right balance by cleverly and subtly suggesting the erotic possibilities."[28]

As the Miller spots demonstrate, sex is working itself back into beer advertising. Some blame it on the laddie-mentality, a macho male backlash characterized by *The Man Show* and the stunning success of magazines like *Maxim, FHM,* and *Stuff.* One such ad, a print ad for Labatt's Ice beer, shows a woman from neck to hips in a tight, metallic-colored top that reveals her navel ring. Most striking, however, are her very prominent nipples, reminiscent of a scene in the film *Kingpin.* Labatt's was using the shot visually to demonstrate a selling point—that it is "Brewed 4[0] Below Zero." The ad also won a facetious *Adweek* honor in 2001 as "Best Temperature-Related Excuse for a Cheesecake Photo."[29] Other, more recent ads include Miller Lite's "Catfight" and Coors Light's "Twins." Perhaps it's safe to say that the bimbos are back—for now.

ROUSING SPIRITS

To forestall any outside regulation, a meeting in 1998 of producers and marketers of liquor, the Distilled Spirits Council of the United States, adopted a code of good practice. Part of that code was an agreement to advertise spirits in a dignified and responsible manner, while avoiding citizens who were underage. Another tenet was adopted: "No distilled spirits advertising or marketing materials should claim or depict sexual prowess as a result of beverage alcohol consumption."[30]

Yet the headline of an 2001 *Advertising Age* article announced: "Spirited Sex: Alcohol Ads Ratchet Up the Sex to Woo Jaded Consumers." The article described the increase in sexual content in spirit advertising.[31] The article's author, Hillary Chura, correctly observed that despite the code of good practice, ads for whiskey, gin, vodka, rum, and liqueurs have supple-

Figure 10.2: Svedka is an up-and-coming premium vodka (2002). Used by permission of Spirits Marque One, LLC.

mented their usual double entendres and romantic couples with increasingly sexual images. Open a magazine and see Bacardi women showing their underwear, drops of Disaronno moving tantalizingly down the bodies of naked women, and a woman giving a man—and viewers—a lap dance in a Revelstoke whiskey ad. Because of a self-imposed ban on television advertising, most spirits marketers rely on magazines, billboards, and various promotions to market their brands. That's changing, however, and television commercials for spirits go as hardcore as networks will allow them.

Through the years, many liquor ads have contained attractive women and sexually loaded double entendres. An ad for J&B in the 1970s showed a man's hands on the cheeks of a young woman and the headline, "Whatever you've got going, keep it going with J&B." A Johnnie Walker ad in the 1960s showed an image of an attractive woman and a Johnnie Walker bottle with the headline, "I buy it for the man who has me." Ads for Chateau Martin Wine featured a blonde lip-syncing the brand's slogan, "Had Any

Lately?" And commercials for Pink Champale's "The Ultimate Experience" campaign featured an array of sexy yet innocent images.[32] Some campaigns have drawn criticism however.

Johnnie Walker Red's "Assets"

Although sexual images and innuendo have been used for years to sell spirits, sex can ignite the critic's ire. That is what happened with the "Good Taste is Always an Asset" campaign developed for Johnnie Walker Red Label Scotch Whiskey. Well-remembered for its "tush" shots, the campaign resulted in at least a few people calling a phone number on a billboard to talk to an anonymous woman in a red bikini. Even more remember the tagline, "*And* he drinks Johnnie Walker."

Introduced in 1988, the goal of the advertising campaign was to reposition Johnnie Walker as a premium brand for two reasons: problems of market share cannibalization and profitability.[33] At the time, Johnnie Walker was competing in the same mid-level tier with category leader and sister brand, Dewar's. Executives wanted to raise Johnnie Walker to top-level status so it wouldn't eat into Dewar's sales. In addition, premium labels are more profitable, an important positioning strategy at the time since category sales of whisky were shrinking. Johnnie Walker is owned by Schieffelin & Somerset, a joint venture between parent company Guinness PLC and Louis Vuitton Moet Hennessey.

Smith/Greenland had handled the brand's account for over twenty-five years. It planned to spice things up with an image campaign. Agency executives decided to move away from the current campaign that featured shots of the bottle. One ad featured a pair of young women on a ski lift looking over their shoulder. "I just saw what I want for Christmas. And I bet he drinks Johnnie Walker Red." Overall there were twelve print ads in the campaign. The target was twenty-five- to thirty-nine-year-olds, somewhat younger than the traditional whiskey drinker. The ads were designed to create an image of desirability. You wanted to be seen as a drinker of Johnnie Walker if you wanted to be associated with these women (or men).

The first print ad featured two women strolling down the beach in revealing swimsuits. The visual emphasis of the ad was on their backsides. "He loves my mind. *And* he drinks Johnnie Walker." Another ad featured two women jogging together with the same headline. One questionable ad contained an image of two men checking out a woman who was walking away from them. "She looks even better when she's walking toward you," said one man to another.

Although some considered the ads sexist, the campaign revolved around an aspirational sex appeal. Readers knew who these women were—beautiful, athletic, smart, playful, and essentially unobtainable for the average guy. But maybe there was a chance for men if they drank Johnnie Walker. Right? Regarding ads like the "Great Assets" campaign, advertising professor Sid Levy said, "If an ad implies an enhancement of our desirability, part of our minds may say, 'Baloney!' The other part will always say, 'It couldn't hurt.' "[34]

Billboards were introduced in the summer of 1989. The boards featured the backside of a tan woman in a high-cut red patent-leather-looking swimsuit stretched across the billboard as she talked on the phone. The headline contained nine words and seven numbers: "My new number is 259-0373. *And* I drink Johnnie Walker." The number was localized depending on what market it was running in. According to one report, over 100,000 people called the number. Those who did listened to a prerecorded forty-second message from one of the "girls"—she had a different name and personality in each market—talking about her preferences, and a short message about drinking and driving.[35]

Adweek's Barbara Lippert was one of the campaign's biggest critics. According to brand historian William Baue, Lippert devoted at least two columns to the campaign, chastising everything from the art direction to the copywriting to the slogan. She called the ads "creepy," and described the campaign's first image in the following manner: "It's the most gratuitous use of two female tushes to sell scotch I've ever seen."[36] Jonis Gold, co-creative director of Smith/Greenland, and creator of the ads, defended the campaign as being modest: "They don't show great big [breasts] hanging out, they're not really saying anything salacious or suggestive at all. They're meant to be light-hearted."[37] The campaign ended in 1991, however.

IN CANADA, THE AVERAGE PAY CHECK RARELY LASTS TWO WEEKS. IT'S MORE LIKE TWENTY SONGS.

Strong, smooth whisky from a country that requires it.

The Revelstoke Canadian Spiced Whisky, 40% Alc./Vol. (80 Proof), imported from Canada by Phillips Beverage Co., Minneapolis, MN

Figure 10.3: Revelstoke Whiskey. Courtesy of Holmes and Lee.

Recent Liquor Advertising

Current ads for whiskey make the "Good Assets" campaign look like a Disney movie. For instance, strip bars appear to be a recent theme in many whiskey ads. Jim Beam ran one in 2000. Its ads featured a group of (male) friends at a table next to the stage: "Your lives would make a great sitcom. Of course, it would have to run on cable." Revelstoke took it a step further in 2001 (see fig. 10.3). Trying to boost its image and sales with a $1 million budget, the Canadian whiskey featured an image rarely seen in public.[38] The image was a close-up shot of a man in a Hawaiian-print shirt receiving a lap dance from a surgically enhanced women in a g-string. The headline read: "In Canada the average paycheck lasts two weeks. It's more like twenty songs." Although they're not set in a strip club, recent ads for Cutty Sark Whiskey feature a simple pinup shot of a blonde with scrunched boobs and hot pants. The image is a clever lure to get consumers to the brand's Web site: "See more of Nikki at www.cuttysarkusa.com."

The liqueur Disaronno is one of several spirit marketers beginning to advertise on television.[39] In an ad running on cable in May 2001, a woman douses her tongue in Disaronno to seal a letter for her lover. When he opens the empty envelope, catching a whiff of the amaretto aroma, he can't help but remember her. "We worked off the idea of Disaronno as a catalyst for passion," Lisa Shimotakahara, McKinney & Silver creative director, told *Adweek*.[40] The agency is attempting to appeal to young males instead of its traditional market of older women. The approach is obvious when examining recent Disaronno print campaigns. Several of these ads in the late 1990s contained black-and-white vignettes of couples in passionate embraces, glasses of Disaronno in hand. The men are Italian-types with dark hair and dark skin, and the women show their share of cleavage. The copy accentuates the passion appeal: "Disaronno Originale. Italian. Sensual. Warm. Light a Fire." The latest iteration of the campaign features close-up shots of women's necks or shoulders with a drop of Disaronno on them. These ads also encouraged the viewer to go to the brand's Web site: the drop was the "dot" in "Disaronno.com."

Ads in the 1990s for Remy Martin Cognac contained images of the bottle and witty double entendres ("Want to come up for a drink sometime?"). The brand received criticism in 1994, however, for a blatant sug-

Figure 10.4: "Only Remy." Remy X0. Courtesy of Remy Amerique and DBB.

gestion in an ad heavily targeted toward Blacks. The ad featured a picture of the bottle and the headline, "Mistletoe gets you a kiss. Imagine what this will bring." The buy included *Essence, Ebony,* and *Black Enterprise,* as well as *Sports Illustrated* and *GQ.* Recently, Remy Martin ads have moved away from images of quipping bottles to images with a lot more spice. Devilish centaurs (the product logo) appear from the ends of cigars smoked by beautiful women, or dripping down the crease between their breasts. In one ad, for instance, a man rubs an ice cube along a woman's neck. The water trickles down her chest to form the cognac-colored centaur—"Only Remy" (see fig. 10.4).

White or clear liquors are also marketed with sexy campaigns—most notably Bacardi with its "Bacardi By Night" campaign. The campaign features images of women loosening up with a glass of Bacardi. In the ad "Buttoned up by Day. Bacardi by Night," a woman shot from her nose to her hips is flashing a sultry smile while her blouse is unbuttoned except for one lone fastening. The "Banker by Day" ad features a midriff shot of a woman's navel ring. "Pussy Cat by Day" features another shot of a woman from neck to hips with an opened blouse this time. She's also pulling down her pants to reveal her leopard print string bikini bra and panty set. Perhaps the campaign is capitalizing on the sexual glamour of "vampire chic"—the models are "constrained" during the day but "unleashed" after dark. In addition, the models' figures do resemble those of the bloodthirsty vixens in campy Dracula movies.

Other liquors are matching Bacardi's sex appeal. In the premium market, Grey Goose instituted a marketing approach with print ads and "vodka-ettes." The magazine ads, running in 1997, featured a couple in a passionate embrace at the bar (see fig. 10.5). The man is nuzzling his girlfriend's neck, while she—eyes closed in rapture—stabilizes her martini on her propped-up bare knee. The headline reads: "If the French can do this with a kiss...(Imagine what they can do with a vodka!)." The ads appeared about the same time a group of young women were hired to tout Grey Goose in cigar bars. The goal of the integrated campaign, according to *Advertising Age's* James Arndorfer, is that "a little sex and a $3.2 million campaign will distinguish [the] high-end vodka from other brands in the crowded niche."[41]

Other premium vodka brands include Absolut, Belvedere, Skyy, and

Figure 10.5 Grey Goose Vodka. Courtesy of Sidney Frank Importing Co, Inc.

Svedka. Absolut has included but not harped on a few nude but playful shots in its long-running image campaign. One ad shows the backsides of John Lennon and Yoko Ono, and the headline, "Absolut John and Yoko." Another ad headlined, "Absolut Au Kurant," shows a bottle-shaped garter clip. And most recently, "Absolut Tom Ford" is a multi-page layout that parodies the Gucci's designer's advertising: young, slinky, and long-haired Euro-types clubbing amidst bubbles in a surrealistic dance scene. Skyy has also run some very sexual ads including #49 "Riviera Rendezvous": a man with a blue bottle of Skyy and two martini glasses stands over a woman whose breasts are barely contained by her platinum top. Currently, Sauza brand tequila is running a campaign featuring a man with either one or two slender beauties. Headlines and images work together to suggest a ménage à trois in one ad: "You still look for trouble on Friday nights. Just not with a bunch of guys." Another Sauza ad shows the man smirking as one of the women tries to lick his ear: "The tequila is pure. Your intentions don't have to be." For many spirit marketers, their intentions are clear. Sex will continue to be a fundamental tool to maintain share and increase sales.

BABES (AND BEEFCAKE) IN POPLAND

Americans love their soft drinks, spending over $55 billion on them each year. They buy the beverages for refreshment, thirst, a kick, or as a substitute for alcohol. Despite the various reasons for consuming soda, many Americans are fiercely loyal to their brands. They identify themselves as members of the "Pepsi Generation" or as die-hard Coca-Cola drinkers. What separates the brands in the minds of consumers despite the similarity of taste and ingredients?

Like beer and spirits, advertising and promotion is a primary tool for positioning brands in consumers' minds. Soft drink marketers associate their beverages with popular celebrities and emotional imagery. Common elements also include slender, attractive bodies. These elements were evident one hundred years ago in ads for Moxie and Excelsior that contained attractive women in low-cut bodices. For much of the twentieth century, Coca-Cola campaigns featured so-called "Coca-Cola Girls"—beautiful women in swimsuits and figure-enhancing dresses intentionally designed to "have sex appeal," but wholesome enough so "a man can take her home to Mother."[42] More recently, Diet Pepsi ads featured "girl-watchers" in the 1960s, and slender swimsuit-beauties in Tab commercials in the 1970s. These elements are still present in contemporary soft drink advertising, perhaps with a few hunks thrown in for good measure.

Pepsi's "Just One Look"—At Cindy Crawford

Of the thousands of Pepsi commercials featuring attractive models and sexy celebrities, two are notable for their use of sexual imagery (at least three if you include Sierra Mist). In 1991 the "Just One Look" spot starred supermodel Cindy Crawford sensually guzzling a Pepsi from its new-fangled can. Ten years later, teen sensation Britney Spears strutted her stuff in a "Joy of Pepsi" commercial/music video.

In 1991 Pepsi wanted a commercial to coincide with its most recent logo change.[43] Not just any commercial would do, however. The spot needed to reinforce the new look of Pepsi cans in a dramatic way, while also associating the brand with an attractive image. Enter Cindy Crawford. Known for her beauty and sex appeal, Crawford had appeared as a cover model on hundreds of magazines. Stunningly beautiful and sensually striking, Crawford was a way to draw attention to the ad while also differentiating the product.

As a celebrity and popular sex symbol, Crawford was a perfect match for Pepsi's marketing approach. The use of celebrity endorsers was nothing new for Pepsi. The company had been using independent, vibrant, and talented celebrities to define Pepsi and hawk its products for many years.[44] Michael Jackson starred in a groundbreaking advertising campaign for Pepsi in 1984. Other celebrates included Lionel Richie, Tina Turner, Madonna, Michael J. Fox, Joe Montana, Billy Crystal, and Ray Charles.

To support the logo change, the campaign "Just One Look" was developed by BBDO Worldwide, New York. The campaign consisted of only one commercial, however. The thirty-second spot, often referred to as "Two Kids," aired during prime-time programming in 1991, culminating its run during the Super Bowl in 1992. Unlike most Super Bowl ads, the spot ended its run during the big game instead of premiering on it. As a result, the campaign gained additional media attention for its unorthodoxy.

The commercial began with Crawford pulling up to a Pepsi vending machine outside a run-down rural gas station—in her red Ferrari.[45] Clad in a pair of cutoffs and a white tank top, Crawford hops out of the car and walks over to the Pepsi machine. Two boys, leaning against a wooden fence, watch the action take place. As Crawford gets her soda and takes a long refreshing drink, the song "Just One Look" plays—an obvious reference to the boys falling in love at first sight. Filmed in a slow-motion, Crawford's gulp is really a glamour shot accentuating her physical attributes.

The commercial concludes when one of the wide-eyed, gawking boys says to the other: "Is that some new Pepsi can—or what?" After a brief voice-over about the new look of Pepsi, the other boy says, "It's beau-ti-ful."

Viewers responded favorably to the ad. The spot was one of five top Super Bowl commercials, according to viewer voting. Critics claimed it was the perfect blend between the innocence of youth and supermodel imagery, with an unexpected plot twist thrown in for good measure. It's no surprise the ad played well, especially with audiences of different ages.[46] The music track, "Just One Look," a song popular in the 1960s, was chosen to appeal to a generation first targeted with youthful Pepsi campaigns—the baby boomer "Pepsi Generation." Overall the ad was a success because it appealed to old and new alike and emphasized Pepsi's new look.

Diet Coke's Beefcake Break

Soft drink advertising—indeed most advertising—shows attractive people having fun. In 1994, a commercial for Diet Coke took the attractive-body, good-time genre a step further. In its now famous "Diet Coke Break," a group of working women engage in their own version of voyeuristic sex-role reversal: "beefcake" ogling.

The spot was one of six in the "This is refreshment" campaign aired in 1994. Lowe & Partners, New York, had just won the Diet Coke account, and wanted to take a different tact from the glitz and celebrity shine of earlier campaigns. The six ads featured everyday people enjoying their Diet Cokes. Although past ads had contained pretty people (Paula Abdul), Diet Coke wasn't known for overtly sexual advertising. As an interesting twist, about the same time as the agency switch, Lee Garfinkel, one of the creators of Pepsi's Cindy Crawford ad, was hired as a creative director by Lowe & Partners to work on the Diet Coke account.[47]

A lot was riding on the new campaign. Diet Coke's long-running "Just for the taste of it" campaign was replaced in 1993 by the ill-fated "Taste it all" campaign. After running only six weeks in the first quarter of 1993, "Taste it all" was canceled, leaving Diet Coke with no advertising support for most of the year.[48] As a result, Diet Coke was losing share to its feisty competitor, Diet Pepsi. Overall, Diet Coke ranked third in total soft drink share behind Coke and Pepsi, with about 9.7 percent of the $50 billion soft drink market, but Diet Pepsi was gaining ground.

The signature spot begins with women in an office whispering to each other, "It's 11:30." "It's 11:30." "Diet Coke break." "Diet Coke break." Smiling with anticipation, the women hastily gather at the windows of their third-story office to peer down at the street below. One woman waves for her compatriots to hurry to the window, a sign they might miss the action.

The women are gathering to catch a glimpse of a handsome, well-built construction worker, model Lucky Vanous, take his Diet Coke break. We see the construction worker hop down from a bulldozer, pull off his hard hat and shirt, pop the top of his Diet Coke, and guzzle down a thirsty sip. All the while, the music track features Etta James singing her sultry lyrics "I just wanna make l-o-v-e to you." The women look at Vanous, then at each other, then back to Vanous. It's obvious the women are enjoying the show.

As the construction worker slowly lifts back his head to take his first long sip of Diet Coke, the camera cuts back to images of the women looking both intently and longingly at Vanous. One women pulls off her eyeglasses to get a better look.

When he releases an "A-h-h-h-h" after a refreshing sip, one women says to another, "Oh, that was great." Without taking her eyes off him, the other woman responds in a winded, catch-your-breath-voice, "See you tomorrow?" "At 11:30," the other woman confirms.

"Diet Coke Break" is notable for its steaminess. It's almost as if the viewer is a voyeur, privy to a group's voyeuristic excitement. Judging from the women's gaping eyes and satisfied smiles, it's clear they enjoyed the view during their Diet Coke break. *Newsweek* writer Michele Ingrassia wrote, "When it's over, you almost feel the need for a cigarette ad."[49]

The commercial was a creative way of combining humor with sexuality. More important, the commercial was a reflection of consumers and their Diet Coke needs identified through research. Testing revealed that people think of drinking Diet Coke as a relaxing break to be taken during the day. Consumers didn't associate Diet Coke with high-paid celebrity endorsers. Nancy Gibson, Diet Coke's worldwide brand director, asserted in the *Wall Street Journal* that consumers felt that Diet Coke was a "brief, important, refreshing moment to their day."[50]

Women across America may have found it easy to identify with the women in the commercial. The women represented a cross section of "women at the office." Some of the women in the ad were attractive, but not threateningly so. On-air testing of the commercial proved successful; test audiences were favorable toward the ads. Gibson told *Beverage World*, "In a fun and engaging way, the campaign encourages all consumers, especially women, to take a Diet Coke break."[51]

Besides the sexiness of the spot, the ad was popular for its reversal of sex roles. Women, usually the object of male gazing and ogling, may have found the commercial empowering, or at least a light-hearted instance of turning the tables. According to the unwritten "ogling" double standard in America, men can publicly view women they find attractive, but women must view in private, or in this instance, from a window. In the Diet Coke spot, the women do view from a distance, but they clearly enjoy it. Tickling another taboo, one of the women in the commercial—she appeared to be the supervisor—is wearing a wedding band. The spot intimates that women can get pleasure from watching men even if they are married.

Another spot in the "This is refreshment" campaign contained playful sexual innuendo. The ad featured a bellhop making four trips to a honeymoon suite to deliver two Diet Cokes in an ice bucket. Each time he knocked, the door would open slightly and a man's hand would reach out to grab the soft drinks. The inference was that the "newlyweds" needed the sodas for as a "refreshing break" from their lovemaking.

Overall, the campaign met with mixed success. "This is refreshment" lasted less than a year: It was replaced in 1995 with a rendition of the 1982 to 1991 "Just for the taste of it" campaign, even though Diet Coke sales did show improvement. According the Gibson, over three million households returned to Diet Coke in 1994.[52] In addition, Diet Coke showed greater growth than Diet Pepsi in 1994, a turnaround from previous years.

If the success of "Diet Coke Break" is measured by its staying power or by sales, the jury is mixed. If the spot is assessed for its notoriety and creation of "buzz," the commercial was a hit—the spot is referred to in a countless number of articles and academic essays. The spot also successfully matched the message (enjoy your Diet Coke break) to the research, especially for female consumers. The biggest achievement may have been a reluctant nod from Barbara Lippert. In 2001, *Adweek*'s Lippert remarked that the ad was a classic: "The ogling ad was one of Coke's all-time hits."[53]

Britney Spears and "Joy of Pepsi"

In keeping with its tradition of signing celebrity endorsers to market its brands, Pepsi signed teen pop-star Britney Spears in 2001 to a $7 million multi-year, global marketing pact. In the cross-promotion agreement, Spears would promote Pepsi—primarily by appearing in its advertising—and Pepsi would sponsor Spears's worldwide music tour. Pepsi chose Spears for her massive teen appeal. She was nineteen years old and had two top-selling albums when she was signed. Her third album was released in 2001. Spears's popularity with youth was especially important considering that twelve- to twenty-four-year-olds are a large segment of the soft drink market.

The first ad produced by the Spears-Pepsi union is especially notable for its titillation. Titled "Performance," it features Spears tailoring the "Joy of Pepsi" theme song to a melody characteristic of her own style of music. In the video/commercial, Spears makes a warehouse come alive with provocative movements and revealing clothing. Spears does most of her dancing in a crop top and pair of low-cut faded jeans. A quick shot to her bare midriff gives viewers an opportunity to see her Pepsi-logo navel ring. Slow motion shots capture Spears as she swings her arms above her head. There are also several extreme close-ups of Spears looking wantonly into the camera, although the shots only last for a split second. Barbara Lippert characterized the filming as: "Head shots of Britney as a sweet-faced, smiling ingénue with major moments of midriff and crotch bumping."[54]

The sexy moves that emphasized her body are intermixed with outtakes of people watching her video. The outtakes create a commercial-within-a-commercial effect. The camera returns several times to a young, short-order cook in a fast-food restaurant watching Spears on a television screen. He's so captivated by Spears that he's unaware of burgers burning on the grill behind him. Firemen arrive to put out the flames, but the young man remains transfixed.

In another outtake, a group of seniors watch the commercial in a retirement home. One man passes an oxygen mask to another man. Former Senator Bob Dole even makes an appearance. Dole is watching Spears's performance in a dark room with his dog. In the video—with obvious symbolism—a Pepsi bottle-cap blasts off a huge billboard-size Pepsi bottle. The camera cuts back to Dole and his dog who is barking at the explosion. Dole says, "Easy, boy," a not-so-veiled reference to his arousal. Barbara Lippert commented, "The Viagra people went to excruciating lengths to make him [Dole] seem dignified; for Pepsi, he mascots as Mr. Penis."[55] She also says, "And in case hormonally charged teen boys weren't teased enough, the spot ends with a neon Pepsi bottle blowing its cap. Was it good for you?"

The spot is an obvious instance of sex in advertising. Several surveys of college students indicate that the students found the commercial to be sexually appealing. Although the imagery was not much different from a Spears music video, it was sexually charged for a soda commercial likely to be viewed by grandmas across the country. The outtakes did provide a tension (or arousal) release by allowing viewers some comic relief.

The spot was also notable for its hype. It first aired during the Academy Awards in March 2001. As part of a weeklong media buzz buildup, the ad was available on Yahoo! two hours before being aired on network television. In addition, Pepsi purchased all the advertising on Yahoo! for a week leading up the airing. Spears was also an omnipresent force on the Pepsi Web site. The Web site contained images of Spears, Spears singing "Joy of Pepsi," and a wealth of information about her. Pepsi's $7 million investment would be returned many-fold if young drinkers associated the brand with Spears's hip, sexy, and cool image.

As previously mentioned, choosing Britney Spears was not happenstance. She was chosen because she represented the youthful and sensual image Pepsi is trying to portray. "Britney is on the cutting edge of popular entertainment. She's youthful, inventive, optimistic and fun-loving—the ultimate fit with the Pepsi brand," said Dawn Hudson, senior vice president, strategy and marketing, Pepsi-Cola North America.[56] Longtime

Pepsi agency BBDO created the Spears commercial. The momentum generated by the ads was one of the reasons BBDO was selected as *Advertising Age*'s 2001 Agency of the Year. Coca-Cola signed young pop star Christina Aguilera, possibly in response to Pepsi's signing of Spears. At any rate, overall Pepsi-Cola sales increased in the first quarter of 2001.

COMMERCIAL ROMANCE: THE TASTER'S CHOICE SERIAL

Romance and sensuality occasionally find their way into advertising for beverages other than soft drinks and alcohol. One of the most popular and successful instances occurred in November 1990 when Taster's Choice initiated it's "Soap Opera Couple" campaign in the United States. The campaign, its lead couple, and Taster's Choice were immediate hits. Within a year Taster's Choice rocketed from third to first in the instant coffee category, as American audiences were engaged in the romantic intrigue and subtle passion between the two lead characters, Michael and a woman whose name was never mentioned.

The campaign was a serial consisting of thirteen episodes, debuting in 1990 and running until 1997. *New York Times* writer Janet Maslin characterized the serial as "a flirtatious woman (played by Sharon Maughan) and her flirtatious neighbor (Tony Head) develop a mating dance based entirely on coffee's aphrodisiac possibilities."[57] In the first episode, a forty-five-second spot referred to as "Doorbell/First Meeting," the two actors meet for the first time. Maughan rings her next door neighbor's doorbell. "Hello. I'm sorry to bother you but I'm having a dinner party and I've run out of coffee." It's obvious she's pleased to discover her neighbor to be a good-looking man.

"Would, uh, Taster's Choice be too good for your guests?" Michael asks. He goes to the kitchen to fetch his jar of Taster's Choice. When he returns to the door and hands her the coffee, she says, "Oh, I, uh, think they could get used to it."

It's obvious from the beginning the characters share a mutual attraction. The repartee is playful and slightly mischievous, with an occasional double entendre thrown in for good measure. *Newsweek* called the couple "those lusty Taster's Choice love birds."[58] Another ingredient was the formula. The

Figure 10.5: From the Taster's Choice commercial "Tell Me About Dad?" Courtesy of Nestle USA, McCann-Erickson, Sharon Maughan, and Anthony Head.

campaign was often referred to as soap opera or serial because it simulated soap opera themes and left viewers hanging until the next episode. The cliff-hangers, mysterious men, and twists and turns in the relationship helped to maintain interest as viewers came to identify Taster's Choice with the sophisticated characters and the evolving relationship.

The Taster's Choice campaign was a British import. The London office of McCann-Erickson was charged with developing several commercials for Nestlé's Gold Blend coffee brand, on what they considered a meager budget.[59] To save money, one of the agency executives developed the idea of introducing a romantic serial. Two British stage actors, Sharon Maughan and Tony Head, were recruited to appear in the commercials.

Running from 1987 to 1993, the campaign was a big success. Articles about the couple appeared in tabloids, and a romantic novel, *Love Over Gold*, based on the romance between the couple in the Gold Blend commercials, sold over 150,000 copies. By the end of the six-year campaign sales of Gold Blend had increased 40 percent.

Based on the success of the British series, the same concept was chosen for Nestlé's Taster's Choice brand in America. After test ads in California and New York which featured other actors fell flat, Maughan and Head were chosen to star in the U.S. campaign. The campaign was an immediate sensation in terms of popularity and sales. By 1993, television viewers ranked the campaign eighth in popularity among television commercials (up from sixteenth in 1990).[60] By 1992 sales of Taster's Choice had surpassed those of Proctor and Gamble's Folgers and Philip Morris's Maxwell House to become number one in the instant coffee segment. Considering that Taster's Choice had been slugging it out with other instant coffees since the late 1960s, the campaign was a catalyst for Taster's Choice.

According to ad tests, one of the most popular episodes was "The Kiss," when the couple met in Paris. Michael says, "I got your telegram." She responds, "I just had to come to Paris." "This is wonderful...the view, the Taster's Choice...," "Is that all?" she asks? "No," he says as he embraces her and gives her a tender kiss. Another memorable plot device was at the end of a "Mystery Man" episode when a young man makes an unexpected appearance, making Michael jealous. In the following spot, it's discovered the young man is her son, Jeremy. Maughan calls Michael to tell him that Jeremy enjoyed meeting him. Michael promptly asks, "Is there anything else you forgot to tell me?" "Volumes," she says.

As romances often fade, so did the campaign's popularity. By the end of 1996, sales for Taster's Choice had dropped 16 percent and attention to the commercials had waned. While devotees still loved the soap opera couple, Americans were beginning to love gourmet and specialty coffees even more, and Starbucks and other hot beverages encroached on sales of instant coffee drinks.[61] Although Americans were drinking more coffee in 1996, sales of instant coffee as a whole declined more than 9 percent.

After seven years of tease, the romance ended without a dramatized resolution. The last episode featured Michael stopping by Maughan's apartment to pick her up for a date, only to meet her ex-husband. Michael wasn't pleased. The commercial ended with the ex-husband phoning her the next day to apologize. "I'm sorry about last night," he said. "I'm not," she interrupted. In an interactive promotion, viewers voted for the serial's resolution—should she pick the ex-husband or Michael—by mailing in Taster's Choice coupons. The outcome, reported in *Soap Opera Digest*, gave Michael overwhelming support. Unfortunately for those hooked on the serial, no more spots were aired. According to *Sun-Sentinel's* Tom Jicha, the lack of a climactic ending had more to do with lack of sales than entertainment value: "Perhaps America had become more concerned with the progress of the romance than the brand of coffee that inspired it. It's a reminder that TV's purpose is not to entertain but to move product."[62]

The campaign stimulated sales of Taster's Choice by creating a new, desirable, image for the brand and enthusiasm for its advertising. For several years viewers were enmeshed in the romance's dramatic action. Some say the campaign was doomed by its own sexual appeal, however. Dave Vadehra, president of Video Storyboards Tests, an advertising testing service, noted that viewers lost interest after the "Kiss" episode.[63] The observation suggests that viewers are often more interested in the rising action—the "tease"—than the romantic aftermath.

CONCLUSION

The commercials for Sierra Mist and Jolt Cola described at the beginning of the chapter are not anomalies. Sexual content in soft drink advertising, while often playful and laced with subtle innuendo, is making its way into national promotional efforts for an increasing array of beverages. As beer marketing has taken a hiatus from sexual themes and imagery, soft drinks have stepped in to fill the void. Although Pepsi maintains that Spears has a "wholesome" image, it's an image that partially consists of a cultivated school-girl eroticism.

In an effort to stay competitive, other beverages have created energetic campaigns to maintain sales. For example, the "Milk Moustache" campaign was initiated by dairy industry groups to salvage decreased milk consumption. Talking about beverages popular with teens, a book about the moustache campaign noted: "These other products are fun to drink and, until recently, had more exciting advertising than milk."[64] Marketers wanted to give milk a contemporary image that would boost sales. So far it has worked; the campaign has "changed the way people think about milk.... In fact, more people remember seeing milk ads than they do ads for Coke and Pepsi."[65]

Perhaps they remember the ads because several have contained images of female models in bikinis, swimsuits, and low-cut blouses. Some of these women include *Sports Illustrated* swimsuit model Rebecca Romijn-Stamos, *Baywatch*'s Yasmine Bleeth, and Victoria's Secret model Tyra Banks. The Banks image was particularly provocative. She was shown in an orange two-piece with her hands on her hips: "Stop drooling and listen." The ad was designed to reach men with a message about their vulnerability to osteoporosis. I won't even get into the issue of the white moustache.

As a last note, the trend in the spirits industry is especially interesting. The images are increasingly lascivious, the appeals more blatant, and the innuendos more brazen and titillating. One reason is that marketers have more outlets than before. Many of the most explicit ads are appearing in men's magazines such as *Maxim* and *Stuff* where the acceptance policies are as liberal as the editorial content is sexual.

11
One Degree of Separation
Condoms, Videos, and VD

Not all sex in advertising is designed to sell fragrance, designer clothing, and innerwear. Consider the following commercial produced in 2000. The forty-five-second spot opens with a slow-moving shot of a young woman's backside. Her hips move rhythmically as she walks to the electronic-lounge music of the commercial's soundtrack. The camera's view moves upward, from the backs of her exposed legs, right above her knee-high socks, to her swaying plaid skirt.

Cut to a shot of a young blonde running her hand along a fence. Cut to a close-up of another blonde drinking water from a fountain, the camera focusing on her open mouth and parted lips. A wisp of long hair falls across her face as she lifts her eyes to look at the viewer. Cut to another young woman on a playground swing, moving back and forth in slow motion. Cut again, this time to a woman seductively licking a lollipop as she stands in front of the trunk of a big tree. With bedroom eyes and a sultry smile, she looks right at the camera, a free hand lifting her hair up from over one eye. Like the other young women, she too is dressed in a parochial school uniform.

A line of text flashes on the screen: "This is how some people see your 6 year old daughter." The text disappears, replaced with the image of a little girl, dressed in a white cotton shirt and plaid skirt, stepping out from

Figure 11.1: "The Park" Public Service Announcement produced by Dieste & Partners (2000). Courtesy of Dieste & Partners.

behind a big tree. The commercial ends with the words: "Talk to your kids before they talk to strangers."

This award-winning public service announcement (PSA), called "The Park," was produced by the Dallas-based Hispanic advertising agency Dieste & Partners. The spot uses sexuality to reach parents with a powerful message about child molestation. Led by Executive Creative Director Aldo Quevedo, the agency attempted to illustrate a dark side of the old adage, "Don't talk to strangers." They achieved it by showing how little girls appear through the eyes of a pedophile.

The PSA is intriguing because it uses sex as a central element in an awareness message about pedophilia, a morally reprehensible and unlawful sexual behavior. The sexual images serve to attract attention, drawing viewers into the ad to discover what product is being advertised. The ad was made to resemble a sensual fashion or fragrance commercial, said Quevedo. "It was meant to have a sexy sophistication—a sexy feel—to draw people in."[1] The twist at the end, that these women are really little girls, hits viewers with an emotional punch. The spot effectively makes its point by tricking viewers with sexual content. The ad demonstrates that sex in advertising can be used for topics that deal directly with sexuality, albeit perverted sexuality in this instance.

Thus far, the discussion has centered on sex in advertising for products that are at least two degrees of separation from the sexual act, if not more. Cigarettes, beer, coffee, and so many other products are touted as part of the beauty/sexual attraction formula. But in reality, sex is not inherently relevant to these products. In these instances, sexual appeals are made to the product through marketers. Some of these products, such as liquor and fashion, are associated with social interactions, of which sex is often an outcome, but these products are not directly involved in or necessary to lovemaking.

Sex is also used to sell products and promote issues that are directly involved with sex and the sex act. For example, condom advertising, long based on informational appeals, has turned sexual with provocative images and compelling text. Here we will touch on two products and a set of issues that have a natural connection with sex in advertising: condoms, sexual self-help videos, as well as PSA's (public service announcements) for sexual health concerns including: birth control, HIV transmission prevention, and education about venereal disease. For both the products and the social issues, sexual content is used to make the intended point, much like the PSA developed by Dieste & Partners.

CONDOM ADVERTISING AND DUREX'S "SET YOURSELF FREE" CAMPAIGN

Condom advertising is, and always has been, a sensitive topic in America. Relegated to print advertising for most of the century and faced with declining sales after the introduction of the pill in the 1960s, condom use experienced a resurgence as herpes and HIV/AIDS became national health issues in the 1980s. Whereas condoms can now be advertised on television, there is plenty of controversy regarding when and what is shown.

Condom advertising on American television, especially network television, is a dicey issue. Currently, three networks, ABC, WB, and UPN, do not allow condom advertising.[2] NBC, CBS, and Fox allow condom spots, but only during late-night time slots. In addition to relegating prophylactic commercials to time spots past most people's bedtimes, NBC and CBS are both very sensitive about the "eroticism" of the commercial. Tom Conley, marketing vice president for Durex, observed that "I've seen very risqué ads for a lot of different categories—clothing, fragrances... [but] if you put a condom in the very same ad, you'd have a clearance issue."[3]

Condom advertising was restricted in the 1960s and 1970s by the National Association of Broadcasters' voluntary Code of Conduct. The Code, which was dropped in 1979 in response to an antitrust lawsuit, prohibited contraceptive advertising, as well as ads for astrologers, fortune tellers, and hard liquor.[4] A local station in San Jose, California (KNTV) violated the ban when it aired the first condom television commercial—a spot for Trojan condoms—in 1975. In 1986, ABC was the first network to air PSAs that mentioned condoms as a way to prevent HIV/AIDS transmission. And in 1991, Fox was the first broadcast network to air nationally a condom ad, on the condition that the spot emphasized disease prevention.

Despite sexually provocative commercials for other brand categories, not to mention increasingly provocative programming, network executives continue to exercise extreme caution concerning the airing of condom ads. As a result, most condom advertisers find cable channels more welcoming than networks. For example, ESPN aired a Lifestyles condom ad in 1985. In some instances, media buyers bypass the networks and work directly with affiliate and independent stations. A Lifestyles ad, for example, initially ran in only two local markets in 1986. The spot, created by Della Femina Travisano & Partners, New York, featured a female talking head making the point that AIDS was a sexually transmitted disease (STD). She said she used Lifestyle condoms because, "I do a lot of things for love, but I'm not ready to die for it."[5] In 1998, Lifestyles once again bypassed network censors to air its "Condoms shaped for 2" campaign on CBS-owned television stations in New York and Los Angeles. This time, however, the campaign consisted of three playfully sexy condom ads involving couples.

Running during the debut of the *Howard Stern Radio Show*, the ads came very close to being yanked in response to criticism from the American Family Association.[6] The $1 million campaign did air in the late-night time slot opposite *Saturday Night Live*, as well as on MTV and Comedy Central.

Condoms advertisers have had to resort to creative media planning because conservative groups, like the American Family Association, don't want their children exposed to condom ads. For these groups, condom advertising implies that promiscuous sex is "okay." In addition, some religious groups, especially Catholics, strongly object to the use of prophylactics as well as other forms of birth control. Others simply don't think network TV is an appropriate venue for sexual matters as close to the surface as condom use. As HIV/AIDS became a public issue, a battle raged between the anti-condom forces and those wanting to promote condoms to stop infectious diseases. A 2001 study found that most adults are supportive of condom advertising. The Henry J. Kaiser Family Foundation asked over 800 adults their opinions about condom advertising on television. They found that 71 percent think that condoms should be advertised on television.[7] The survey also revealed that few television viewers would harbor negative reactions toward the network, program, or other advertisers if they saw a condom ad. Despite shifting attitudes, primetime network television is still devoid of condom ads.

Small media budgets are another reason networks are reluctant to run condom ads. If the category represented tens of millions of dollars, network executives might be more amenable. For networks, the small revenue condom marketers represent is not worth the complaints the network would receive. Bruce Silverman, CEO of a media agency, told *Adweek*: "For a relatively small amount of revenue, is it worth the headache? Even in a soft economy, some things are not worth the pain."[8] As a result of television clearance issues, condom advertisers resort to print and radio to get their messages across. For example, Trojan, the largest advertiser in the category, invested $6 million in advertising in 2000, but only 7 percent went to network television.[9] In contrast, Anheuser-Busch invested over $225 million to promote Budweiser and Bud Light in 2000, with over 70 percent going to the networks.

As a result, print ads have to be effective, and Trojan ads usually are.

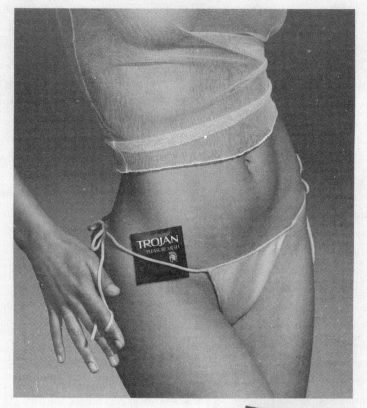

Figure 11.2: Trojan Condoms. Courtesy of Church & Dwight Co., Inc.

Consider recent ads for Trojan that contain enticing images of women posing with a Trojan condom packet. In one of the ads, the packet is tucked inside a woman's bra. In another Trojan ad, a condom packet is tucked under the hip string of a woman's string-lingerie (see fig. 11.2). The headline reads, "What everyone will be wearing this year."

Condom marketers concentrate their efforts on the eighteen- to twenty-four-year-old demographic. Males are a primary buying group, but Durex condoms has been taking a different approach because they recognize the growing influence of women as condom buyers. A recent survey indicated that 35 percent of condoms are bought by women, up from 30 percent just a few years ago. Jim Cowsert, a Durex brand manager, told *Advertising Age* that "we've seen a shift in attitudes, where women are feeling that they have to play a greater role in their own protection."[10] Consequently, Durex is making sure its ads appeal to both men and women. Gone are ads appealing to male egos such as "the big score." *In* are ads emphasizing pleasure, romance, intimacy, and good sex.

Condom advertising hasn't always emphasized the hot and steamy aspects of condom use. Until the mid-1980s, condom ads took a rather bland tact to emphasize sensitivity and performance. For example, a 1977 ad for Stimula condoms contained a large illustration of a ribbed condom accompanied by the headline, "The ribbed-head condom stimulates orgasms deeper." Despite the reference to orgasm, the ad was far from sexy. It resembled an ad for industrial equipment. Another prototypical condom ad, this one in 1980, contained the headline: "The Strong Sensitive Type." The only image in the copy-heavy ad was boxes of Sheik condoms. These ads, and many other condom ads, were relegated to the back pages of magazines.

In response to the HIV/AIDS epidemic, the 1980s saw condoms move from the back of magazines to more prominent positions. Condom advertising increased as editors gave their reluctant approval, but only if the ads passed standards of good taste and emphasized prevention, not pleasure. It wasn't until 1987 that several major publications, including the *New York Times*, Time Inc. publications, *Newsweek*, and *U.S. News & World Report*, reversed their policies against birth-control advertising, thus opening the door for condom advertisers. As a strange twist of fate, the *New York Times* had been the first American newspaper to run a condom ad. The ad for Dr.

Power's French Preventatives ran in the *Times* in 1861.[11] Soon after the ad appeared, the Comstock Law, passed in 1873, made birth-control advertising illegal. The law was repealed in 1972.

Although recent prophylactic ads have taken an informative approach (copy-heavy ads with images of condom boxes), some condom advertisers push the boundaries of acceptable sexuality. Durex condoms is one brand taking such an approach. The company's "Set yourself free" print campaign in 1998 practically placed the viewer in the midst of a lovemaking scene. Durex, a subsidiary of United Kingdom conglomerate London International Group, is a leader in worldwide condom sales. In the United States, Durex represents 15 percent of the prophylactic market with its High Sensation and Avanti brands.[12] Globally, Durex has promotional efforts in over 140 countries, often sponsoring beach parties in Spain and humorous commercials in Asia and Europe that would fail to get broadcast clearance in the U.S.

The Durex campaign evolved from hawking condoms with "safe-sex" themes to using messages that demonstrated the pleasurable benefits of its condoms with the ads featuring steamy images of couples engaging in sex (see fig. 11.3). Metaphorical headlines illustrated the sensitivity of Durex condoms. For example, the copy for one magazine ad reads: "The human body has over 45 miles of nerves. Enjoy the ride. Set yourself free. In a new Durex condom." The ad features a sepia-toned image of a svelte naked couple. We see the woman's back as she sits in her lover's lap, straddling him. He has one hand behind her back, supporting her, as he appears to be kissing her breast. The ad, along with other similar ads in the campaign, is sexy by any standard. If the creative team's purpose was to place the viewer in the midst of the couple's lovemaking scenes, they achieved it.

Executives at Durex felt that consumers knew about the risks of HIV/AIDS, and that condoms were a way to prevent infection. Carolyn Donegan, an agency account supervisor working with Durex, said, "We're trying to normalize condom use, to talk about it is an important and pleasurable part of sex because the groundwork is there in everyone's heads. Everyone knows they are supposed to use condoms."[13]

Another ad says: "During lovemaking, sexual stimuli travel to the brain at 170 miles per hour. Fly first class." The couple in this ad are as equally engaged as in other Durex ads. It's clear Durex is selling heightened

Figure 11.3: Durex Condoms. Photography © Michele Clement Studios, Inc.

pleasure instead of anxiety. It's a smart move. Studies in health communication show that message strategies using fear as motivation to get people
to do what they're told may backfire. If the appeal is too strong, people turn
away from it. If the appeal is too weak, the message fails to conjure up

enough anxiety to motivate people. On the other hand, emotional appeals that promise pleasurable outcomes draw in readers.

If you consider the proposed audience's attitudes and proclivities, it's also clear the sexy condom ads are right on target. While some people are offended by pictures of passion-filled couples, people who engage in sex necessitating condoms aren't likely to be turned off by them. In addition to Durex, other condom marketers run advertising campaigns based on the pleasure principle. For example, a 1997 ad for the Reality Female Condom featured a near-naked couple in a conjugal embrace. The headline adds pizzazz, however: "They both swear the Earth moved.... and so did their neighbors downstairs. The Female Condom."

In addition to advertising, Durex promotional efforts also include global surveys. Durex conducts polls of sexually active respondents in several different countries. In 1998, for example, Durex surveyed over 10,000 sixteen- to forty-five-year-olds about sexual issues. The Durex Global Sex Survey reported both good news and bad news. The good news is that 71 percent of respondents claim they use condoms with new partners.[14] The bad news is that only 15 percent report using condoms consistently with their new partners. Tom Grant, a spokesperson for Durex, told *AIDS Weekly Plus* that "The survey indicates that 80 percent of this audience [young people] is still not using condoms during every sexual encounter, highlighting the vital need to promote safe sex practices directly to this audience, especially in light of HIV/AIDS."[15] In addition, the survey revealed that young adults are having sex earlier.

At this point, Durex is once again transitioning its advertising this time away from sensual appeals. According to Leigh Taylor, SSL global category director for Durex, "We've moved away from the preaching campaigns that create anxiety. And we've moved on from sexual ads because they are not effective anymore."[16] Durex is now using humor. A reason for the change, according to Taylor, is that sex has lost its effectiveness because teens are inundated with sexual ads for so many products. As a result, Durex condom ads may cease to depend solely on sex to appeal to horny teens. It's likely the company will combine sex and humor in the future to reach young adults.

Whatever approach Durex takes, one thing is for sure. Condom manufacturers have made inroads into mainstream advertising and will continue to run their ads regardless of the approach they use. Nudity and blatant sex appeals in condom ads are de rigueur in consumer magazines these days. Racier ads are finding their way onto radio waves, cable, and late-night television. It's only a matter of time before condom commercials make the leap to primetime network advertising.

EDUCATING LOVERS: SINCLAIR INTIMACY INSTITUTE

If you read men's or women's lifestyle magazines with any regularity, it's difficult for you to miss the ads in the back. Ads relegated to the last few pages hawk psychic services, caffeine pills, French ticklers, and erotic-product catalogs. One such advertiser, Sinclair Intimacy Institute, is very successfully running full-page ads for its "Better Sex" video series. Since the early 1990s, Sinclair has sold millions of sex-education videos with its staid formula of touting the benefits of "better sex" reinforced with images of good-looking, near-naked couples in the midst of passion. For Sinclair's founder, Phil Harvey, there is probably little doubt that sex sells sex. Harvey is also president and founder of Sinclair's parent company PHE Inc., the largest erotic mail-order company in America.

Welcome to the world of the Sinclair Intimacy Institute, a leading sex-education company. In the summer of 1991, ads began appearing in *Playboy* for Sinclair's "Better Sex Video Series," a best-selling adult sex education video collection for couples to improve their sex lives. Since then Sinclair has developed a collection of more than fifty titles and sold more than four million videos in twenty-four countries. According to one source, the privately owned Chapel Hill-based company grosses over $8 million annually.[17]

According to the headline of one of its ads, Sinclair is a place where "Women are always interested in a well-educated man (especially when it comes to sex)." Although the subject matter of its videos is sexual and eroticism is present, how to please your lover (and yourself) is the primary message. Some of the titles include: *Sex After 50*, *Sexual Positions for Lovers*, *Better Oral Sex Techniques*, *A Man's Guide to Stronger Erections*, and *Becoming Orgasmic*. *Village Voice* writer John Thomas described the company as a "leader in what might be described as the adult self-help sex-ed industry, producing explicit how-to-screw (and suck and lick...) guides."[18]

Figure 11.4: Sinclair Intimacy Institute's "Better Sex for a Lifetime" series. Used by permission from the Sinclair Intimacy Institute.

If consumers want hard-core erotica, however, they had better go someplace else. Sinclair strives to keep its reputation on the up-and-up by marketing sex education, not sexual arousal. Legitimate sex therapists and sex researchers help to create the content; they also appear in the videos. Allan Schwartz, an executive with Sinclair Productions, told *Electronic Media*, "This is top-quality programming, featuring sex education with top doctors and sex therapists, such as the chief of urology at the University of North Carolina."[19]

Although the company takes sex education seriously, its roots are in adult entertainment marketing. Several of its executives worked for adult content providers and marketers such as Playboy Entertainment Group. In addition, Phil Harvey, the president of Sinclair's parent company PHE, Inc., has a history of marketing sex products and content. Harvey, a 1961 Harvard graduate, got his start selling condoms through the mail. Adam & Eve, the largest seller of mail-order erotica in America, and the main division of PHE, grosses over $80 million each year.[20]

Similar to its sister company, Sinclair Intimacy Institute is a direct response marketer. In addition to a substantial e-commerce presence, Sinclair stimulates sales by advertising in a variety of high-circulation magazines. Some of the more high-brow publications include the *New York Times Book Review*, *Psychology Today*, *Harpers*, and *USA Today*. Ads have also appeared in *Playboy*, *Esquire*, *POV*, *Men's Health*, *Maxim*, and *Stuff*, to name a few. Ads also consistently appear in women's magazines such as *Cosmopolitan*, *New Woman*, and *Redbook*. According to Kathy Brummitt, Sinclair's marketing director, the company invests anywhere from $2.5 to $4 million dollars to support the company's advertising program.

Ingredients in Sinclair print advertising are surprisingly similar. For instance, the full-page ads are all designed to be attention getting. They consistently feature images of half-dressed men and women cozying up to each other. Conspicuous headlines read: "Great Lovers Are Made, Not Born," and "Sex Education For Me? Know-how is still the best aphrodisiac." A 1998 *Esquire* ad promoted "The Advanced Sexual Fulfillment Series" with the headline, "Advanced Chemistry Lessons For Me?" Readers can order the entire set (usually three to five videos) or buy one video.

Despite little deviation from its tried-and-true formula, Sinclair's ads have gotten spicier over the years. The raciest ads appear in *Playboy*. These

Figure 11.5: The bra in this ad was airbrushed onto the woman to gain editorial approval. Used by permission from the Sinclair Intimacy Institute.

ads feature naked or topless women with their backs to the camera. In a recent ad, a woman clad only in a thong causes her man, busy at the computer, to look up with a knowing smile. In this ad, as with most ads, both sexes show off their healthy bodies. Men are well defined with muscular chests, shoulders, and arms. Women are slender, curvaceous, and busty. They are often topless, but their breasts are covered with an arm or by their man as they lean into him. In other ads women wear bras or tank tops without bras. Most models wear wedding bands that are visible when their left hands are showing. Brummitt asserts: "Some of the models in our ads are actually married to each other. It usually works out, but not always. There needs to be a chemistry between the models. Sometimes married couples are uncomfortable revealing intimacy with their actual partners."[21]

Chemistry is readily apparent in recent Sinclair ads. In a August 1999 ad in *POV* magazine for example, the man appears to have kissed his way up to his partner's thigh so as to be only inches from her crotch. The headline again proclaims that "Women Are Always Interested In a Well Educated Man." Other ads feature a great deal of breast kissing, as well as kisses to the woman's neck as her head is thrown back in pleasure. Petting is also evident. In a black-and-white ad appearing in the May 1995 issue of *Esquire*, the woman, as well as the man, is cupping her left breast as her strap falls off her shoulder.

Recent ads also feature women making moves on men. For example, a recent ad shows a topless woman astride a man sitting on his home gym— a simple case of workoutus-interruptus (see fig. 11.6). Wearing only a thong, the woman is straddling her lover, pressing her breasts against his chest. There is no wedding ring in this ad, but then again, who wears their band when engaging in heavy lifting? Another ad appearing in 1999 also shows a women straddling her partner. Her hand is around her lover's neck as she begins to kiss him. Her other hand is resting on the top of his thigh.

As a direct marketer, Sinclair ads are copy intensive. The words describe the benefits that accrue to Sinclair video watchers. For example, the first paragraph of copy in a recent ad reads as follows: "When your lover tells you, with a word or a sign—that this is the place to touch, then you have just learned a powerful sexual secret that can be used again and again." The headline for a piano-themed ad reads "Learn to Strike the Right Chords in Just Three Easy Lessons." The man is sitting on a piano

Figure 11.6: A workout distraction? Used by permission from the Sinclair Intimacy Institute.

bench leaning against the piano keys. In another ad, an attractive women, wearing unbuttoned short shorts and a low-cut tank top, sits on a guy's lap. Her eyes are closed and she's tightly clutching a pool cue between her legs as he begins to pull down her shorts. The scene could be a subtle reference to the sexual fantasy of having sex on a pool table—although no pool table is present.

As with all effective direct response and mail-order advertising, Sinclair adheres to the fundamentals. The ads provide pricing information along with sufficient descriptions of the products offered. All material is 100 percent guaranteed. The materials can be purchased through a toll-free number or over the Internet. In addition, there is usually a worthwhile inducement to motivate action. An ad in 1997 stated that if you ordered the five-video package, you would get two additional free videos, *Advanced Oral Sex Techniques Part 2* and *Great Sex 7 Days a Week*. It's a fairly enticing offer as far as direct-marketing incentives go.

With so many ads featuring a range of subtle to provocative sexual imagery, are there any lessons regarding what resonates best with consumers? Brummitt says that the level of eroticism makes a big difference in terms of sales. "The more seductive the image, the more effective the response in terms of sales," said Brummitt.[22] "However, we're less likely to run highly seductive images because of clearance issues. We want to successfully market our product, but we want to do it responsibly."

Based on Sinclair's continued success, it's evident the company has found the right intensity of sexual provocation without creating a backlash to its marketing efforts. It's also clear that marketers can successfully utilize sexy advertising to sell sex-related products. Despite the obvious connection, there is at times a double standard for sexual products. "You can use sex to sell anything in mainstream media—but sex," says Brummitt.[23] Sinclair's marketing manager argues that it's easier to use sexual imagery to sell fragrances and clothing than sex education videos: "Comparatively speaking, any time sex is used to sell videos, or condoms for instance, it's harder to get clearance." Brummitt's comments suggest that American culture tolerates, if not encourages, titillation but is less tolerant with open discussion of sexual issues. As a strange twist of fate, the proliferation of Sinclair's videos may help liberate America's attitudes and openness about sex.

SEXY SOCIAL MARKETING

Sex in advertising isn't only used for branded commercial products such as condoms and sex education videos. Sexual content is also used to talk *about* sex—especially risky sex. Sexual themes and suggestive visuals are used to promote social causes related to sexual health and sexually transmitted diseases. These public health campaigns are designed to educate, to inform, and to promote safer sex practices such as using condoms.

In 1997 and 1998, the Kaiser Family Foundation teamed up with MTV and Black Entertainment Television (BET) to educate teens about sexual health. The MTV partnership, titled "Be Safe," consisted of PSAs that addressed sexual issues and several promotional efforts such as news specials, booklets, a "campus invasion" tour, and inserts in MTV CDs and videos. The PSAs were "designed to speak to young people in a bold and direct manner about STDs, HIV and teen pregnancy."[24] The media campaign was designed to educate and inform young people about the risks associated with sex. Teens, for example, are often uninformed or misinformed about sexual issues, such as the incidence of STDs and the odds of contracting one.[25] So far the campaign has been a success. Millions of teens have seen the PSAs, and after the first twenty-two months of the campaign, over half a million teens called a toll-free number to request information.

Most PSAs containing messages about STDs are based on fear appeals, messages designed to scare people into doing the right thing. Fear is an effective persuasive tool, but not always. People in high-risk groups—those people who need the information the most—practice selective vigilance. They avoid PSAs and discount scary information designed to frighten them. Trying to evoke fear in people also can be tricky. Too much gory detail, and people become overwhelmed or they turn away in disgust. Too little gore, and people don't feel threatened. As a result, it's often difficult to find the middle ground that is most effective. Even if viewers are appropriately scared, however, research shows that they need to believe that the threat is real, or at least likely to happen to them, before they can be persuaded. If not, people feel anxious but don't know what to do about it. Mass communication researchers Charles Atkin and Alicia Marshall made the following observation: "In health campaigns, there has been an over reliance on fear appeals that threaten physical harm; these should be sup-

Figure 11.7: "Dad" Public Service Announcement produced by Dieste & Partners (2000). Courtesy of Dieste & Partners.

plemented with positive arguments and with economic, social, or psychological incentives."[26]

In fact, people sometimes purchase goods for the same reasons they engage in risky or detrimental health behaviors. According to Mara Adelman, a sexual health researcher, emphasizing the rewards and positive advantages of safe-sex behavior may be just as motivating, if not more so, as evoking fear and emphasizing negative consequences.[27] If sexy appeals can communicate sexually relevant benefits, or influence people by evoking a favorable reaction, they should be as apt to induce change in the advocated direction. Indeed, many sexual appeals in commercial advertising argue that sexual pleasure, and romantic or physical intimacy, is associated with products.

Consider a particularly hot PSA, produced by the same agency that produced "The Park" (Dieste & Partners). The spot illustrates a different slant on how condoms can save lives. The scene begins with two teenagers making out on a couch (see fig. 11.7). The girl is shown unzipping her boyfriend's pants. They go back to kissing, but not for long. Soon she raises up and pulls off her turtleneck. The boy is so excited by his girlfriend's behavior that he's wheezing. They go back to kissing just as the girl's father walks in on them. Surprised, the couple jumps up, scrambling with their clothes. As the father comes closer, his daughter pleads for his restraint, "Papa, no. Papa no!" As a last resort, the boy holds up a condom as if to say, "At least I was going to protect her." The spot ends with the message, "A condom could save your life. Use it."

The PSA, titled "Dad," consists almost entirely of the couple's sexual adventures. It was created for the Nelson-Tebedo Clinic, a community health center with HIV testing in Dallas. Quevedo described the PSA as "a fresh way of showing you that a condom can really save your life."[28] At the very least, the spot's heavy sexual content attracted attention among viewers. In addition, the spot was sure to generate talk about condoms among members of the target audience. It contained sex, conflict, humor, and a pro-health message: good ingredients for a creatively produced PSA.

Adelman maintains that HIV/AIDS prevention methods have relied to such an extent on fear-oriented, safe-sex messages that their effect has diminished. Based on the results of her analysis of safe-sex talk among couples, Adelman recommends alternative strategies to promote condom use. "We must target research and interventions that question, serve, and enhance perceptions of personal pleasure with condom use as a way of motivating safe-sex behavior."[29] If PSAs can show people that condom use can help them get more pleasurable things in life, it can grab their attention and provide sufficient motivation so that they can adopt the recommendation.

The use of sex for safe-sex social marketing is effective even when the advocacy is very sexually explicit. Consider a condom-use media campaign developed by the French in 1998. The French Ministry of Health commissioned several short films to promote condom use to curb HIV/AIDS transmission.[30] The vignettes were very overt, showing condom-use procedures that American audiences could only imagine. The vignettes were shown on a pay-television channel and run right before a highly rated hard-core pornography program. As people tuned in to get aroused, they also got a spicy dose of a safe-sex message. It was an inventive idea and a way to reach high-risk groups with promotion on a par with programming content. Even if the audience didn't learn a thing about condom use, it's

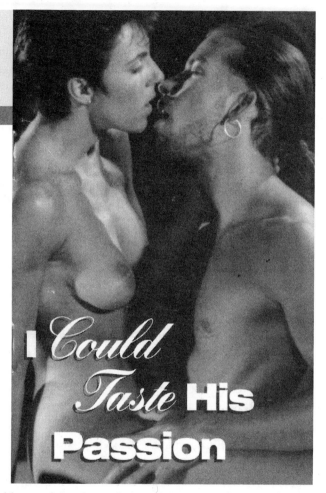

Figure 11.8: "I Could Taste His Passion." Courtesy of Tucson AIDS Project.

doubtful they would complain about the explicitness of the PSAs. They were, after all, watching porn. Leave it to the French to really incorporate sex to sell sexual health.

Advocacy groups in the United States have not run explicit ads on television, but they have produced sexually explicit promotional information. Usually in the form of posters, brochures, or hand cards, the explicit condom-use information is available in bookstores and distributed at seminars or bars and nightclubs. For example, a series of explicit brochures was created by The Tucson AIDS Project in the early 1990s. Designed to educate about safe sex and about HIV/AIDS, the slogan for the brochures was

"Sex without fear. Sex without guilt." The brochures were designed to educate couples about sex, but designed to do so with erotic copy—using the vernacular—and nude images. One brochure titled, "I could taste his passion," contained an image of a bare-chested woman passionately kissing a man while sitting on his lap (see fig. 11.8). This particular brochure was about oral sex. The first two pages contained an erotic vignette, very similar to that of a sex novelette: "We fell on the bed together, our bodies naked, hot with passion. I kissed him, plunging my tongue deep inside his mouth. He moved slowly down my body, his tongue beginning a trip from my neck, across my breasts where he lingered for a moment, down my belly, across my hips, and to my tuft of hair. He licked my thighs slowly and continued to toward my wetness."[31]

I'll stop there, but the story continues on until both lovers are satisfied. The vignette is followed by four pages of advice and facts about oral sex and HIV transmission, and safe-sex choices. A similar brochure contained a vignette describing how—using her mouth—a women put a condom on her male lover. In these brochures, descriptions of sexual acts and sexual body parts eschewed technical jargon (semen, fellacio). To enhance comprehension, language was intended to match the lingo of the target audience (cum, going down).

What's really fascinating is that safe sex was woven into the erotic story. The brochures—handed out at bars and health clinics—introduced dental dams, condoms, and withdrawal: ways of pleasuring one's partner that are safe(er). It provided a frank discussion of the risks of HIV transmission from oral sex. It's obvious that sexual content in mainstream mass media PSAs, like the MTV sex-education effort, will never match the level of explicitness in these brochures, but these promotional efforts may help to educate and save lives.

The Tucson AIDS Project also produced a series of brochures for gay men. The booklets contained fairly explicit images on the front cover (see fig. 11.9). For example, one featured simulated fellatio, and another anal contact. The series was called "Men Aloud" and brochure titles ranged from "Oral Sex" to "Sex Options." The brochures lacked the explicit prose of the heterosexual pieces, but did contain slang for sexual activities.

Explicit PSAs are equal opportunity purveyors of information; safe-sex promotional materials also exist for lesbians. Several woman-to-woman

Figure 11.9: "Oral Sex." Courtesy of Tucson AIDS Project.

safer sex videos were produced in the early 1990s. They contained titles such as "Safe Soap," "Safer Sister," and "Safe Sex Is Hot Sex." It's not clear if they were ever aired, but the PSAs represented an opportunity for everyone, regardless of sexual orientation, to be educated with explicit safe-sex appeals. There is evidence that explicit appeals do work. Several research studies have shown that explicit discussions, with an emphasis on sexual pleasure instead of scare tactics, can be effective in transmitting information about venereal disease information.[32]

One of the reasons sexy PSAs are effective is that—similar to the reason marketers use sex in advertising—they attract attention. Getting attention was the reasoning behind a recent teen pregnancy campaign developed by Ogilvy & Mather, New York. Each ad featured a teenager with a big, bold provocative word superimposed over him or her (see fig. 11.10). Some of the words included "Dirty," "Cheap," and "Prick." The provocative words grabbed attention and viewers were motivated to read the smaller print to understand why the word was used. "All it took was one

Figure 11.10: "Cheap." Courtesy of National Campaign to Prevent Teen Pregnancy. Photo: Christian Witkin.

prick to get my girlfriend pregnant. At least that's what her friends say." In that particular ad, "Prick" was used with the image of a teenage male.

Marisa Nightingale, director of media programs for the National Campaign to Prevent Teen Pregnancy, the organization that hired Ogilvy & Mather, said, "I think these do the best a print ad can do. They grab attention, spark discussion and reach teens who otherwise might not get the message."[33] The words in the copy were uttered by teens in focus groups conducted for the campaign. The headline "Cheap," accompanied by the image of a female teenager, reads "Condoms are cheap. If we'd used one, I wouldn't have to tell my parents I'm pregnant."

MARCH OF DIMES

Sexy PSAs can be used for topics other than STD prevention. For example, a 2001 March of Dimes PSA contained a sexy shot of celebrity Daisy Fuentes. She posed in a revealing black crop top. Her revealed stomach and shoulders, as well as the way she gazed at the camera, lent a sexy feel to the PSA. Even a sexy gold chain wrapped around her belly.

The PSA's headline reads, "Daisy Fuentes is not pregnant." Confused readers had to examine the copy to make the connection between the headline and the image of Fuentes. "But she is taking folic acid just in case…to prevent birth defects of the brain and spine. Start now." The PSA was meant to appeal to young women, especially those who might be considering pregnancy. Perhaps the point was that Fuentes could be pregnant, but still look sexy. Whether she was pregnant or not, she was taking folic acid to ensure that if she did become pregnant, her children would receive the prenatal nutrients necessary to sustain health. The ad's slogan was: "Saving babies, together."

The ad is clearly attention getting. Fuentes is appealing in her own right, but she was shot in a pose that accentuates her body. The image is obviously meant to appeal to a younger audience, especially those familiar with Fuentes. Although the ad contains subtle sexuality, there is a disconnection between the image and the topic. Focus group members may have responded favorably to Fuentes, regardless of the topic. Nonetheless, the sexy shot gets attention for The March of Dimes, and the headline draws in readers so that they see the intended message.

THE BREAST CANCER FUND

A series of shocking images in a breast cancer campaign put a real twist on sex in advertising. The Breast Cancer Fund, a San Francisco-based nonprofit, ran its "Obsessed with Breasts" public awareness campaign in January and February 2000. Three provocative images were designed for placement in bus shelters in the San Francisco Bay area. The models in the PSAs were attractive and posed in a manner similar to other sexy ads. The difference, however, was that these models were revealing their mastectomy scars.

The campaign was created by BBDO West, a talented creative office of BBDO Worldwide. With digital technology, images of mastectomy scars were transposed onto the models' images, so the models looked like they had had mastectomies. Overall, three ads were produced. One looked like a Victoria's Secret ad, another like an Obsession ad, and the third image resembled a *Cosmopolitan* magazine cover. The headline in the simulated Victoria's Secret ad read, "It's no secret" (see fig. 11.11). The copy continued, "Society is obsessed with breasts. But what are we doing about breast cancer?" The model, clothed in Victoria's Secret signature burgundy innerwear, pulled down the left side of her bra to reveal a scar.

The scar raises the question, is revealing a mastectomy scar as taboo as revealing a breast? Some viewers seemed to think so. Outdoor Systems, the largest transit company in the Bay area, refused to accept the PSAs. The director of its San Francisco office told the *San Francisco Chronicle*, "In good conscience, we just couldn't let these ads through. They're just too tough. You can't force people to look at rough stuff like this. They are very shocking."[34] After receiving complaints, other transit companies removed the PSAs after running them only a few days.

According to the nonprofit's Web site, one of the campaign's goals was to show graphically what happens when a woman has a mastectomy. The organization wanted to raise public awareness of breast cancer by showing surgical scars. A second goal was to raise awareness of the organization. A spokesperson for the American Cancer Society added additional insight into the purpose of the campaign. "The point they're making is breasts are viewed as playthings and sexual things, and to deliberately do something so opposite to that is going to be very shocking. I think it is daring and risky, but if it works well, then I congratulate them for doing it."[35]

Figure 11.11: "It's No Secret." Courtesy of the Breast Cancer Fund. Image taken from the Breast Cancer Fund's *Obsessed with Breasts* campaign, www.breastcancerfund.org, Photographer: Heward Jue.

The success of the PSAs isn't entirely clear. Considering the amount of attention the campaign received in local media, as well as feedback from Bay Area residents, the images were noticed. At the very least, the images turned the tables on traditionally sexy images, many of which appear in commercial advertising. The images caused some viewers to consider the culture's sexual preoccupation with breasts, and their presence, or absence, in the breast cancer campaign.

CONCLUSION

If you change Kevin Bacon to *sex act*, and play the Six Degrees of Kevin Bacon game, you'll see that there is only one degree of separation between the products discussed in this chapter and sex. Sex in advertising isn't a requirement when advertising condoms. And as strange as it may seem, sexy images aren't absolutely necessary when selling sex-education videos. Either of these products can be advertised through straightforward approaches that emphasize facts, instead of relying on sexy images and provocative promises. Elaborate make-out scenes aren't necessary to convince sexually active teens that condoms can save lives.

But sex is used to sell condoms, videos, and safe sex for the same reasons marketers use sex to sell cars, beverages, tobacco, and fashion. They use it because sex gets attention, and sex is a motivating emotion, and *good* sex can be an outcome of using the product. If advertising can somehow link a product to a favorable sexual outcome, it can be sold. Try telling advertisers of sex-related products they don't need to use sex. According to Kathy Brummitt, Sinclair's marketing director, the sexier the ad, the better the response.[36] Regarding condoms, social science research shows that sexy ads are more persuasive than strictly informative ads.[37] Sexy condom ads can be especially effective when combined with other appeals such as fear and humor.

All products aren't treated equally, however. Are the "rules" different when sex is used for a sex-related product or issue? If you ask those involved in the process, the answer is "yes." Brummitt says a double standard exists for sexual products. "Sometimes we have to tone down our advertising to get it approved. But other ads in the same magazine, for perfumes and underwear, are much more racy."[38]

In the recent past, while other advertisers like Calvin Klein and Guess were using scintillating images, condoms advertisers were unable to break into network advertising until it was discovered they helped to save lives. Carol Carozza, Ansell's director of marketing, told *Advertising Age* that a lot of commercials on TV are more explicit than condom ads, but "the networks won't even put our ads into the VCR to look at."[39] Richard Buckley, president of Buckley Broadcasting and board chair of the Radio Advertising Bureau, described how the industry reacted to condom spots. "Years ago people were just as horrified about running spots for Preparation H. This is the same sort of situation."[40] Buckley was talking about radio ads, but his point is applicable to all forms of prophylactic ads and PSAs.

Last, who would have guessed a sexual ad could have been produced, much less aired, to guard against pedophilia? It was a gutsy move on behalf of Dieste & Partners. It's doubtful any other agency would have taken such a risky approach with such blatant sexual images. More than likely, the topic would have been handled with kid gloves and an informational approach. Instead, Dieste created a provocative commercial that drew people in and communicated its message in a powerful manner—because of sex, not in spite of it. As a result, the agency won several prestigious awards and convinced some parents in Texas to talk to their children. "We received a lot of positive feedback," said Quevedo.[41] "The only criticism was that there wasn't a phone number at the end of the spot so viewers could call for more information."

As for condoms and PSA's, using sex to sell "safe sex" makes a lot of sense. If you consider that most PSAs are ignored, an appeal that doesn't shy away from sexual frankness may make a difference. The only concern—and it's a big one—is the same concern faced by condom and sex-education companies: the objections by network censors and editorial boards who don't want to risk offending audiences. As sexual content becomes more prevalent in media programming, it's likely that sex in advertising for sex-related goods—with only one degree of separation from sex—will increase as well.

12
PC Envy
Internet Advertising and Beyond

I
n the spring of 2001 an Internet marketer tweaked one of its online banner and pop-up ads by changing an image and adding a couple of words. The result was a sharp increase in sales of one of its products—the Xcam2—primarily by driving people to the company's Web site. The company was X10 and its product was a small video camera. What it did differently was include "bedroom" to the list of suggested areas where the camera could be used. When coupled with a newly added image of an attractive blonde in revealing clothing, the camera and its potential functions had a whole new set of meanings. *Adweek* reported that in the month of May 2001, "X10.com has registered a huge jump in traffic...by one measure becoming the fifth most-visited site on the Internet."[1]

After several viewer complaints, the online edition of the *Los Angeles Times*, LATimes.com, asked X10 to remove the inference from its banner ads posted on the news site. The company complied, but X10 continues to sell its mini-cam with images of sultry women in bikinis and low-cut dresses, most likely because it discovered sexual content to be so effective.

ONLINE SEX IN ADVERTISING

X10 is not alone. There are a multitude of marketers using sexy images to market their wares online. Aside from the untold number of intensely explicit sexual ads for pornographic Web sites selling peepshows, photographs, live-sex, and so on, sexual images also appears in ads for more mainstream products. Some of these online ads hawk investment services, brokers, long-distance phone service, debt reduction, electronics, muscle-building supplements, and clothing. According to Internet scholar Jacqueline Lambiase, "The 'sex sells' advertising mantra—right or wrong—has migrated from other media forms and is being tested in the new media environment."[2]

Sex is used in online advertising content for the same reasons it is used in traditional forms of advertising. For one, it's attention getting. With banner and button click-through rates at less than 1 percent, images that particularly attract attention serve only to enhance the probability of a click—just ask X10. In addition, sexual content can be motivating. For consumers who like seeing sexual imagery, catching a glimpse of a provocative image—with the hope or promise of seeing more—will motivate clicks that other images cannot. For instance, a pop-up window for SpiceTV.com pictured a lascivious image of an open-mouthed woman holding her bared breasts. She was accompanied by the action-based text: "Hot pix – sizzling video. Free Look. *CLICK NOW.*"

There several different forms of Internet promotion. Regarding advertising there are banner and button ads as well as pop-up windows and interstitials. Site or content sponsorship is another form of promotion. Even home pages are a form of corporate promotion. Many of these promotional messages contain images as simple as attractive women in short skirts. Often the images are only parts of women: a pair of wanton eyes or a sultry smile. A pop-up window for a wireless mp3 player contained the headline/selling point: "listen to PC music anywhere." The visual demonstration of the selling point consisted of a sensually posed, bikini-clad woman by the pool.

Sexual content in the form of enticing images and playful innuendo is not uncommon, even for respected organizations. In 1997 the Internet portal Yahoo! ran banner ads with an attractive pair of female eyes and the slug line: "I don't show My Yahoo! to just anyone. Click here to take a

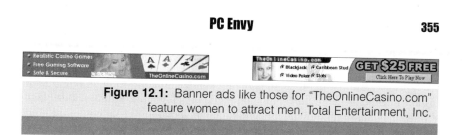

Figure 12.1: Banner ads like those for "TheOnlineCasino.com" feature women to attract men. Total Entertainment, Inc.

peek." A banner ad on an Excite search site contained a wanton image of a woman's square-jawed face and wet hair. Words in an online Courier font read, "Cindy: Hi, I'm an 18 year old female. Anyone wanna chat?"

Company home pages, especially for on- or offline marketers, are a form of promotion because not only do consumers buy the product from the site, but impressions are created about the brand. Several home pages contain subtle and not-so-subtle forms of sexual content. For example, the home page for the cellular phone manufacturer Nokia USA contained images of Calvin Klein model Christy Turlington in a little black dress. Smiling and looking good, she adorned the Web pages of Nokia's site.

In 2000 the home page for *Baywatch* was beefed up with more images of its attractive female stars. The organization wanted to attract males eighteen to thirty-four to the site so it could sell online advertising to marketers wanting to reach that demographic. "The changes online were designed to attract a wider—and more financially attractive—demographic," said *Adweek*'s Erik Gruenwedel.[3] Marketers planned to appeal to men by altering the site to emphasize the bikini-clad women on the program. "The 18-to-35 male demo is pretty hard to reach these days. *Baywatch Hawaii* has the advantage of beautiful babes. So we decided to focus on that," said Stern O'Connor, a director of an Internet services company working on the site.[4] Why the focus on young males? Gruenwedel said, "Madison Avenue continues to covet the concept of young male browsers, flush with disposable income and testosterone, in front of their PCs drooling over images of beautiful women sprinkled among ad-supported pages."[5]

Men's lifestyle magazines often contain sexual imagery of women. *Playboy*'s Web site is a model for many online versions of these magazines, according to *Adweek*'s Brett Forest. He characterized the look and feel of *Playboy*'s site as: "High-class smut where anything's possible."[6] The site isn't as sexually graphic as one might think. "Playboy's long-standing soft-core fare has been shunted to the side online, into a separate pay-per-view site. In its place is a vastly inhabited world of free content: articles, videos, advice, auctions, Webcasts and reviews. Other men's magazines are in varying stages of trying to measure up to Playboy.com's, um, depth."[7] That's not to say there aren't *any* sensual images. In fact, enticing images of voluptuous women abound. They appear throughout the home page and its links, as well as in sexual pop-up ads and banners. Much of it is self-promotion. For example, one banner contained the image of a woman's enhanced breasts and the headline: "A treasure chest of sex products. Playboystore.com."

SEXY ONLINE ADS FIND YOU

Whereas online sex in advertising is similar to its manifestation in traditional forms of mass media, there are some interesting differences. The most significant dissimilarity, other than for home pages, is that online sexual promotion finds the consumer. If you are not a member of a target audience deemed to be "favorable to sexual imagery," you may never see it. A notable exception is "spam." The onslaught of sexual e-mail has caused anger and annoyance among many Web users.

Aside from sex-charged "subject lines," promotion for consumer products is relegated to certain sites. For example, Jacqueline Lambiase, who co-edited a book with me, was writing an essay about sex online when she initially observed that sex in advertising is absent from the Internet for mainstream products. My advice was to see what she could find by going to sites popular with eighteen- to thirty-four-year-old men instead of those most frequented by, say, a forty-year-old mother. What she found surprised her. She discovered a wide array of online sexual ad content. Her conclusion was that Web ads find the people who are most predisposed to their use, again, with the exception of spam.[8]

As people surf the Net, they leave imprints that are stored in databases. The information is later used to construct patterns of usage and visitation. Surfers can be tracked through cookies and other identifiers so it's known if a viewer has visited that site before, when, and for how long. If something is purchased online, or an online survey is completed, information about the consumer is stored on the database so that when that person comes back, a tailored message can be sent to that person.[9]

As an example, I once purchased equity in a foreign company. Later, as I surfed the site of my online broker, I noticed banner ads touting overseas and international mutual funds. Those ads weren't there before. Based on my past usage, the broker was able to direct advertising to me that I would be most predisposed to view. Because they knew I purchased foreign stocks, they sent me appeals for funds many users would spurn. The same thing happened to the 2 million visitors to Victoria's Secret online fashion show in 2000. If they logged on, registered, or bought an item, the company—via database marketing—is able to track when they return to the site and direct appropriate promotional content to that visitor.

For online advertising, it means that ads with sexual content will be targeted to those who behave in certain ways, buy certain things, and go to certain sites. Sites with sexually oriented ads are not that far out of reach. They can appear when a surfer goes to any site that might even tangentially be associated with sexual themes or bikini-clad women. Web sites for online gambling are common, as are sports sites such as the World Wrestling Federation and the wwfdivas.com site. Any men's lifestyle magazine's online site has potential to have sexual content on its online ads (maximonline.com, esquiremag.com). Someone shopping for fashionable clothing can come across ads for dating services or intimates' marketers such as Frederick's of Hollywood. Entertainment sites for television programming, movies, and music sites, popular with teens have the potential to contain sex-tinged online advertising for electronics, long-distance service, and entertainment (videos, CDs).

E-mail aside, the consumer-finder approach has a distinct advantage for online marketers who use sex—it cuts down on complaints. Consider the many ads that are altered or denied by network censors because the networks want to avoid offending viewers. Online ads can be more explicit than those traditional media outlets will allow, while resulting in fewer complaints, because those most apt to be offended, like forty-year-old mothers, won't see them. "For users not fitting certain profiles, the absence of sexually oriented advertising may be seen as a benefit of the medium, especially by those who object to such content for a variety of reasons," observed Lambiase.[10]

Other notable differences in online ads include compelling graphics and interactivity. Unlike magazine ads, erotic online ads can contain moving video and animation, as well as sound. Like magazines but unlike television, the erotic ads are often viewed when the surfer is alone. Most important, if viewers like what they see, they can simply click a button to see more or be taken to a site that will help them see more. Instead of picking up a phone or remembering a number, only one relatively insignificant action separates the consumer from the online home page. As such, sexy online ads can motivate that action—just like it did for the consumers who clicked on the Xcam2 banner ad.

SEX IS HERE TO STAY

If its entrée into the net is any indication, sex in advertising will continue as a promotional fundamental. Looking back to the origins of modern media and modern advertising, we can clearly see that sexual themes, content, and promises surface repeatedly as marketers have tried to position their wares. Often companies have been at the brink of bankruptcy, or discontinuing a brand, only to survive by implementing a sex-tinged marketing promotion strategy. As *Inside Print*'s Maureen Goldstein observed, sex will continue because "the fact remains that sex in advertising beats out the business lunch as an effective sales tool hands down."[11]

Sex in advertising will continue as long as small advertisers strive to get attention and be competitive. Often the budgets of minor-league national advertisers are dwarfed by corporations with massive promotional resources. In 1987, executives for Travel Fox, a brand of sports shoe, ran very provocative ads—a nude woman straddling a nude man (although both were wearing Travel Fox shoes). Management rationalized its approach by saying it was extremely difficult to compete one-on-one with Nike and Reebok. According to Margaret Muir, Travel Fox's director of business development, "We had a tiny budget [$1 million] compared to the other guys, and in competing against Reebok and other big-name companies, we knew we had to do something that everyone was going to remember."[12] The approach worked. Soon after the award-winning campaign was initiated, sales at Travel Fox increased 300 percent.

Travel Fox is not an anomaly. Agency executives on the Miller Genuine Draft account said they implemented a sexier approach because they

GUESS
Rinse Denim

Figure 12.2: Guess associates its brand with attractive supermodels because it works. Guess? Inc., Creative Director: Paul Marciano, Photographer: Daniela Federici.

couldn't compete on the same level as other brands with much larger advertising budgets. What alternatives are left when beer humor is dominated by brands with advertising budgets in the hundreds of millions? A similar situation existed for Revelstoke whiskey. With only $1 million, a meager advertising budget compared to major distillers, Revelstoke went sexual with a gentleman's club approach. In addition to "edgy" ads, sex provides these companies a way to get noticed, a way to appeal to men (especially young men), and a way to position their brands with a wink and nod to those who appreciate the gesture.

Sex in advertising will continue as long as other long-time advertising strategies need updating. In 1989 Sansabelt, a men's clothing manufacturer, initiated a very attention-getting campaign that didn't show any of its men's clothing. The campaign, "What Women Look for in Men's Pants," did feature attractive women imparting playful wisdom—laced with double entendre—about what they found attractive about men's slacks: "All men

Has he been reading your Harlequin® books?

Figure 12.3: An inventive way to sell Harlequin romance novels. Courtesy of Harlequin Enterprises Limited.

Figure 12.4: Buffalo Jeans (2002). Buffalo by David Bitton.

are alike until they put their pants on," "I always lower my eyes when a man passes. To see if he's worth following," and "I've always considered a man's lower half his better half." Sansabelt implemented the strategy because its previous advertising had failed to register with consumers. "We tested the ads and got a lot of positive response," said an executive for HartMarx, Sansabelt's parent company. "We had discovered that we had very low awareness among younger men, and we also knew that [ads with] the conventional handsome men in nice slacks had not done much."[13]

Sex in advertising will continue as long as marketers want to imbue their brand with sensual identities. For instance, a set of fashion and fragrance marketers can always be counted on to position their brands as sexual, or with promises of sexual attraction. But sex will also be used for different products, perhaps to put a sexy shine on the product's image. Rockport, a shoe brand known for comfort (and a fairly nonsexual image), recently initiated a campaign containing an unmistakably sexual commercial. The spot shows a woman's foot rubbing up against a man's bare neck and torso, just before he gives her a foot massage. As ad columnist Art Ross said, "Every TV writer, producer, and art director considers sex appeal as a legitimate tool of the trade." The only challenge, said Ross, is deciding when to use it.[14]

Similarly, sex in advertising will be used to market products not traditionally associated with sex. Who would have guessed that Uncle Ben's Rice Bowls or Dannon's La Crème yogurt commercials could be marketed with steamy images of couples necking over their noodles or wives wearing French maid outfits? Sex hasn't been a strategy for high-ticket items such as computers, but as prices fall and computers become a commodity product that may change. Several years ago in London, a billboard contained a sexy image of a woman with a low-cut blouse and the headline, "Lap Power." Sales were reportedly very high. Over time, it appears that sex will be used not only for sex-relevant products—the tried-and-true—but for an increasing array of products.

Last, sex in advertising will continue to be used to tap new markets. Candie's fragrance is attempting to parlay its popularity with young women into a lucrative fragrance business. As a result, its sexually irreverent ads are meant to be seen by teens and young adults. In addition, mainstream companies don't always limit their sexual advertising to mainstream audiences. For example, several brewers are using sex to target the

Zippo. It works or we fix it free.™ Made in USA. @zippo.com

Want a Zippo? You can find one at select Spencer Gifts stores or Meijer Fine Jewelry Departments.

zippo Use it to start something.

Figure 12.5: "Use it to start something." New possibilities for Zippo? Zippo.com.

gay community. Media scholar Gary Hicks has written about beer advertisers appealing to homosexuals with sex-tinged advertising.[15] Many of these ads for Miller, Anheuser-Busch, and Coors appear in *Out, Instinct,* and the *Advocate.* Often, the themes of these ads are sexual, revolving around images of sexual attraction. Hicks described an interactive Miller Lite ad in a 2000 issue of the *Advocate.* "[The ad] asks for reader participation in bringing two handsome gay men together. In a bar scene, one model is posed on the far left of the ad while the other is on the far right. The model of the left has a line marked A next to him, while the model on the right has one marked B next to him. The ad's copy reads, "Connect A to B and Celebrate with Miller Lite. The reader who actually goes so far as to follow these directions ends up making the models touch bodies, one model's hand rubbing against the other's."[16] By targeting gay readers, beer markets can feature sexy ads without women.

SEXY SPIN (RE)CYCLE

What will change, however, is the look of sexual content, both in terms of intensity and form. Over time, the general trend appears to be that sexual content in advertising has (and continues to) become more intense and more explicit, albeit marked by periods of ebb and flow. Talking about the intensity of sexual content, *New York Times*'s Stuart Elliott speculated, "What is not clear is just how perverse, erotic or naughty ads will have to be to sell products next year, the year after that and the year after that…"[17]

Despite the erosion of standards, there is only so far it can go. For example, it's doubtful that the taboo against frontal nudity will be broken in the near future. As advanced as Europeans are with regard to sex in advertising, there still are few, if a handful, of examples of Old World nudity below the waist. The swimsuits and lingerie will become ever more skimpy, but they aren't going away anytime soon. As such, sex in advertising will continue to be used, but its packaging will vary as it recycles themes.

As advertisers hit the limits of what they can show, they package sex differently to keep it fresh. Pornography research has shown that viewers experience wear-out: the more they see scintillating sex, the more scintillating it needs to be to evoke the same effect. One way that erotic films maintain arousal is the introduction of new themes or scenarios. The same is true for advertising as marketers position their advertising as sluttish, offensive, affluent/patrician, trashy, playboy, or lesbian chic. Although Victoria's Secret has taken women in intimates about as far as it can go, it has positioned its look with a high-class, glamour appeal. Frederick's of Hollywood's models, also clothed in intimates, are positioned not quite as elegantly. Some advertisers even employ a mock-pornographic look. For example, a recent ad for Porn Star clothing borrows from the pornography motif to sell its garments. The ad features a woman spanking a topless woman in front of what appears to be a grade-school class (see fig. 12.6).

Even packaging sex with an emotion works. For example, much contemporary sexual content is interwoven with humor. Lee Garfinkel, the advertising creative who's worked on many sexual ads, once said that humor and sex work well together in advertising. When asked about a sensual Mercedes ad he produced, he said: "Wit and humor let you do a lot."[18] On the opposite end of the spectrum, sex can also be effectively packaged with a bit of fear for use in public service announcements, especially for publicizing issues such as sexually transmitted diseases. The sexual content draws people in and then delivers a message that is relevant to the topic.

As public attitudes change, so does the intensity and explicitness of sexual content in advertising. It will be as explicit as the public allows it to be. If it becomes too out of hand, there will be a backlash and it will recede, only to resurface as citizens become more complacent. For example, beer-bimbos in bikinis reached a fevered pitch in the 1980s until the confluence of several events moved public attitudes: the sexual harassment suit against Stroh Brewery, the Surgeon General's call for modesty, and the Clarence Thomas hearings. Only recently are viewers seeing an increase in the eroticization in beer advertising for brands like Coors Light, Miller Lite, Michelob, Bacardi Silver, Skyy, and Jack Daniel's Hard Cola. Some of the relaxation is evident in other indicators such as laddie-magazines, *The Man Show*, *The Howard Stern Show*, and public marketing of videos such as *Girls Gone Wild*.

As advertising becomes more sexual (and sexist), people will respond and interest groups will become more vocal. For example, the women's advertising organization, Advertising Women of New York, both rewards and shames advertisers for the way they portray women in the organiza-

Figure 12.6: Ads for Porn Star Clothing push against the boundaries of acceptability. Courtesy of Porn Star Clothing.

tion's annual the Good, the Bad, and the Ugly Awards. Many Bad and Ugly award winners earn the distinction for sexual objectification: Del Taco ads with women in bikinis, moaning in Clairol's Herbal Essences commercials, and rockets shooting between women's legs in Candie's ads. Even a Doritos ad that features a woman walking through a library as men worship her was a dubious award-winner. The woman (and chips) were so "hot" that the sprinklers go off when she bites a snack chip. Advertising creators, at least those working at larger agencies, are responsive to the negative publicity.

Other groups are watchful as well. For example, a recent ad in *Linux Journal* for computer hardware products featured the face of an attractive woman and the headline: "Don't feel bad, our servers won't go down on you either." Although the company's president said the advertisement had a sizable impact on sales, he discontinued running the ad after complaints from GraceNet.[19] The group is a high-tech organization that provides support to women in that industry. The ad earned the organization's "DisGraceful Award." Sylvia Paull, the group's founder, said, "The ad implies that its customers are men, and that these men aren't desirable enough to get a blow job." She also said, "It's offensive both to women and to potential male customers—not to mention servers, which are gender neutral."[20]

From the examples of titillating images to sell tobacco in the 1870s to the CNN promo of Paula Zahn's news show, it's clear that products will be sold through sexual themes and sex appeal will only continue. The use of sex will ebb and flow, but it will never disappear. University of Maryland's advertising instructor, Erik Zanot, said: "There is always going to be sex in advertising for the simple reason that it's just one of our basic strong emotions. And advertisers are always looking for basic emotions to attach to products in order to sell them."[21] Zanot's observation suggests that sex will continue as a mainstay in advertising for an increasing array of products, perhaps even if that product turns out to be the news.

Notes

PREFACE

1. Natalie Angier, *Woman: An Intimate Geography* (Boston: Houghton Mifflin, 1999).

INTRODUCTION

1. Norman Douglas, "Norman Douglas," *TCPN-Great Quotations* [online], www.cyber-nation.com/victory/quotations/authors/quotes_douglas_norman. html [10 October 2002].

CHAPTER 1

1. Matt Kemper, "'Sexy' Ad Stirs Up a Storm at CNN," *Tuscaloosa News*, 10 January 2002, sec. D, p. 1.
2. "Fox News Channel's Bill O'Reilly Said Zahn Was Being Politically Correct When She Said She Was Offended," *Tuscaloosa News*, 15 January 2002, sec. A, p. 2.

3. David M. Buss, *The Evolution of Desire: Strategies of Human Mating* (New York: Basic Books, 1994).

4. Bob Coen, "Bob Coen's Insider's Report," *McCann-Erickson WorldGroup* [online], www.mccann.com/insight/bobcoen.html [12 October 2002].

5. Charles Goodrum and Helen Dalrymple, *Advertising in America: The First 100 Years* (New York: Abrams, 1990); Juliann Sivulka, "Historical and Psychological Perspectives of the Erotic Appeal in Advertising," in *Sex in Advertising: Perspectives on the Erotic Appeal*, ed. Tom Reichert and Jacqueline Lambiase (Mahwah, N.J.: Lawrence Erlbaum Associates, 2003), pp. 39–63.

6. James Twitchell, *Adcult USA: The Triumph of Advertising in American Culture* (New York: Columbia University Press, 1996); Sivulka, "Historical and Psychological Perspectives."

7. Tom Reichert, "Sexy Ads Target Young People," *USA Today* 129 (May 2001): 50–52.

8. Tom Reichert, "What is Sex in Advertising? Perspectives From Consumer Behavior and Social Science Research," in *Sex in Advertising: Perspectives on the Erotic Appeal*, ed. Tom Reichert and Jacqueline Lambiase (Mahwah, N.J.: Lawrence Erlbaum Associates, 2003), pp. 11–38.

9. Tom Reichert and Artemio Ramirez, "Defining Sexually Oriented Appeals in Advertising: A Grounded Theory Investigation," in *Advances in Consumer Research*, vol. 27, ed. Stephen J. Hoch and Robert J. Meyer (Provo, Utah: Association for Consumer Research, 2000), pp. 267–73.

10. Ibid.

11. Ibid.

12. Jacqueline Lambiase and Tom Reichert, "Promises, Promises: Exploring Erotic Rhetoric in Sexually Oriented Advertising," in *Persuasive Imagery: A Consumer Perspective*, ed. Linda Scott and Rajeev Batra (Mahwah, N.J.: Lawrence Erlbaum Associates, in press).

13. Wilson Bryan Key, *Subliminal Seduction: Ad Media's Manipulation of a Not So Innocent America* (New York: Signet, 1973); Wilson Bryan Key, *The Clam-Plate Orgy and Other Subliminal Techniques for Manipulating Your Behavior* (New York: Signet, 1986).

14. Charles Trappey, "A Meta-Analysis of Consumer Choice and Subliminal Advertising," *Psychology & Marketing* 13 (1996): 517–30; Key, *Subliminal Seduction*.

15. Wilson Bryan Key, interview by author, 12 June 2002.

16. Twitchell, *Adcult USA*, pp. 111–16.

17. Ibid.

18. Wilson Bryan Key, "Subliminal Seduction: The Fountainhead for America's Obsession," in *Sex in Advertising: Perspectives on the Erotic Appeal*, ed. Tom

Reichert and Jacqueline Lambiase (Mahwah, N.J.: Lawrence Erlbaum Associates, 2003), pp. 195–212; Key, *Subliminal Seduction*; Key, *Clam-Plate Orgy*; Dennis L. Rosen and Surendra N. Singh, "An Investigation of Subliminal Embed Effect on Multiple Measures of Advertising Effectiveness," *Psychology & Marketing* 9, no. 2 (1992): 157–73; William J. Ruth, Harriet S. Mosatche, and Arthur Kramer, "Freudian Sexual Symbolism: Theoretical Considerations and an Empirical Test in Advertising," *Psychological Reports* 64 (1989): 1131–39; Kathryn T. Theus, "Subliminal Advertising and the Psychology of Processing Unconscious Stimuli: A Review of Research," *Psychology & Marketing* 11 (1994): 271–90; Trappey, "Meta-Analysis."

CHAPTER 2

1. William F. Arens, *Contemporary Advertising* (New York: McGraw-Hill), p. 25.

2. Ann Maxwell, "Advertising & The Business of Brands," in *Advertising & The Business of Brands*, ed. Bruce Bendinger (Chicago: The Copy Workshop, 1999), p. 40.

3. Joseph Straubhaar and Robert LaRose, *Media Now: Communications Media in the Information Age* (Belmont, Calif.: Wadsworth/Thomson Learning, 2002), p. 118.

4. Maxwell, "Advertising & The Business," p. 43.

5. Marilyn Miller and Marian Faux, eds., *New York Public Library American History Desk Reference* (New York: Macmillan, 1997), p. 371.

6. Maxwell, "Advertising & The Business," 46.

7. Charles Goodrum and Helen Dalrymple, *Advertising in America: The First 100 Years* (New York: Abrams, 1990).

8. Ibid.

9. Patrick G. Porter, "Advertising in the Early Cigarette Industry: W. Duke, Sons & Company of Durham," *North Carolina Historical Review* 48, no. 1 (1971): 31–43.

10. Ibid., p. 35.

11. Ibid.

12. Ibid., p. 34.

13. Ibid., p. 12.

14. Washington Duke to James Buchanan Duke, 17 October 1894, in Benjamin N. Duke Letterbooks, Benjamin N. Duke Papers, Rare Book, Manuscript, & Special Collections Library, Duke University, Durham, North Carolina.

15. "Cigars and Cigarettes," *Display Advertising* 1, no. 6 (1898): 10.

16. Ibid., pp. 9–11.

17. Ibid., p. 9.

18. Valerie Steele, *Fashion and Eroticism: Ideals of Feminine Beauty from the Victorian Era to the Jazz Age* (New York: Oxford University Press, 1985), p. 75.

19. "Corset Advertising," *Display Advertising* 1, no. 4 (1897): 5–8.

20. M. D. C. Crawford and Elizabeth A. Guernsey, *The History of Corsets in Pictures* (New York: Fairchild Publishers, 1951).

21. Ibid., p. 27.

22. "Corset Advertising," p. 5–8.

23. Lucian T. Warner, *Always Starting Things: Through Seventy Eventful Years* (Bridgeport, Conn: Warner Brothers Co., 1944), Warshaw Collection, Corsets, Archives Center, National Museum of American History, Smithsonian Institution.

24. "Corset Advertising," pp. 5–8.

25. Crawford and Guernsey, *The History of Corsets*.

26. "Corset Advertising," pp. 5–8.

27. Ibid.

28. "A Censorship at Mt. Vernon," *Display Advertising* 1, no. 6 (1897): 13.

CHAPTER 3

1. Marilyn Miller and Marian Faux, eds., *New York Public Library American History Desk Reference* (New York: Macmillan, 1997), p. 445.

2. Ibid., p. 285.

3. Ibid., p. 106.

4. Ann Maxwell, "Advertising & The Business of Brands," in *Advertising & The Business of Brands*, ed. Bruce Bendinger (Chicago: The Copy Workshop, 1999), p. 47.

5. Havelock Ellis, *The Love Rights of Women* (New York: The Birth Control Review, 1918), p. 4.

6. "Account Histories: The Andrew Jergens Company-Woodbury's Facial Soap," Andrew Jergens Company, Domestic Advertising Collection, J. Walter Thompson Company Archives, Hartman Center for Sales, Advertising & Marketing History, Rare Book, Manuscript, & Special Collections Library, Duke University, Durham, North Carolina.

7. Tom Pendergast, "Jergens," in *Encyclopedia of Consumer Brands*, vol. 2, ed. Janice Jorgensen (Detroit: St. James Press, 1994).

8. "Account Histories: The Andrew Jergens Company."

9. Ibid.

10. Ibid., p. 1.

11. "Market Studies and Research: Woodbury's Facial Soap National Campaign 1926," Andrew Jergens Company, Domestic Advertising Collection, J. Walter Thompson Company Archives, Hartman Center for Sales, Advertising &

Marketing History, Rare Book, Manuscript, & Special Collections Library, Duke University, Durham, North Carolina.

12. "Account Histories: The Andrew Jergens Company."

13. Ibid.

14. "Market Studies and Research," p. 3.

15. "Account Histories: The Andrew Jergens Company."

16. Ibid., p. 3.

17. Howard Henderson to Stanley Resor, 4 January 1929, in Andrew Jergens Company, Domestic Advertising Collection, J. Walter Thompson Company Archives, Hartman Center for Sales, Advertising & Marketing History, Rare Book, Manuscript, & Special Collections Library, Duke University, Durham, North Carolina.

18. Henderson to Resor, p. 1.

19. "Market Studies and Research."

20. "Account Histories: The Andrew Jergens Company."

21. Ibid.

22. Pendergast, "Jergens."

23. Ibid.

24. 1985 Chesebrough-Ponds ad, "Horse Epidemic," Domestic Advertising Collection, J. Walter Thompson Company Archives, Hartman Center for Sales, Advertising & Marketing History, Rare Book, Manuscript, & Special Collections Library, Duke University, Durham, North Carolina.

25. Evelyn S. Dorman, "Pond's," in *Encyclopedia of Consumer Brands*, vol. 2, ed. Janice Jorgensen (Detroit: St. James Press, 1994).

26. Ibid.

27. Ibid.

28. J. W. Pike, *Directory of the Hosiery & Knitting Goods Manufacturers of the United States* (Philadelphia, PA: J. W. Pike, 1883), Warshaw Collection, Hosiery, Archives Center, National Museum of American History, Smithsonian Institution.

29. *The Hosier*, no. 19 (November 1910): 10–11, Warshaw Collection, Hosiery, Archives Center, National Museum of American History, Smithsonian Institution.

30. Charles Goodrum and Helen Dalrymple, *Advertising in America: The First 100 Years* (New York: Abrams, 1990).

31. "Schemes for Selling," *The Hosier*, no. 17 (September 1910): 8–9, Warshaw Collection, Hosiery, Archives Center, National Museum of American History, Smithsonian Institution.

32. Lucian T. Warner, *Always Starting Things: Through Seventy Eventful Years* (Bridgeport, Conn.: Warner Brothers Co., 1944), p. 13, Warshaw Collection, Corsets, Archives Center, National Museum of American History, Smithsonian Institution.

33. Ibid., pp. 18–19.

34. Ibid.

35. Ibid.

36. Edward A. McCabe, "Sex in Advertising," *Playboy* (August 1992): 76–83.

37. Michael Gaines, personal communication, 25 September 2002; see also, Michael Gaines, *The Shortest Dynasty* (Bowie, Md.: Heritage Books, 2002).

CHAPTER 4

1. Charles Goodrum and Helen Dalrymple, *Advertising in America: The First 100 Years* (New York: Abrams, 1990).

2. Marilyn Miller and Marian Faux, eds., *New York Public Library American History Desk Reference* (New York: Macmillan, 1997), p. 289.

3. Ibid., p. 290.

4. Ann Maxwell, "Advertising & The Business of Brands," in *Advertising & The Business of Brands*, ed. Bruce Bendinger (Chicago: The Copy Workshop, 1999), p. 63.

5. Ibid.

6. Ibid.

7. "MacPherson Sketch Book," Warshaw Collection, Archives Center, National Museum of American History, Smithsonian Institution.

8. Edward A. McCabe, "Sex in Advertising," *Playboy* 39, no. 8 (August 1992): 76–83.

9. "The History of Lux Flakes," *Lever Standard* 22, no. 10 (October 1950): 2–8. Lever Brothers, Domestic Advertising Collection, J. Walter Thompson Company Archives, Hartman Center for Sales, Advertising & Marketing History, Rare Book, Manuscript, & Special Collections Library, Duke University, Durham, North Carolina.

10. Ibid.

11. "History of Lux Toilet Soap, 1925–1951," Lever Brothers, Client Files, J. Walter Thompson Collection, Rare Book, Manuscript, & Special Collections Library, Duke University, Durham, North Carolina.

12. F. A. Countway to Stanley Resor, 27 January 1925, p. 3, Lever Brothers, Domestic Advertising Collection, J. Walter Thompson Company Archives, Hartman Center for Sales, Advertising & Marketing History, Rare Book, Manuscript, & Special Collections Library, Duke University, Durham, North Carolina.

13. "History of Lux Toilet Soap."

14. Ibid.

15. Alan Joyce, "Works Like Listerine, Tastes Like Cool Mint Campaign," in

Encyclopedia of Major Marketing Campaigns, ed. Thomas Riggs (Detroit: Gale Group, 2000), p. 1918.

16. Gillian Wolf, "Listerine," in *Encyclopedia of Consumer Brands*, vol. 2, ed. Janice Jorgensen (Detroit: St. James Press, 1994), pp. 336–38.

17. Joyce, "Works Like Listerine," pp. 1918–20.

18. Wolf, "Listerine."

19. Joyce, "Works Like Listerine," p. 1918.

20. "Listerine Antiseptic Historical Review," (1962), Warner-Lambert, Domestic Advertising Collection, J. Walter Thompson Company Archives, Hartman Center for Sales, Advertising & Marketing History, Rare Book, Manuscript, & Special Collections Library, Duke University, Durham, North Carolina.

21. Wolf, "Listerine."

22. "Research and Copy Strategy 1937–1938," General Cigar Company, Domestic Advertising Collection, J. Walter Thompson Company Archives, Hartman Center for Sales, Advertising & Marketing History, Rare Book, Manuscript, & Special Collections Library, Duke University, Durham, North Carolina.

23. "Confidential Case History of The General Cigar Co.," March 1961, Domestic Advertising Collection, J. Walter Thompson Company Archives, Hartman Center for Sales, Advertising & Marketing History, Rare Book, Manuscript, & Special Collections Library, Duke University, Durham, North Carolina.

24. Ibid., p. 6.

25. "Research and Copy Strategy," p. 1.

26. David A. Munro, "Sex & Cigars," *Space & Time* (21 November 1938): 1, General Cigar Company, Domestic Advertising Collection, J. Walter Thompson Company Archives, Hartman Center for Sales, Advertising & Marketing History, Rare Book, Manuscript, & Special Collections Library, Duke University, Durham, North Carolina.

27. "Research and Copy Strategy," p. 1.

28. Ibid.

29. "Confidential Case History."

30. General Cigar Company to W. J. Ryan, 22 November 1937, General Cigar Company, Domestic Advertising Collection, J. Walter Thompson Company Archives, Hartman Center for Sales, Advertising & Marketing History, Rare Book, Manuscript, & Special Collections Library, Duke University, Durham, North Carolina.

CHAPTER 5

1. Judson Knight, "Virginia Tourism Corporation," in *Encyclopedia of Major Marketing Campaigns*, ed. Thomas Riggs (Detroit: Gale Group, 2000), p. 1873.

2. Ann Maxwell, "Advertising & The Business of Brands," in *Advertising & The Business of Brands*, ed. Bruce Bendinger (Chicago: The Copy Workshop, 1999), p. 68.

3. Lawrence R. Samuel, *Brought to You By: Postwar Television Advertising and the American Dream* (Austin: University of Texas Press, 2001).

4. Ibid., p. 75.

5. Ibid., p. ix.

6. Maxwell, "Advertising," p. 72.

7. Ibid., p. 84.

8. Charles Goodrum and Helen Dalrymple, *Advertising in America: The First 100 Years* (New York: Abrams, 1990), p. 74.

9. Ibid., p. 76.

10. Ibid., p. 80.

11. Ibid., p. 74.

12. *Maidenform Mirror* 32 (July–August 1962): 14, Maidenform Collection, Archives Center, National Museum of American History, Smithsonian Institution.

13. Louise Anita Coryell, "The Dream Campaign," in *Encyclopedia of Major Marketing Campaigns*, ed. Thomas Riggs (Detroit: Gale Group, 2000), p. 988.

14. Kitty D'Alessio, transcript of interview, New York, 8 August 1990, Maidenform Collection, Archives Center, National Museum of American History, Smithsonian Institution.

15. *Maidenform Mirror*, p. 4.

16. Ibid.

17. Ibid., p. 5.

18. Joe Sacco, "Dreams for Sale: How the One for Maidenform Came True," *Advertising Age* (12 September 1977): 63.

19. Coryell, "The Dream Campaign," p. 988.

20. Ibid.

21. Ibid., p. 991.

22. "Maidenform 50th Anniversary: The Golden Dream," Maidenform Collection, Archives Center, National Museum of American History, Smithsonian Institution.

23. Coryell, "The Dream Campaign," p. 990.

24. D'Alessio, interview.

25. Ibid.

26. Ibid.

27. Ibid.

28. Ibid.

29. "Advertising Program," Maidenform Collection, Archives Center, National Museum of American History, Smithsonian Institution.

30. Sacco, "Dreams for Sale," p. 63.

31. Coryell, "The Dream Campaign," p. 992.

32. *Maidenform Mirror*, p. 14.

33. Sally Cobau, "A Diamond is Forever Campaign," in *Encyclopedia of Major Marketing Campaigns*, ed. Thomas Riggs (Detroit: Gale Group, 2000), p. 450.

34. Donna J. Bergenstock and James M. Maskulka, "The De Beers Story: Are Diamonds Forever?" *Business Horizons* 44, no. 3 (2001): 37.

35. Cobau, "Diamond is Forever," p. 452.

36. Nicholas Stein, "The De Beers Story: A New Cut on an Old Monopoly," *Fortune* 143 (19 February 2001): 186.

37. Bergenstock and Maskulka, "De Beers Story," p. 37.

38. Ibid.

39. Cobau, "Diamond is Forever," p. 452.

40. Ibid.

41. Allison J. Porter, "Shadows Campaign," in *Encyclopedia of Major Marketing Campaigns*, ed. Thomas Riggs (Detroit: Gale Group, 2000), p. 456.

42. Ibid., p. 460.

43. Bergenstock and Maskulka, "De Beers Story," p. 37.

44. Cobau, "Diamond is Forever," p. 455.

45. Deborah Mack, "Take It Off, Take It All Off Campaign," in *Encyclopedia of Major Marketing Campaigns*, ed. Thomas Riggs (Detroit: Gale Group, 2000), p. 1468.

46. Ibid., p. 1471.

47. Angela Woodward, "Clairol," in *Encyclopedia of Consumer Brands*, vol. 2, ed. Janice Jorgensen (Detroit: St. James Press, 1994), p. 127.

48. "Clairol's Influence on American Beauty and Marketing," *Drug & Cosmetic Industry* 159 (August 1996): 28.

49. Ibid.

50. Malcolm Gladwell, "True Colors," *New Yorker* 75 (March 1999): 73.

51. Ibid.

52. Robyn Griggs, "Clairol's Off-Color Campaign Produced Lots of Green," *Advertising Age* 70, no. 14 (1999): 24.

53. Woodward, "Clairol," p. 128.

54. Yumiko Ono, "Can Racy Ads Help Revitalize Old Fragrances?" *Wall Street Journal*, 20 November 1996, sec. B, p. 1.

55. William Safire, "Name Your Poison," *San Francisco Chronicle*, 27 October 1985, p. 18.

56. Anita Louise Coryell, "I'm Going to Have an Aviance Night Campaign," in *Encyclopedia of Major Marketing Campaigns*, ed. Thomas Riggs (Detroit: Gale Group, 2000), p. 1306.

CHAPTER 6

1. Joe Sacco, "Dreams for Sale: How the One for Maidenform Came True," *Advertising Age* (12 September 1977): 63.

2. Robin Kamen, "Underwear Sales Now Unmentionable," *Crain's New York Business* (14 November 1994): 4.

3. Jay P. Pederson, "Jockey International," *Encyclopedia of Consumer Brands*, vol. 2, ed. Janice Jorgensen (Detroit: St. James Press, 1994), p. 294.

4. Ibid.

5. Ibid., p. 296.

6. Steven Gaines and Sharon Churcher, *Obsession: The Lives and Times of Calvin Klein* (New York: Avon), p. 317.

7. Ibid.

8. Ibid., p. 319.

9. Ibid.

10. Barbara Lippert, "Advertising's New Hunks: A Post-Feminist 'Tat for a Tit,'" *Adweek* (26 October 1987): 60.

11. Joshua Levine, "Fantasy, Not Flesh," *Forbes* (22 January 1990): 119.

12. Gaines and Churcher, *Obsession*, p. 414.

13. Ibid., p. 413.

14. Hermann Vaske, "I Wanna Say More," *Archive* 4 (2001).

15. Bernice Kanner, "Undressed for Success," *New York* (12 September 1983): 24.

16. Ibid.

17. Ibid.

18. Art Ross, "The Sexual Imperative," *Back Stage* (3 February 1984): 10.

19. Dorchen Leidholdt, "Sexual Values in Advertising," *Ads Magazine* (March–April 1984): 48.

20. Deborah Mack, "Playtex Apparel, Inc.," in *Encyclopedia of Major Marketing Campaigns*, ed. Thomas Riggs (Detroit: Gale Group, 2000), p. 1403.

21. Ibid., p. 1402.

22. Pat Sloan and Carol Krol, "Underwear Ads Caught in Bind Over Sex Appeal," *Advertising Age* 67 (8 July 1996): 27.

23. Mack, "Playtex Apparel," p. 1404.

24. Ibid.

25. Sara Pendergast, "Calvin Klein," in *Encyclopedia of Consumer Brands*, vol. 2, ed. Janice Jorgensen (Detroit: St. James Press, 1994), p. 100.

26. Mariko Fujinaka, "The One and Only Wonderbra Campaign," in *Encyclopedia of Major Marketing Campaigns*, ed. Thomas Riggs (Detroit: Gale Group, 2000), p. 1583.

27. Cyndee Miller, "Bra Marketers' Cup Runneth Over with, Um, Big Success," *Marketing News* 28 (24 October 1994): 1.

28. Fujinaka, "The One and Only," p. 1580.

29. "Leave it to Cleavage," *People* 42 (15 August 1994): 84.

30. Miller, "Bra Marketers' Cup," p. 1.

31. Fujinaka, "The One and Only," p. 1583.

32. Miller, "Bra Marketers' Cup," p. 1.

33. Margaret Carlson, "Less Than Uplifting," *Time* (4 April 1994): 31.

34. "Wonder Stories," *Wonderbra* [online], www.wonderbra.com/frame_funny. htm [March 14, 2002].

35. Fujinaka, "The One and Only," p. 1584.

36. Christopher Palmeri, "Victoria's Little Secret," *Forbes* (24 August 1998): 58.

37. Steve Salerno, "Super Model," *Individual Investor* (June 1999): 56.

38. Paul Miller, "Victoria Reveals Her Secret," *Catalog Age* (February 1999): 18.

39. Salerno, "Super Model," p. 56.

40. Ibid., p. 57.

41. Debbie Then, "Men's Magazines: The Facts and the Fantasies" (paper presented at the annual convention of the American Psychological Association, Washington, D.C., 1992), p. 10.

42. Sandra Dolbow, "Angling for Uplift," *Brandweek* (27 November 2000): 4.

43. Debra Goldman, "Rated X," *Adweek* (15 February 1999): 58.

44. Barbara Lippert, "Indecent Exposure," *Adweek* (15 February 1999): 34.

45. Ibid., p. 36.

46. Ibid., p. 34.

47. Alice Z. Cuneo and Wayne Friedman, "Spreading Secrets," *Advertising Age* (22 October 2001): 3.

48. Ibid.

49. David Bauder, "ABC Getting Heat for Risqué Victoria's Secret Fashion Show," *Tuscaloosa News*, 21 November 2001, sec. A, p. 2.

50. Ibid.

51. Alice Z. Cuneo, "Blue Xmas for Some Retailers," *Advertising Age* (10 December 2001): 70.

52. Lippert, "Indecent Exposure," pp. 34–35.

53. Evelyn Ellison Twitchell, "Barron's Online: Victoria's Beauties," *Barron's* (24 April 2000): 55.

54. Tom Reichert, "Sexy Ads Target Young People," *USA Today* 129 (May 2001): 50.

55. Emily Scardino, "Can the Market Push Up a Flat Bra Business?" *Discount Retailing Today* 40 (5 March 2001): A20.

56. Monica Greco, "Intimate Apparel: Shaping Up the Industry," *Apparel Industry Magazine* (September 1997): 64.

57. "Plus Comfort and Style," *Discount Store News* 36 (18 August 1997): A34.

58. "Plus-Size Finds Support at Retail," *Discount Store News* 37 (26 October 1998): A19.

59. Debby Garbato Stankevich, "The Cover Shot," *Discount Merchandiser* (September 1999): 79.

60. "The Art of Being Sexy," *Vassarette* [online], www.Vassarette.com [7 February 2002].

61. "Available in B, C and D Cartons," *Advertising Age's Creativity* 5 (September 1997): 6.

62. Mack, "Playtex Apparel," p. 1403.

63. Greco, "Intimate Apparel," p. 68.

64. Debby Garbato Stankevich, "Picking the Right Spots," *Discount Merchandiser* (February 2000): 86.

CHAPTER 7

1. Steven Gaines and Sharon Churcher, *Obsession: The Lives and Times of Calvin Klein* (New York: Avon), p. 293.

2. Sara Pendergast, "Calvin Klein," in *Encyclopedia of Consumer Brands*, vol. 2, ed. Janice Jorgensen (Detroit: St. James Press, 1994), p. 99.

3. Barbara Lippert, "'Look' Again," *Adweek* (6 November 2000): 26.

4. Andrew Sullivan, "Flogging Underwear," *New Republic* (18 January 1988): 20.

5. Barbara Lippert, "Dude Ranch," *Adweek* (14 September 1992): 73.

6. Pat Sloan, "I Don't Have Long Term Plans. I Just Act Instinctively," *Advertising Age* (18 May 1992): 60.

7. Pendergast, "Calvin Klein," p. 98.

8. Gaines and Churcher, *Obsession*, p. 277. Much of the description of Calvin Klein commercials comes from Gaines and Churcher.

9. Ibid.

10. Ibid., p. 287.

11. Ibid.

12. Ibid., p. 288.

13. Ibid.

14. Pendergast, "Calvin Klein," p. 99.

15. Gaines and Churcher, *Obsession*, p. 295.

16. Ibid.

17. Barbara Brady, "Calvin Klein, Inc.," in *Encyclopedia of Major Marketing Campaigns*, ed. Thomas Riggs (Detroit: Gale Group, 2000), p. 229.

18. Gaines and Churcher, *Obsession*, p. 406.

19. Stuart Elliott, "Has Madison Avenue Gone Too Far?" *New York Times*, 15 December 1991, sec. F, p. 6.

20. Sloan, "Long Term Plans," 60.

21. Cyndee Miller, "Publisher Says Sexy Ads Are OK, But Sexist Ones Will Sink Sales," *Marketing News* (23 November 1992): 8.

22. Kevin Goldman, "Risk Seems To Have Paid Off In 1992 Print Campaigns," *Wall Street Journal*, 18 May 1993, sec. B, p. 6.

23. Lippert, "Dude Ranch," p. 73.

24. Brady, "Calvin Klein, Inc.," p. 231.

25. Ibid., p. 232.

26. Ibid., p. 230.

27. Elliot, "Madison Avenue," p. 6.

28. Richard Behar, "Guess What's Behind This IPO," *Fortune* (14 October 1996): 133.

29. Fran Sherman, "Guess?" in *The Encyclopedia of Consumer Brands*, vol. 2, ed. Janice Jorgensen (Detroit: St. James Press, 1994), p. 245.

30. Pat Sloan, "Guess? Fall Ads to Emulate Scorsese," *Advertising Age* 68 (13 January 1997): 10.

31. "History," *Guess Online Store* [online], www.guess.com [February 8, 2002].

32. Kathy Tyrer, "Guess? Again," *Adweek* 44 (13 June 1994): 4.

33. Ibid.

34. Alice Z. Cuneo, "Jeansmaker's Spot Wins More Awards Than Any Ad," *Advertising Age International* (June 1997): I4.

35. Elaine Underwood, "Guess on the 'Net," *Brandweek* 37 (May 13 1996): 14.

36. Elaine Underwood, "Guess Again," *Brandweek* 37 (25 November 1996): 1.

37. Ibid.

38. Kirk Davidson, "Guess? Ads Cross Line From Fashion Art to Pornography," *Marketing News* 30 (21 October 1996): 13.

39. Behar, "Guess What's Behind," p. 133.

40. Sandra Dolbow, "Guess Steady on Ad Plans Despite Shortfall," *Brandweek* 41 (2 October 2000): 18.

41. Bob Garfield, "Levi's Latest Strategy Hits Below The Belt," *Advertising Age* (9 August 1999): 33.

42. Barbara Brady, "501 Reasons Campaign," in *Encyclopedia of Major Marketing Campaigns* (Detroit: Gale Group, 1999), p. 960; David P. Cleary, *Great American Brands* (New York: Fairchild, 1981), p. 211.

43. Sandra Dolbow, "Assessing Levi's Patch Job," *Brandweek* (6 November 2000): 34.

44. Ibid.

45. Ibid.

46. Ibid.

47. Garfield, "Levi's Latest," p. 33.

48. Ibid.

49. Alice Z. Cuneo, "Levi's Adds Sexy, Rebellious Tone To Retooled Jeans," *Advertising Age* (2 August 1999): 45.

50. Garfield, "Levi's Latest," p. 33.

51. "Sexy Spots," *Agency* 10 (Spring 2000): 16.

52. Dolbow, "Assessing Levi's," p. 34.

53. Rebecca Stanfel, "Nice Pants Campaign," in *Encyclopedia of Major Marketing Campaigns*, ed. Thomas Riggs (Detroit: Gale Group, 2000), p. 965.

CHAPTER 8

1. William F. Buckley, "Show Your I.D. Before Reading...," *National Review* (23 July 2001): 59.

2. Ibid., p. 58.

3. Ibid.

4. Lauren Goldstein, "The Alpha Teenager," *Fortune* (20 December 1999): 201.

5. Mercedes M. Cardona, "Perry Ellis Effort Accents Style," *Advertising Age* (24 January 2000): 6.

6. "Abercrombie's Beefcake Brigade," *Time* (14 February 2000): 62.

7. Goldstein, "Alpha Teenager," p. 201.

8. Adam Bryant and Anjali Arora, "Fashion's Frat Boy," *Newsweek* (13 September 1999): 40.

9. Goldstein, "Alpha Teenager," p. 201.

10. "Abercrombie's Beefcake Brigade," p. 62.

11. Ibid.

12. Bryant and Arora, "Fashion's Frat Boy," p. 40.

13. Ibid.

14. Barbara Lippert, "Body Heat," *Adweek* (4 October 1999): 32.

15. Michael Wilke, "Gay Overtones Seen in Abercrombie Ads," *Advertising Age* (16 September 1996): 20.

16. Corinne Wood to Michael Jeffries, June 13, 2001, copy available from the author.

17. Bryant and Arora, "Fashion's Frat Boy," p. 40.

18. Daryl F. Mallett, "Tommy Hilfiger Corporation," in *Encyclopedia of Major Marketing Campaigns*, ed. Thomas Riggs (Detroit: Gale Group, 2000), p. 1768.

19. Robin Kamen, "Underwear Sales Now Unmentionable," *Crain's New York Business* (14 November 1994): 4.

20. "Annual Report," Polo.com: Ralph Lauren [online], www.corporate-ir.net/media_files/NUS/RL/reports/00ar/polo2000-gatefold1-8.pdf, p. 3. [October 17, 2002].

21. "The 100 Top Brands," *Business Week* (6 August 2001): 60.

22. Barbara Lippert, "Here's the Beef," *Adweek* 36 (19 April 1999): 34.

23. Margaret Carlson, "Where Calvin Crossed the Line," *Time* 146 (11 September 1995): 64.

24. Tray LaCaze and Tom Reichert, "From Polo to Provocateur: Ralph Lauren's Evolving Brand Image," in *Proceedings of the 2002 Conference of the American Academy of Advertising*, ed. Avery Abernethy (Austin, Tex.: American Academy of Advertising, 2002), p. 110.

25. Carlson, "Calvin Crossed Line," p. 64.

26. Ellen Neuborne and Katherine Kerwin, "Generation Y," *Business Week* (11 January 1999): 82.

27. Faye Rice, "YSL Looks to Rebound," *Advertising Age* (14 August 2000): S6.

28. Ibid.

29. Tim Nudd, "Burn, Baby, Burn: Fashion Ads Drive Publisher Wild," *Adweek* (4 September 2000): 50.

30. Rice, "YSL Looks," p. S6.

31. Barbara Lippert, "Trick or Treat," *Adweek* (9 October 2000): 32.

32. Jane L. Thompson, "Risqué Business: The Fashion Industry Has Always Sold Sex and Style," *National Post*, 12 October 2000, sec. W, p. 12.

33. Valli Herman-Cohen, "Is Fashion Too Forward?" *Los Angeles Times*, 6 September 2000, sec. E, p. 1.

34. John Fetto, "Where's the Lovin'?" *American Demographics* (February 2001): 10.

35. Tom Reichert, "'Lesbian Chic' Imagery in Advertising: Interpretations and Insights," *Journal of Current Issues & Research in Advertising* 23, no. 2 (2001): 9.

CHAPTER 9

1. Stuart Elliot, "Has Madison Avenue Gone Too Far?" *New York Times*, 15 December 1991, sec. F, p. 6.

2. Robert Crooke, "Why Love, Sex, and Desire Still Dominate Fragrance Ads," *Magazine Age* (October 1980): 50.

3. Ibid., 49.

4. Ibid., 52.

5. Anita Louise Coryell, "I'm Going to Have an Aviance Night Campaign," in *Encyclopedia of Major Marketing Campaigns*, ed. Thomas Riggs (Detroit: Gale Group, 2000), p. 1308.

6. Ibid., p. 1306.

7. Ibid., p. 1307.

8. Ibid., p. 1306.

9. Ibid., p. 1307.

10. William D. Baue, "Share the Fantasy Campaign," in *Encyclopedia of Major Marketing Campaigns*, ed. Thomas Riggs (Detroit: Gale Group, 2000), p. 278.

11. Ibid.

12. Ibid., p. 279.

13. Rebecca Johnson, "Scent of a Woman," *Adweek* (29 November 1993): 32.

14. "They Built a Business on Musk," *Chemical Week* (7 July 1976): 28; Sharon Strangenes, "Men's Fragrances are Soaring," *Women's Wear Daily* (31 March 1978): 30.

15. "They Built a Business," p. 28.

16. Ibid.

17. "Jovan, Nini Ricci, Puig are Top Fragrance Award Winners," *Advertising Age* (9 June 1975): 1.

18. Lorraine Baltera, "Jovan Moves Out New Fragrances, Steps Into After-Bath Product Area," *Advertising Age* (13 September 1976): 40.

19. Barbara P. Johnson, "Jovan Using Packaged Goods Strategy To Market Cosmetics," *Product Management* (September 1976): 32.

20. Ibid.

21. Strangenes, "Men's Fragrances," p. 30.

22. Johnson, "Jovan Using Packaged," p. 32.

23. Pat Sloan and Nancy F. Millman, "Jovan Maneuver catapults Beecham Onto World Scene," *Advertising Age* (3 September 1979): 1.

24. Joshua Levine, "Fantasy, Not Flesh," *Forbes* (22 January 1990): 118.

25. Crooke, "Love, Sex, and Desire," p. 50.

26. Levine, "Fantasy Not Flesh," p. 118.

27. Dottie Enrico, "Flouting Taboo, Sexy New Ads Raise Eyebrows and Ire," *Adweek* (26 October 1987): 52.

28. Maureen Goldstein, "The Big Chill," *Inside Print* (March 1988): 44.

29. Levine, "Fantasy Not Flesh," p. 119.

30. Enrico, "Flouting Taboo," p. 58.

31. Goldstein, "Big Chill," p. 42.

32. Sara Pendergast, "Calvin Klein," in *Encyclopedia of Consumer Brands*, vol. 2, ed. Janice Jorgensen (Detroit: St. James Press, 1994), p. 101.

33. Ibid.

34. Barbara Lippert, "Advertising's New Hunks: A Post-Feminist 'Tat-for-Tit'," *Adweek* (26 October 1987): 60.

35. Andrew Sullivan, "Flogging Underwear," *New Republic* (18 January 1988): 23.

36. Ibid.

37. Steven Gaines and Sharon Churcher, *Obsession: The Lives and Times of Calvin Klein* (New York: Avon Books, 1994), p. 374. Much of the information on Calvin Klein's fragrance advertising is from Gaines and Churcher.

38. Glenn O'Brien, "Like Art," *Artforum* (April 1989): 17.

39. Pendergast, "Calvin Klein," p. 101.

40. Ibid.

41. Gaines and Churcher, *Obsession*, pp. 381–82.

42. Ibid., p. 383.

43. Kevin Goldman, "Risk Seems to Have Paid Off in 1992 Print Campaigns," *Wall Street Journal*, 18 May 1993, sec. B, p. 10.

44. Pendergast, "Calvin Klein," p. 101.

45. Levine, "Fantasy Not Flesh," p. 119.

46. Gary Levin, "More Nudity, But Less Sex," *Advertising Age* (8 November 1993): 37.

47. Rincker Buck, "10 Trends to Watch," *Brandweek* (26 July 1993): 58.

48. O'Brien, "Like Art," p. 17.

49. Dana Ritter, "Nudes in Ads: What Are They Selling?" *Magazine Age* (May 1982): 64.

50. Stuart Emmrich, "'Himbo' Flexes His Pecs in U.K. Ads," *Adweek* (12 August 1991): 16.

51. Lippert, "Advertising's New Hunks," p. 60.

52. Elliot, "Madison Avenue," p. 6.

53. Emmrich, "'Himbo' Flexes," p. 16.

54. Ellen Graham, "Buying the Simple Life in an Age When Success is Defined by Intangibles, Aspirational Marketing Doesn't Work," *Wall Street Journal*, 17 October 1996, sec. D, p. 4.

55. Pendergast, "Calvin Klein," p. 101.

56. Barbara Lippert, "Picture Imperfect," *Adweek* (22 February 1999): 32.

57. Angela Dawson, "All in the Family," *Adweek* (3 January 2000): 2.

58. Pendergast, "Calvin Klein," p. 101.

59. Elliot, "Madison Avenue," p. 6.

60. Pendergast, "Calvin Klein," p. 101.

61. Rebecca Stanfel, "Calvin Klein Cosmetics," in *Encyclopedia of Major Marketing Campaigns*, ed. Thomas Riggs (Detroit: Gale Group, 2000), p. 225.

62. Nora Kiley, "Lucky You Fragrance Campaign Debuts," *Adweek*, (14 August 2000): 20.

63. Ibid.

64. Luisa Kroll, "Like My Shoes," *Forbes* 159 (7 April 1997): 70.

65. Ibid.

66. Ibid., p. 71.

67. "Alyssa Milano and Candie's Jeans Make a Perfect Fit: Company Introduces New Jeans Collection with Campaign Featuring 'Charmed' Star," [online], www.corporate-ir.net/ireye/ir_site.zhtml?ticker-cand&script=410&layout=11& item_id= 39320 [July 6, 1999].

68. "Sexy Spots," *Agency* 10 (Spring 2000): 16.

69. Christine Bittar, "Condoms, Candie's to Romp," *Brandweek* 41 (1 January 2000): 16.

70. "Candie's Announces Major Advertising and On-line Partnership With Rock Megastar, Mark McGrath," [online], www.corporate-ir.net/ireye/ir_site. zhtml?ticker-vand&script=410&layout=11&itme_id=97041 [June 6, 2000].

71. Ibid.

72. Crooke, "Love, Sex, and Desire," p. 52.

73. Lippert, "Advertising's New Hunks," p. 60.

74. Heather Chaplin, "Smell My Candie's," *American Demographics* 21 (August 1999): 65.

75. Crooke, "Love, Sex, and Desire," p. 55.

CHAPTER 10

1. Jodi Duckett, "Cold Patrol Warms Up Beer Sales," *Portland Oregonian*, 25 January 1992, sec. C, p. 1.

2. Kathy DeSalvo, "Tarsem Creates Good Vibrations for MGD," *Shoot* (8 December 2000): 14.

3. Joanne Lippman, "Farewell, at Last, to Bimbo Campaigns?" *Wall Street Journal*, 31 January 1992, p. B2.

4. William D. Baue, "Spuds MacKenzie Campaign," in *Encyclopedia of Major Marketing Campaigns*, ed. Thomas Riggs (Detroit: Gale Group, 2000), p. 82.

5. Beth Ann Krier, "Those Good Looks, That Square Jaw Put Spuds Right Up There With Stars Like Joan Collins," *Toronto Star*, 19 July 1987, sec. D, p. 8.

6. Shelly Garcia, "Brews, Bozos, Bikinis: New Times For Old Milwaukee," *Adweek* (20 May 1991): 4.

7. Ibid.

8. Patrick Scullin, "The Swedish Bikini Team Hub-Bub: From Fame to Infamy in Six Months," press release, Ames, Scullin, O'Haire, p. 2.

9. Garcia, "Brews, Bozos," p. 4.

10. "Stroh Brewery Settles Sexual Harassment Suit," *Atlanta Journal*, 2 December 1993, sec. E, p. 6.

11. "Battling The Bimbo Factor," *Time* (25 November 1991): 70.

12. Ibid.

13. Henry J. Reske, "Stroh's Ads Targeted," *ABA Journal* (February 1992): 20.

14. Duckett, "Cold Patrol," p. C1.

15. "Brewers Can Help Fight Sexism," *Advertising Age* (28 October, 1991): 28.

16. Cyndee Miller, "Babe-Based Beer Ads Likely to Flourish," *Marketing News* (6 January 1992): 1.

17. Ibid.

18. Lippman, "Farewell, at Last," p. B2.

19. John M. McGuire, "Brews and Babes—Ad Strategy Losing Its Fizz, Many Say," *Seattle Times*, 18 February 1992, sec. F, p. 1.

20. Duckett, "Cold Patrol," p. C1.

21. Ibid.

22. DeSalvo, "Tarsem," p. 14.

23. Ibid.

24. Ibid.

25. Ibid.

26. Ibid.

27. Bob Garfield, "Bad Beer: Miller's New MGD Effort is Weak and Tasteless," *Advertising Age* (19 February 2001): 35.

28. DeSalvo, "Tarsem," p. 14.

29. "Mixed Blessings," *Adweek* (2 July 2002): 20.

30. "Code of Good Practice," The Distilled Spirits Council of the United States, 18 October 2002.

31. Hillary Chura, "Spirited Sex: Alcohol Ads Ratchet Up the Sex to Woo Jaded Consumers," *Advertising Age* (9 July 2001): 72.

32. Art Ross, "The Sexual Imperative," *Back Stage* (3 February 1984): 10.

33. William D. Baue, "Schieffelin Somerset & Company," in *Encyclopedia of Major Marketing Campaigns*, ed. Thomas Riggs (Detroit: Gale Group, 2000), p. 1602.

34. Joshua Levine, "Fantasy, Not Flesh," *Forbes* (22 January 1990): 120.

35. Baue, "Schieffelin Somerset," p. 1605.

36. Ibid., p. 1602.

37. Jeffry Scott, "The Old Thrill is Gone From Some Ads: Advertisers Split on Using Sexy Images to Attract Consumers," *Atlanta Journal and Constitution*, 29 October 1989, sec. G, p. 1.

38. Chura, "Spirited Sex," p. 72.

39. Alicia Griswold, "Liqueur TV Spot as Foreign Film," *Adweek* (14 May 2001): 6.

40. Ibid.

41. James B. Arndorfer, "Models to Troll Taverns for Pricey French Vodka," *Advertising Age* (5 May 1997): 8.

42. Charles Goodrum and Helen Dalrymple, *Advertising in America: The First 100 Years* (New York: Abrams, 1990), p. 92.

43. Rebecca Stanfel, "Just One Look Campaign," in *Encyclopedia of Major Marketing Campaigns*, ed. Thomas Riggs (Detroit: Gale Group, 2000), p. 1329.

44. John Simley, "Pepsi-Cola," *Encyclopedia of Consumer Brands*, vol. 1, ed. Janice Jorgensen (Detroit: St. James Press, 1994), p. 441.

45. Stanfel, "Just One Look," p. 1330.

46. Ibid.

47. Kevin Goldman, "Refreshment Bears New Weight In New Campaign For Diet Coke," *Wall Street Journal*, 13 January 1994, sec. B, p. 6.

48. Larry Jabbonsky, "With Diet Segment In Need Of A Boost, New Diet Coke Ads Stress Refreshment," *Beverage World* 113 (31 January 1994): 1.

49. Michele Ingrassia, "Going One Step Ogle The Line?" *Newsweek* 123 (14 March 1994): 66.

50. Goldman, "Refreshment," p. B6.

51. Jabbonsky, "Diet Segment," p. 1.

52. Karen Benezra, "Diet Cola Daze," *Brandweek* 36 (17 April 1995): 32.

53. Lippert, Barbara, "Sex Appeal," *Adweek* 42 (9 April 2001): 21.

54. Ibid.

55. Ibid.

56. Rob Eder, "Pepsi Signs Britney to Global Marketing Deal," *Drug Store News* (5 March 2001): 31.

57. Janet Maslin, "Steamy TV: Coffee Opera," *New York Times*, 22 November 1992, sec. V, p. 9.

58. Annetta Miller and Seema Nayyar, "Ads of Our Lives," *Newsweek* 124 (26 September 1994): 48.

59. Sally Cobau, "Soap Opera Couple Campaign," *Encyclopedia of Major Marketing Campaigns*, ed. Thomas Riggs (Detroit: Gale Group, 2000), p. 1220.

60. Dave Vadehra, "Taster's Choice Ads Lose Flavor With Consumers," *Advertising Age* 67 (5 August 1996): 21.

61. Stephen Levine, "Tony, Sharon on the Outs?" *Adweek* 38 (10 March 1997): 2; Leah Rickard, "Taster's Choice Rolls Love Potion No. 9," *Advertising Age* (13 June 1994): 70.

62. Tom Jicha, "TV Minisoap Ends as Taster's Choice Unveils New Ad Campaign Thursday," *Sun-Sentinel*, South Florida, 8 April 1998, (no page number).

63. Vadehra, "Taster's Choice Ads," p. 21.

64. Bernie Hogya and Sal Taibi, *Milk Moustache Mania* (New York: Scholastic, 2001), p. 5.

65. Ibid., p. 7.

CHAPTER 11

1. Aldo Quevedo, phone interview by author, 2 July 2002.

2. Eleftheria Parpis, "Risky Business," *Adweek* 38 (13 August 2001): 18; Michael Wilke, "Changing Standards: Condom Advertising on American Television," June 2001, *A Special Report of the Kaiser Daily Reproductive Health Report*, p. 8. Much of the information on past condom advertising comes from Wilke's report.

3. Parpis, "Risky Business," p. 18.

4. Wilke, "Changing Standards," p. 8.

5. "Condom Ads Gaining Wider Acceptance," *Broadcasting* (2 February 1987): 85.

6. Michael Wilke, "Condom Ads Will Debut Along with Stern Show," *Advertising Age* (10 August 1998): 8.

7. Parpis, "Risky Business," p. 18.

8. Ibid.

9. Ibid.

10. Ibid.

11. "Brief History of Condoms," *ABC Postal Condoms* [online], *www.postal condoms.co.uk/history.htm* [April 15, 2002].

12. David Goetzl, "Durex: Good Sex, Not Just Safe Sex," *Advertising Age* 70 (5 July 1999): 12.

13. Ibid.

14. Alessandra Galloni, "Is the Condom Industry Ready for a Little Comic Relief?" *Wall Street Journal* [online], 27 July 2001; Sandra W. Key and Daniel J. Denoon, "Research Reveals Alarming Rate of HIV/AIDS Complacency," *AIDS Weekly Plus* (7 December 1998): 14.

15. Key and Denoon, "HIV/AIDS Complacency," p. 14.

16. Galloni, "Condom Industry."

17. Tim Gray, "The XXX Files," *Business-North Carolina* (1 March 1999): 40.

18. Amy Taubin and John D. Thomas, "Softcore Sex Ed," *Village Voice*, 28 July 1998, p. 49.

19. Anna Carugati, "Sinclair Finding Success with Sex Videos" *Electronic Media* [online], 20 June 1994.

20. Gray, "XXX Files," p. 40.

21. Kathy Brummitt, interview by author, Chapel Hill, North Carolina, 25 March 2002.

22. Ibid.

23. Ibid.

24. "Kaiser Family Foundation Sexual Health Public Education Campaigns," June 1999, p. 5. Available online at www.kff.org/docs/sections/entmedia/MTV-BETCmpgnSumm.Mar2000.PDF.

25. Ibid.

26. Charles Atkin and Alicia Marshall, "Health Communication," in *An Integrated Approach to Communication Theory and Research,* ed. M. B. Salwen and D. W. Stacks (Mahwah, N.J.: Erlbaum, 1996), p. 479.

27. Mara B. Adelman, "Sustaining Passion: Eroticism and Safe-Sex Talk," *Archives of Sexual Behavior* 21, no. 5 (1992): 481.

28. Quevedo, interview.

29. Adelman, "Sustaining Passion," p. 492.

30. *Details* (July 1998): 42.

31. "I Could Taste His Passion," Tucson AIDS Project brochure, Tucson, Ariz., 1992.

32. K. Siegel, P. B. Grodsky, and A. Herman, "AIDS Risk-Reduction Guidelines: A Review and Analysis," *Journal of Community Health* 11, no. 4 (1986): 233; Mildred Z. Solomon and William DeJong, "Recent Sexually Transmitted Disease Prevention Efforts and Their Implications for AIDS Health Education," *Health Education Quarterly* 13, no. 4 (1986): 301; Cindy Struckman-Johnson, David Struckman-Johnson, Roy C. Gilliland, and Angela Ausman, "Effect of Persuasive Appeals in AIDS PSAs and Condom Commercials on Intentions to Use Condoms," *Journal of Applied Social Psychology* 24, no. 24 (1994): 2223.

33. Mallore Dill, "Pregnant Pause," *Adweek* (6 November 2000): 24.

34. Jonathan Curiel, "Graphic Breast Cancer Ads Taken Down," *San Francisco Chronicle*, 29 January 2000, sec. A, p. 13.

35. Ibid.

36. Brummitt, interview.

37. Tom Reichert, Susan E. Heckler, and Sally Jackson, "The Effects of Sexual Social Marketing Appeals on Cognitive Processing and Persuasion," *Journal of Advertising* 30 (Spring 2001): 13; Struckman-Johnson et al., "Persuasive Appeals," 2223.

38. Brummitt, interview.

39. Wilke, "Condom Ads," p. 8.

40. Reed E. Bunzel, "Radio Executives Open to Condom Spots," *Broadcasting* 121 (25 November 1991): 48.

41. Quevedo, interview.

CHAPTER 12

1. Tim Nudd, "Basic Instinct," *Adweek* (2 July 2001): 26.

2. Jacqueline Lambiase, "Sex Online—And in Internet Advertising," in *Sex in Advertising: Perspectives on the Erotic Appeal*, ed. Tom Reichert and Jacqueline Lambiase (Mahwah, N.J.: Lawrence Erlbaum Associates, 2003), p. 247.

3. Erik Gruenwedel, "Dude, Surf's Up!" *Adweek* (13 November 2000): 94.

4. Ibid.

5. Ibid., p. 95.

6. Brett Forest, "Boys to Men," *Adweek* (27 March 2000): IQ58.

7. Ibid., p. 50.

8. Lambiase, "Sex Online," p. 251.

9. Ibid.

10. Ibid., p. 257.

11. Maureen Goldstein, "The Big Chill," *Inside Print* (March 1988): 39.

12. Ibid., p. 43.

13. Jeffry Scott, "The Old Thrill is Gone From Some Ads: Advertisers Split on Using Sexy Images to Attract Consumers," *Atlanta Journal and Constitution*, 29 October 1989, sec. G, p. 1.

14. Art Ross, "The Sexual Imperative," *Back Stage* (3 February 1984): 14.

15. Gary R. Hicks, "Media at the Margins: Homoerotic Appeals to the Gay and Lesbian Community," in *Sex in Advertising: Perspectives on the Erotic Appeal*, ed. Tom Reichert and Jacqueline Lambiase (Mahwah, N.J.: Lawrence Erlbaum Associates, 2003), p. 229.

16. Ibid., p. 237.

17. Stuart Elliot, "Has Madison Avenue Gone Too Far?" *New York Times*, 15 December 1991, sec. F, p. 6.

18. Sally Goll Beatty, "Critics Rail at Racy TV Programs, But Ads Are Often the Sexist Fare," *Wall Street Journal*, 28 May 1996, sec. A, p. 26.

19. Tim Nudd, "Nerd Humor," *Adweek* (11 December 2000): 78.

20. Ibid.

21. Elliot, "Madison Avenue," p. 6.

The author would like to thank the organizations (manufacturers, advertising agencies, and archives) who permitted use of the ads in this book. Additional permissions are gratefully acknowledged below. In all cases, the publisher has made every effort to contact all copyright holders. Should there be any oversight, we would be pleased to update our information.

Grateful acknowledgement is made for permission to quote from the following work:

Ad text (Chapter 9): 1985 Paco Rabanne ad, Paco Rabanne 20 East 55th Street, New York, NY 10022.

Index